FRONTIERS

By Archer Butler Hulbert

THE MAKING OF THE AMERICAN REPUBLIC
THE PATHS OF INLAND COMMERCE
TRANSCONTINENTAL TRAILS
WASHINGTON AND THE WEST
THE OHIO RIVER: PATH OF EMPIRE
PILOTS OF THE REPUBLIC
HISTORIC HIGHWAYS OF AMERICA
FRONTIERS: THE GENIUS OF AMERICAN NATIONALITY

FRONTIERS

The Genius of American Nationality

BY

ARCHER BUTLER HULBERT

BOSTON

LITTLE, BROWN, AND COMPANY

1929

Published April, 1929

PRINTED IN THE UNITED STATES OF AMERICA

TO

MARIAN AND KATHARINE

And all the memories reflected in the camp fires
we have built between Lake Champlain
and Puget Sound.

The frontiers are not east or west, north or south, but wherever a man fronts a fact.

— Thoreau

Destiny . . . is nothing more than the unforseen coincidence of events, the emergence into action of hidden forces which, in a complex and disordered society such as that of Rome or of our own day, no contemporary can be expected to discern.

— Ferrero

NOTE

THERE is a blaze of golden-red glory which, once seen, you would long remember, on the floor of a living room in a quaint American house high up on the Continental Divide in one of our southwestern States. It is a Navajo rug of the largest size, made of wool, fully an inch in thickness; and the patterns on the two sides are wholly unlike. The color is that of a strange red mingled with gold. The splendor of its brightness matches well the enchantment of those southwestern skies; it might have flown in the window from the Painted Desert near by!

My friend, the owner of this brilliant heirloom of ancient days, is the only American ever adopted into the tribe of the Navajos. They are his children. And about his house stand their *hogans* where some of them weave their rugs and fashion their jewelry. But never, even by chance, can one of these swarthy somnambulists of a vanished dream recall the art by which such masterpieces as this Red-Gold Rug was made.

Every effort has been put forth to compel the oldest of their race to recall the process of coloring and of weaving which gave to the rugs of the far-off Navajos their luster and distinction. Before my very eyes I watched old Schu-ma's gnarled fingers at work in her task of *trying to remember!* The woof went in; the fingers paused; then the head dropped, sometimes with a shamefaced laugh, sometimes with a sigh, and the thread was withdrawn and the work renewed. That struggle — the task to remember arts which were the glory of other generations — will go on until my white Navajo friend follows his children "to hunt the souls of the beaver and buffalo in the Soul-Land, walking on the souls of their snowshoes on the soul of the snow." But will he obtain his desire here? Will any Navajo ever remember?

When, at times, I hear men speak disconsolately of the future of our American Republic, or of democracy, and prophesy all the fearsome things which anxious or distraught minds can fancy, I sometimes wonder if a day will come when men will ask what was the method of weaving that this nation of ours could have been built out of discordant, quarrelsome, petulant colonies? Ask how — when people were continuously planting fresh colonies on far distant frontiers; when leagues upon leagues of desert and mountain separated the frontiers which men said could only "pretend" to form a single nation; when sectionalism once violently burst even the nearest and most contiguous distinct province of the nation away from the central government; when, in fact, every centrifugal influence of geography, racial complexity and political antipathy conceivable had spent its force — the United States proved to consist of the most perfectly united people, occupying an equal region of territory so quickly, that the world had ever known.

One explanation of this enigma of the centuries is contained, I believe, in the word *Frontiers* — the frontiers of yesterday, frontiers of to-day, and the spirit of frontiering in a nation's blood. The meaning of this word must be qualified, or rather interpreted, by the ideas of five great thinkers, Bagehot, Royce, Bryce, Sumner and Turner. Bagehot bequeathed to us those perennially stimulating concepts of developing civilization involving "the principle of originality", "the hidden impulse of extrication", "the delicate principle of progress" and "the partial permission of selected change which improves nations." To Royce we owe the thought that in diversity of geography and personnel are found the seeds of stability and freedom; to Bryce, the theory that the growing strength of our government may be attributed to sentimental forces — the "fixed traditional sentiments which are the stays of human nature", as Bagehot puts it. To Sumner we owe the exegesis of those soul-made laws of men, folk ways; and to Turner an understanding of the influence upon our nation of the backlash of the leaven of restlessness accruing from the process of far-off frontiering; he also showed us how true it was to all life that the interior of an organism (or wilderness) when, exposed by a cut, as the physiologist would say, "acquires the characteristics of the surface layer."

Men have always been confused because the strands by which civilization was woven were wholly unlike and ran counterwise. That zigzagging may be called "frontiering." Doctor White of St. Elizabeth's Hospital expresses the tenet when he says: 'We must look upon . . . society . . . as made of tendencies that are disruptive, to an extent, in character, and therefore the final result is based upon a series of compromises . . . of displacements, substitutions and repressions or inhibitions of varying strengths and importance at various times." I have also quoted, as you may see, strange bedfellows for the well-known students just mentioned; and if you find here Wister and Remington, Andy Adams and Willa Cather, Kephart and Cactus Pete, account it to me for righteousness' sake — the righteousness which holds that all real things are inherently interesting. Sumner, Bagehot, Bryce, Royce or Turner would rather have known "Joe, the Desert Rat", poet of the alkali, than you or me.

A text has been fashioned for us. It was proposed by that good churchman, the Planter of Mount Vernon, in his farewell message to the people he had patiently led to freedom: "Be a Nation; Be American, and Be True to Yourselves." The first command, I take it, called for political and commercial solidarity. To get the inspiration that ought to be ours we must see the "disruptive" strands a-weaving which first made a civilization possible on these shores; then, if ever, the centrifugal and centripetal forces — tearing down, building up — played such havoc that some one said that it would be no more difficult to form a nation by annexing Neptune to the moon than to unite America's colonies into one. By "Be American" our first president doubtless meant that his people should not shun distinctiveness, not ape Old World types — be neither English, French, Hottentot or Whatnot. He wanted them to be national in spirit even if provincial in individuality. By being "True to Yourselves" I fancy he meant for them to dare to work out their own problems in the spirit of unity, with verve and boldness; to create an industrial nation by developing the resources of the land and fashion new ethical ideals for new industrial and intellectual frontiers.

I am indebted to Professor Allan Nevins of Columbia University for constructive criticisms.

ARCHER BUTLER HULBERT

Casita Del Jardin
CLAREMONT, CALIFORNIA

CONTENTS

PART ONE: "BE A NATION"

I The Harlequin Platoon of the Longitudes 3
II The Provincial Basis of Patriotism 13
III The Soil Factor in American Unification 34
IV A Vision of Opportunity and Power 58
V "Growing Up in War" 69
VI The Promise of Statehood 86
VII When Faith Removed Mountains 96

PART TWO: "BE AMERICAN"

VIII The Emergence of Hidden Forces 113
IX Frontiers Breed Frontiers 127
X The Pateran of Your Lincolns 150
XI Strands of Dusty Trails 161

PART THREE: "BE TRUE TO YOURSELVES"

XII Bands of Tempered Steel 181
XIII A Road Made Rough with Bayonets 201
XIV The Frontiers of Business Efficiency 220
XV The Integrity of the Old Frontiers 232
XVI The Responsibility of Frontiering 244
Index 257

PART ONE

"BE A NATION"

I

THE HARLEQUIN PLATOON OF THE LONGITUDES

WE were pounding across the Yellow Sea. As daylight faded, a distracted passenger spoke anxiously to the captain. Although busy with affairs of the night and the storm, that officer courteously found time to offer the laconic explanation, "No, it is not that the ship is unsound, but that the road is rough."

Often, in recent days, has that calm answer come back to me when I have heard distraught persons speak gloomily about the future of our Republic. "It is not," I have echoed, "that the ship is unsound, but that the road is rough." If such forebodings were entertained only by the professional ranter and bemoaner, dependent on rant and moan for a pitiful livelihood or more pitiful reputation, one might rest easy. The wolves following any herd can be sure of snatching off some foolish calves, some locoed grown-ups and some decrepit ancients. But there are signs of despondency in our splendid country among respectable folk who make no pretense of "taking in" the soiled public linen to wash — who would disdain to exploit its filth for profit and never by any chance to clean it.

At first through mere boyish enthusiasm, but later of a set purpose, I came to think a little about our national epic from an unusual angle — by following the paths of our pioneers from sea to sea. With something of the glee of an explorer I tracked Champlain and La Salle, Washington and Boone, Lewis and Clark, Astor, Carson and Fremont across the Alleghenies, Rockies and High Sierras. But in the end the tracks and trails themselves sank into insignificance beside an alluring conception of the frontier-building processes which those pathways revealed. For, strung like so many jewels on those dim strands, I found an unlimited assortment of provinces of value — dukedoms of Aroostook potatoes; empires of cotton and of rice; bishoprics of Burley tobacco and of maple forests; grand duchies of blue grass; kingdoms of wheat and of citrus fruit; principalities of lumber and of sugar beet and princely fiefs of gold, silver, iron and copper. I caught something of the bewildering mystery of the finding and the planting of those imperial countries by the "harlequin platoons" of men which surged so restlessly across those trails. I saw "Babel" towers erected proudly in Massachusetts and Virginia — and disintegrate; rebuilt on new frontiers in Pennsylvania and Kentucky — and go down; reappear in Illinois and Missouri and Iowa — and crumble; and founded again in Texas, Oregon and California.

"What a bizarre picture of inbreeding which preserved type, and outbreeding which strengthened stock," thought I; "the pathways are nothing compared with the impulsive force which broke down those frontier 'towers' and drove forward the breeders — human seed — across so many longitudes in such a brief moment of years." I watched, in imagination, that process, in the hope of understanding the force. I saw tribe-seed, sect-seed and clan-seed drifting westward — hard-woods people, piney-wood folk, blue-grass generations, pennyroyal colonies, human oaks, tumbleweed generations, timothy families, buffalo grass families, like Nature's seed before them, groping in the dark for lands that felt like home, and developing in the struggle with a forbidding wilderness the arts, the very genius, needed to defend themselves and conquer. Chameleon-like, they turned brown on the prairies; they became "alligator horses" on the Mississippi; they ranked themselves close together, — here, like berry bushes, for safety and, there, hardened almost into 'dobe bricks. Now they planted prickly pear settlements, evolved spiny cactus colonies, poison nettle generations, thorn tree tribes — anything, everything to win the fight against winds and tides, floods and droughts, blizzards and sand storms, bronze men and white, land sharks, railroads, revenue officers, red ants and grasshoppers. Talk of rough roads! You could count thousands of dead cattle on desert stretches and the wrecks of hundreds of wagons; and everywhere graves and graves and graves. Not unlike the scientific order of plant migration, human clans and sects, tribes and families, went through a somewhat routine, if irregular, process of "invasion", "competition", "succession" and "climax."

I might not soon have found a key to that wild scramble which we now know to have been genuine empire-building. I discovered it lifted high on the walls of the Chicago Public Library and, paraphrasing Victor Hugo, I read: "Our Republic is an Act of Faith which generations, still in darkness hid, signed in their night in witness of the Dawn." From first to last, what a record of faith in the dark is the epic of our country! "Their night" — all those generations — Captain John Smith's night, Washington's night,

Nathan Hale's, Jim Bridger's, General Lee's, Lincoln's. And those Acts of Faith: forming the New England Confederation; planting a mission on the Willamette; contracting to drive the first cattle north from Texas; a Declaration of Independence; digging a Clinton's "Ditch"; building (amid scoffs) a flat-bottomed steamboat on the Ohio out of the timbers of old Fort Henry; laying an Atlantic cable; constructing an aeroplane; irrigating a Great Salt Lake shore. What a host of men and women thus became witnesses of the Dawn—no, not a millennium; just a dawning of better things and men; of American constitutions to supersede confederations; of New York Centrals to supplant Erie Canals; of Imperial Valleys to displace arid deserts; of Union Pacifics to take the place of Pony Expresses; of "My Antonia"'s wheat fields to stand on a brown Nebraska upland. Is our night blacker than theirs?

For do not suppose that the "night" of other days failed to create its own bevy of mourners and ranters. Those witnesses of old heard the same groanings and outcries that assail our ears; the country was always "on the brink of ruin" — always "going to the Devil." It matters nothing how patent was the earnestness of witnesses; nor how very clearly the "wise" and "learned" were outguessed by exceedingly plain and simple individuals to whom the unseen really was the eternal. The road was always rough. Did not Increase Mather bemoan the fact, two hundred and fifty years ago, that "conversions are becoming rare", just as we do to-day? You who writhe to-day over the fretful "Charleston" — did not the Albany *Patriot* say, a century ago, that it would not trust the moral purity of any woman who would *waltz* with a man to whom she was not married? You who sigh over attention given to-day to athletic prowess — did not the Boston *Atlas* cry out eighty years ago for a *former day* when "a taste for intellectual and scientific amusements prevailed over exhibitions of brute force"? Was the road smoother or the ship more staunch in those polite Victorian days of 1843 when the Boston *Bee* said "robberies, murders, rapes, suicides and perjuries are as common as marriages and deaths"? Was the Ship likelier to be piloted safely by the oncoming generation of sedate and pious youth one hundred one years ago when the leading American educational journal said of a great university, "to attempt to stem the torrent of vice and immorality there would be considered by the students a freakish innovation"? Or when, also a century ago, one sixth of the prisoners in the Massachusetts State prison had been thieves at sixteen years of age and one half had been accustomed to strong drink in their 'teens? And ought not those who are so lugubrious over this startling unstockinged age to be somewhat mollified (the while they stare) at the grief of old Stubbs — three hundred and fifty years ago — over the "impudent insolency and shameful outrage" of persons who "tho otherwise very poor, having scarce 40 shillings by the year, will not stick to have 2 or 3 pairs of these silk nether stocks, curiously knit with open seam down the leg, with quirks and clocks about the ancles and sometimes interlaced about the ancles with gold and silver threads as is wonderful to behold."

Nor were some of our wise and patriotic better informed, in many instances, than the mourner and ranter. Singular indeed were some of their impatient, if not very dense, estimates as to the doubtful practices and vain dreams of those who broke down the "Babel Towers" and planted new frontiers. You see some of the latter building a Sault Sainte Marie Canal, in a land which Henry Clay said, discouragingly, was "as far off as the moon." You see others form a constitution in New Mexico, although Daniel Webster pessimistically said that the only constitution that that country could ever have "must be written for it in Washington." You find them settling a noble empire flanked by the Columbia River and Puget Sound, although a learned "blue stocking" of Boston wrote Marcus Whitman that the best that the region could ever hope for was to draw the dregs and refuse of the old centers of culture and wealth. You see the clever editor of the California *Star* (in a city no more conservative than San Francisco was in 1848, with its seething population full of frantic dreams of gold and forty-acre whisky) say editorially of those who were rushing to the Sacramento Valley, "Was there ever anything so superlatively silly!"— and those poor fanatics, half-fed, half-clothed and laid in windrows by the cholera, doubled the whole world's content of gold in twenty thousand hours! You see the New World's greatest wheat empire spring to life out of a bagful of hard wheat seed planted on high uplifted plains, whereas a learned official of the Smithsonian Institution had just said that there the husbandman could "never find tillage or profit."

The roads were always rough — but the Ship was always stauncher. And how did it come by that strength, if not by the Acts of Faith of witnesses in "their night"? The viewpoint has its value for our day, for any day. In that belief, a Vermonter, who did the gist of his life work in Ohio, but is a happy resident of Colorado, writes these pages in a California orange grove — a later atom therefore, himself, in that harlequin platoon of the longitudes. I have a great respect for my friend, this orange-grower, because the perfume of his flowers and the beauty and value of these bright orange discs in the laurel-like, shadowy recesses of his trees inspire him to ceaseless battle against the vermin and insects which never cry quarter or acknowledge defeat. And oh, but I wish we could see in the flower and fruit of our civilization an equal glory, and be inspired with a similar ardor and patience to fight our vermin and pests! For in saying that the Ship is strong I do not mean, by any means, that evils are not present. What I mean is that no constructive building — of a nation, a canning factory or a petticoat — can be done by those obsessed by the untoward ways of men, by the infelicities of every "to-day", by the gluttonous, sordid, criminal facts of life. This friend of mine is never so optimistic over his magnificent orange grove that he does not have telephone extensions so placed that, night or day, he can hear the dread frost alarm. The witnesses who had faith in the night were alert men, eager to battle real wrong; but they were not made hysterical by fakirs. If you build the train and track stronger, in order to make faster time, your momentum must be greater and the crash, in the event of accident, more terrific. Thus it is with civilization; every gain is part loss; our faith holds fast, not because evil and wrong are absent but because of the compensations automatically afforded by what Bagehot calls "the delicate principle of progress."

This grove has associations which blend a little with our point of view touching the processes of nation-building. Suppose these orange trees should fade from sight and the gravelly plain reappear as in the olden time. An uncouth figure strides thoughtfully across the scene. His clothing bespeaks rough roads — but his courage reflects the staunchness of the Ship. It is Wolfskill, the

Kentucky hunter, first of his race to plant a citrus grove beside the Pacific. Perfectly does he typify that flair for the abundant life which broke towers down and created a republic of continental dimensions. In his wake, north and south, drifted the same kind of seed, sons of David Harum, if you please, of the Despot of Broomsedge Cove, of The Gentleman from Indiana, of Huckleberry Finn, of Doctor Sevier, of the Virginian. Do you not see them leaving old homelands, taking the rough road amid doubts and wonderings, like Kipling's staunch "Explorer"?

Then I knew, the while I doubted — knew His Hand was certain o'er me.
Still it might be self-delusion — scores of better men had died —
I could reach the township living, but . . . He knows what terrors tore me . . .
But I did n't . . . but I did n't . . . *I went down the other side.*

Do you not see them on those critical going-down places? They always fascinate me, for here "their night" was blackest; down Laurel Hill, east of Uniontown, Pennsylvania, the last range of the Alleghenies; down the Cumberlands to Rockcastle Creek; down dreaded Ash Hollow into the sands of the Platte, the ropes creaking from the smoking windlass; down the Ratons to the Cimarron; down *La Bajada* to the Rio Grande west of Santa Fé; down jagged South Pass to the Dry Sandy; down the Blue Mountains to the Umatilla; down the Sierras to American Fork; down Cajon Pass to the Santa Ana? We think of "going down" as easy, but usually it was bitter business — all holding on like grim death to save the wagon wheels and hounds—dragging trees behind them to "brake" the descent. Eight tenths of all disasters occurred here. Cabins were built at such points out of wagon wrecks; supply stations, outfitting stations, blacksmith shops here arose; more than a score of towns owe their origin to these *La Bajadas* — the "going-down places."

And once down do you not see them scatter — like seeds blown through a mountain gap? They are lured thither, blocked yonder, react favorably to this climate or altitude and unfavorably to that; retreat; stick; become restless and move on; build log houses, board houses, 'dobe houses, half-faced camps, shanty boats, lean-tos, tepees — tell me, was their success in themselves or in their "Stars" that they should become "God's Whisper" (in Kipling's trenchant words) in the Minnisink Flats in Pennsylvania, at Tinkling Spring near Staunton above the Shenandoah, in Goshen's Hole in Wyoming, in the Grande Ronde in Oregon, in Aubrey's Valley in Arizona, in these sunny valleys of California?

This weird process of frontiering, which I have tried to picture thus in a paragraph, may be likened to the dominant gradient theory of brain-cell development. Physiographically, we had as a nation at the outset a [illegible] number of potential life zones, just as the brain has its fixed number of cells. They were disparate units, isolated from each other by Blue Ridges and Big Horns, by laurel wildernesses, great rivers and lakes, by alkali deserts, Dismal Swamps and Sinks of the Humboldt. The stirring, the "urge" — God's Whisper — gave birth to new connections and these links awoke to life new "cells" (provinces) which, otherwise, were doomed to atrophy. Dominant gradients personified were those Austins, for example. One came from England to Connecticut. Another went from Connecticut to develop Chiswell's mine in Virginia, then to pioneer in the Missouri lead region, then to plant a Texas colony — a "cell" so famous in the annals of American frontiering.

What urge — force — "Whisper" — lured so many strange seeds into so many strange provinces in so short a space of time? Since Abraham's day men have asked the same question. In the case of American pioneering by that medley of human seed, hurrying forward into so many kinds of far-scattered kingdoms and empires, the answers formerly given to the question leave, I think, something to be desired. For with us, as was not so usual elsewhere, together with all the divergent and centrifugal influences, there went, hand in hand, very curious amalgamating forces. Out of the very nature of the distinctive provinces themselves there came to be born an equally distinctive love of section, provincial affection. In American "cell" — provincial — development we find very singular illustrations of a newly created passion for locality, for environment, for "home" — far from home. Once this is glimpsed clearly, the miracle of a divergence and separatism, carrying the truest seeds of future homogeneity and nationality, becomes fascinating. For at last each "cell", so distinctive and individual to the very verge of eccentricity, coöperated to make an astonishingly unified country.

But how shall we see the genius of this process "clearly"? In no way, I think, more satisfactorily than by going back to those centuries of unwritten American history and seeing Nature's seed-children occupy the same mighty territory; seeing them acquire their very evident and very loyal "love of country" and, best of all, seeing them develop in the struggle for mastery the "structure and habits" which made them, if you please, ardent and affectionate "Georgians", "Nebraskans" and "Californians" centuries upon centuries ago.

II

THE PROVINCIAL BASIS OF PATRIOTISM

THE passion for locality introduces to us an American background of American history which has been ignored just as the European background was formerly ignored. Some one playfully said that, as soon as a man of science attains eminence on any subject, he becomes a nuisance upon it. Speaking in a similarly flippant vein one might say with no little tinge of truth that our friends, the geologists, no sooner attained eminence in helping us to interpret American history than they became a "nuisance." Their physical maps showed how our continent was formed; showed its great geological divisions and boundary lines. This was all scholarly and fundamentally correct and you could prove it by digging down anywhere to rock strata below.

But migrating Americans were dealing with the earth's surface, not anticlines; with soil provinces, not "faults." And confusion arose when within one geological division theoretically a unit (judging wholly by its rocky bones) were found many, and often utterly dissimilar, provinces. A single Virginia county lying in one geological zone is divided by a mountain range; and the sections on opposite sides of that height could hardly differ more in soil and products and in the social, political and religious ideals afterwards developed there, if one had been in Maine and the other in Florida. What we have lacked was a proper coöperation between geological map makers and soil-province and climate-province map makers. This lack of coördination has been a real nuisance.

For those harlequin platoons which we have described as sifting across the longitudes found manifold countries, as we have seen. The American background of our history, then, relates to those almost innumerable centuries when those many "countries" began to assume individuality; when the first spears of blue grass found their home and said "We Must March"; when fifty families of oaks occupied the eastern three quarters of our country and another fifty occupied that portion beyond the Rockies, and no member of any of these families was able to cross that mountain barrier; when Orangeburg soils built their empire and Hagerstown and Marshall soils established theirs. When this background picture is ours we are then in a position to catch something of the impossibly beautiful story of seed migration — of tree, plant and flower finding homes and developing a physical type of love of country, a passion for locality. This age-long background is suggestive because of the analogy which it affords between plant and human migration; between the physics of an unconscious predilection which made plants indigenous, and a psychic love of "home" in you or me. For there must be local, provincial pride before there can be national patriotism — before we could "Be a Nation." "A national character," said Bagehot, "is but the successful parish character."

Professor Warming of Copenhagen, in developing his science of ecology, plant migration, affords the hint of the profitable analogy mentioned above. All who may be tempted to lay down even semi-strict laws for human migration may well consider the fantastic assortment of devices adopted by Nature to scatter her seed-children over the earth, as illustrated by the ragweed and tumble-weed and thistle, by the membranous wings of the elm's or maple's seed, by flowers so bright that they lure to them winged vehicles who will spread their seed or pollen abroad. Just as infinite and innumerable were the causes of the dispersal of human seed on all frontiers. The canniness with which plants, when overcrowded, got rid of weaker species is not unlike similar processes employed by humans. The ability of plants to formulate systems of defense against enemies, as in growing in thickets, like the cane-brake or the blackberry, to withstand destruction may be likened to the "compact-making" types of pioneering of those who forged into wildernesses; and, as the acacia puts out a sweet gum on the ends of its leaves to attract colonies of friendly ants who will keep off injurious parasites, so the canny Quakers gave rich borderlands freely to the doughty Irish and Scotch-Irish who would defend them from red-skinned parasites.

Our figure so far, it is readily admitted, has been fanciful; but a lesson to be drawn from it has its serious significance. Professor Bergen has brought out the fact that existing plants to a considerable degree owe their structure and habits "to the operation of the struggle for existence, this term including the effort to respond to the changes in the conditions by which they are surrounded." The analogy here is compelling, and when we see men, like the American pioneers, fighting hard to gain their objectives and meeting every known and unknown peril to build homes in borderlands, we see them like the trees and plants, which came before them, acquire structure and habits from the operation of the struggle for existence.

Some day a super-Warming or super-Fernald will develop this analogy and show the interesting parallelism between migrating plants and migrating men. They will take, perchance, as an illustration, the epic of the replanting of that empire almost obliterated by the mighty ice sheets which moved from the north across a portion of our country. Before those chilling blasts all life fled southward. But at the end of long eons came the order: "Northward March." The reconquest of the despoiled empire was led by those William Pyncheons and Daniel Boones of plant life, the tundra, mat herbage and other hardy growths known only in Arctic regions. Those sturdy pioneers went all the way and never felt at home, never developed a virile, provincial "parish character", until Hudson Bay was left far behind. The sweet gum and persimmon halted at the Hudson; but the oak and maple, the chestnut and hickory strode upward to the Great Lakes and beyond. The imperial integrity of every seed to feel "at home" here, or be warned away there — to become indigenous — was never challenged successfully. In the struggle for existence, and in the conquest, there may have been very strange expedients adopted, cunning ruses employed, tricky deceptions practiced; the nettle may have mimicked a poisonous plant or a stone to escape destruction; ironwood may have hardened to withstand the blows of fate; plants may have developed bristles or thorns or hairs, like the barberry and nightshade, or fashioned a way to emit unpleasant or poisonous odors, like the dog fennel, hound's-tongue, buckeye or tansy, for the same life-saving purpose. In numerous instances, of course, no artifice, no cunning, availed in the "struggle for existence." Some seeds spread into zones where they could not live; the eager vanguards soon felt the forbidding conditions and perhaps attempted a retreat; some blundered headlong into hopeless box cañons from which there was no exit. In such cases stern Nature commanded that the seed change its form or perish; the snow apple died; the Ben Davis gracefully changed into the Arkansas Black; grape seed which bore black grapes near Los Angeles produced white grapes in the Sacramento Valley. Stern laws, never to be ignored in a single instance without peril, determined where the harebell and arbutus and sunflower and daisy and violet might live and bloom.

Idle it would be to urge an analogy of these processes to human migration wantonly — as earnestly, for instance, as did the enthusiastic student who, contemplating such factors, averred that he could tell from an Indiana or Illinois farmer's soil whether he was a Democrat or Republican! But a very genuine satisfaction — and a very interesting problem — arises if we keep in mind this mighty story of the peopling of our great provinces with these seed-families, and remember the response to changes which gave them their "parish character", when we behold races sifting slowly from our Atlantic seacoast into a great continental wilderness; see the Yankee respond in sterile New England and become a singular people; see the German settle fruitlessly in many portions of Atlantic America but develop an astonishingly powerful kingdom on Pennsylvania's limestone soil; see the Scotch-Irish, taught to fear limestone lands in Scotland, hurry on by the German and build an equally famous empire in the slate-and-shale regions of the Alleghenies. It is not that any one law holds true with any regularity — except that men, like plants, on every frontier, acquired structure and habits from the operation of the struggle for existence.

When we acquire this viewpoint we are fully able to appreciate the exceedingly important fact of the great differences which marked our many provinces; we then are in the way of appreciating something of the fundamental principles of their individuality — and therefore understand as never before the intense local patriotism which Americans, in common with other people, have constantly exhibited in the soil-vegetation-climate-topographical factors which makes me "love" Vermont, or you Iowa, or our friend love New Mexico. For, before we could "Be a Nation", this love of section had to show itself, even if in the subtle form described by Manasseh Cutler when he said "There is nothing in nature that a Southern Democrat hates more than a Northern Democrat!"

In essence, this tender regard for province and section partakes of that feeling of "at-homeness" which the pine tree feels in the Black Forest of Colorado but which it could never feel five miles away on the plains. It is a love of material things — the spread of tawny plains in Nebraska; the delicate lacery of elm branches overhanging a Vermont river; an intimate knowledge of soils, woods, frosts and rains which personally attend just your given portion of our country. "The sense to place," says Partridge, "is the core of the love of home . . . the attachment to place has also its biological roots, the sense of familiarity of place being, of course, as a basis of orientation, a deep element in consciousness." You are a patriotic American in proportion as you are a patriotic provincial; and is not he the greatest patriot who feels *true* affection for the largest number of localities? Every year or two I, a Vermonter, quarrel royally with a Mississippian, in a Rocky Mountain cabin, as to which one of us loves our country more. He maintains that if a born loyal Mississippian can honestly say he loves the North and its people the last word in patriotism has been spoken. I hold fast to the cherished whim that I am a real lover of provinces without number. Hundreds of thousands of us would feel this affection more if, despite the automobile, we could be travelers rather than, in Thackeray's poignant word, mere "arrivers."

All delights of touring are, to me, as nothing compared to the sensation of crossing, every now and then, an unseen Tropic of Capricorn, so to speak, and entering a new world. Leave the western gate of Yellowstone, for instance, and cruise southward for a day. From Fire Holes, Mud Pots and Geysers, you pass into the Big Woods, another world; and on to the Henry Lake country; and on to a former desert valley now blossoming as only water can make calcareous soil blossom; and on to magnificent farming lands of northeastern Utah; by eventide you are sliding down into the lovely meadows and orchards and fertile truck gardens about princely Salt Lake City. In the morning the smell of spruce gum was in your nostrils, and mosquitoes, seemingly as big as bats, hummed in your ears. At night boys and girls were offering you from the roadside peaches, plums, pears, grapes — and you are in a new kingdom.

Head north from the "High Tide of the Confederacy" at Gettysburg and you soon enter the more fertile part of the Pennsylvania Dutch country; on nearing the Hudson, farther north, the gates of another land swing open to you on the Divide — a world too busy, almost, for agriculture. Beyond the Hudson your engine tells you that the Berkshires are at hand, and you cross that beautiful barrier which once half-guarded New England from the savage raids of the Iroquois; stone walls, long white houses, codfish and rustless window-screen signs herald the fact that you have, indeed, entered another land.

Strike west from Santa Fé and you cross the Rio Grande and climb up and up to Gallup-land; painted deserts and petrified forests bespeak a strange new frontier; the pines of Flagstaff betoken another; faring south from Ash Fork you cross the rangy Bradshaws into an immense mesa when — look! — as the little boy said, "There are trees with their pants on." Palm trees! Giant cactus! Gila monsters! And from shivering in the cold by the Grand Cañon (in February) in the morning, by night you are star-gazing through the Phoenix palms.

And all that, to me, is my country. I am the heir of my friend on Long Island, with its lovely vistas between glorious roads; princely houses; exquisite gardens; foam-covered rocks white with the spray of the sea. I love the swift tide of his life; the crush and crash of commuting; the intensity of business rush; pleasure rush; contact with men who are moving the world, preaching its great sermons, writing its great books and plays, curing its great maladies, building its Woolworth towers. I revel in his pride of life, sense of power, thrill of victory. But I smile at his conviction that all the world is bounded by his roads, skyscrapers and offices!

I am heir of my friend on his ranch on Wagon Hound Creek. How interminable are those level plains — "Where thar's plenty o' elbow room to spit," as he would say. How he detests cities — where folks live so "hunched up" that you "can't cuss a cat without gittin' hair in yer mouth." How he exults as King of a Royal Domain! How little mere miles mean to him — with a Pharaoh's train of horses! He looks abroad and sees things I will never learn to see; hears things I can never expect to hear; senses changes, signs and wonders on a dead level prairie where I can sense nothing. I am a dullard in his presence because I am only educated, while he has been *educed.* Where I see a gray landscape, broken by a ravine, there appears to him

> "A mudded butte — and shapes that come
> And at the sunset stare;
> For here is the land of forgotten pasts
> Where God plays solitaire."

And when, of the earth, earthy, I am wondering if the recent rain will necessitate our putting on chains, he is strangely dumb with that

> . . . ardent, yearning pain
> Wide sage lands bring when damp with summer rain.

The way buffalo [illegible]ss slants informs him. The piercing notes of birds [illegible]im a story. In vast lands, he tells me, the bird note[illegible]ust carry fa[illegible]r, for flocks are few and far between, [illegible] if mates [illegible] find each other, the call must be loud[illegible] than i[illegible]lly land "where echoes live." The eyes [illegible] wil[illegible]e are, similarly, sharper, he says; because dis[illegible]ances are greater, and foes and prey must be sighted from afar, if at all. There is a sweep, a majesty, in his outlook, in his planning, in his care of loved ones and stock, in the way his latchstring hangs out of his door, in his kingly unconquerableness. The "operation of the struggle for existence" gave him those "Admirable Crichton" qualities. Nothing is more gripping than the spirit of masterfulness of such human plants — the unflinching determination to win, to beat the game, "come Hell or high water", as one of them said. I relish the dogged resourcefulness of Kephart's frontiersman, breast to breast with his bear in the pit:

Then I jumped down into the sink and kicked him loose from the dogs, or he 'd a-killed Coaly. Waal, sir, he wa'n't hurt a bit — the ball had just glanced off his head. He riz up an' knocked me down with his left paw, an' walked right over me, an' lit up the ridge. The dogs treed him in a minute. I went to shoot up at him, but my new hulls [cartridges] fit loose in this old chamber and this one drap [dropped] out, so the gun stuck. Had to git my knife out and fix hit. Then the dad-burned gun would n't stand roostered [cocked]; the feather-spring had jumped out of place. But I held it back with my thumb *and killed him anyhow.*

"Kill it anyhow," cried the ranks of blue grass as they fought their way down the valleys of the Alleghenies; and "Kill it anyhow" was the battle-chant of the cohorts of timothy as they worsted their blue-grass foes on the "balds" in that same country.

Likewise, I am heir of my friend on that old home-stead in Vermont; of my fisherman-friend in an Allegheny cove who knows "hants"; of my poet-friend, "Joe, the Desert Rat", in his Arizona foothills; of my golfing-friend in his California orange grove. No one of these friends would feel much at home in the shoes of another. Each is of his own frontier — knows its peculiar secrets, cherishes the glories and illusions belonging to it, breeds its traditions. Because I happen to know them all well enough to catch at least a glimpse of their happiness and virile pride, I toast myself to my Mississippi friend that I am the patriot *par excellence* because I am proud of so many "nations" within "my" country. In that sense I could fight for "my" Otter Creek in Vermont, for "my" Little Switzerland in California, for "my" Goshen Hole in Wyoming, for "my" Staked Plains in Texas, for "my" Black Pool of the Little Blue country in Kansas, for "my" Sapphire

Land of the Carolinas, for "my" Isle Brevelle in Cane River, for "my" Dillon's Pass in the Dakota Bad Lands.

From every standpoint we must realize the existence of these provinces; get a vision of them; take into account their exceeding number and their almost bewildering variations which makes one the home of the palmetto, another of the pine; one the home of cranberries, another the home of vast, silent acres of somber sage; Indian corn lands, sugar-cane countries; Rocky Ford melon countries; "would to God," as Washington said long ago, "we may have wisdom enough to improve them." Often the most fundamental of things only becomes current by jest. A wealth of suggestion underlies the creation of such nicknames for people as Nutmegs, Jayhawkers, Badgers, Buckeyes, Sooners and Hoosiers. Intercollegiate athletics present many problems and, frequently, are roundly condemned, but they have one merit which I have never seen accorded to them. They, more than any factor save our fiction, keep alive this merriest, most picturesque (if not, indeed, most truly American) fact of our national life — the individuality of provinces. I like to read of the Golden Bears of California fighting the Huskies of Washington; of the Nittany Lions of highland Pennsylvania at grips with the Ohio River Pirates; of the Bob Cats of Montana eating the Arizona Gila Monsters alive; of the Mud Hens of Toledo and the Sage Hens of Pomona. For behind many such names lie whole volumes of provincial history and tradition, throbbing with individuality and yet alive with virile nationalism.

Men love the things for which they have fought. And how these provinces were loved by those who won them against all odds! I went once to a cottage in one of these "countries", carrying to its owner a message that the

Serbian Minister to Great Britain believed him to have a fair claim to the throne of Serbia. Oh, but "no"; he much more preferred those hard-won acres in Minnesota's potato belt to any dream of a European throne! He had fought in his "night" for that Minnesota frontier. No king had so secure a possession of any throne. His father had been "God's Whisper" there. It is only by seeing these many, many provinces, so occupied and so loved, so utterly different and so far separated, that the true romance of the welding of our magnificent realm into one mighty republic can have the thrill for us, the tang, which should be, also, a part of our great heritage.

"Many sorts of Americans live in America," said Owen Wister, "and the Atlantic American, it is to be feared, often has a cautious and conventional imagination. In his routine he has lived unaware of the violent and romantic era in eruption upon his soil." One wonders that Waldo Frank can complain that America has no local colors but is, rather, "one universal drab"; or that Chesterton can be surprised that Americans care little for local traditions or that Chum Frink's soul can be oppressed by the "obliteration of sectional variations", or that Miss Hazard can take evident delight in "the triumph of standardization", a condition to be made possible "only after the passing of the frontier."

A recent writer, following Royce's lead, has hit off the salutary expediency of our refusing to recognize the obliteration of provincial individuality as follows:

To have united the thirteen colonies with their divergent types and interests, their local prides and prejudices, and their differing social, political and religious ideals, into one federated union was an accomplishment made possible only by recognizing and respecting those local differences and giving them full legal protection. . . . These diversities are today not less, but greater; and sound government should continue to recognize them. . . . Our diversification of interests and institutions geographically and socially is itself a guaranty of stability and of freedom. . . .

If politicians forget the potency of the challenge of *E Pluribus Unum*, one powerful class of citizens, our novelists, continually tend to verify it. Consider the work of Hawthorne, Fox, Cable, Garland, Wister, Harte and many others, for, as Bagehot pointed out, "What philologists call a dialectic difference often amounts to a real and total difference." I sometimes hold a mock reception in my classroom; college boys there shake hands, in imagination, with Hester Prynne, Specimen Jones, The Cavalier, Peter Stirling, Ramona, Janice Meredith, Tillie the Mennonite Maid, My Antonia, Tom Sawyer, The Little Shepherd of Kingdom Come and Old Man Enright. How redolent of frontiers innumerable are these and hundreds of other "children of the brain" of our more famous authors! No "local color"? No "local traditions"? "Sectional variations" obliterated? We readily admit that some are caricatures rather than characters; the art varies. And yet how uniquely the success has been achieved is indicated by the fact that not a few of these author-parents are *personae non gratae* in the regions where their brain-children dwelt! It is said that Cable was more berated in New Orleans than it was ever Ben Butler's misfortune to be; the truth Cable thought he depicted hurt more than the loss of the spoons which Butler never stole! John Fox was nearly mobbed at Berea College when he attempted to read his "poor white" stories to poor whites: "Why, that fellar cay n't even spell," they protested; "if he 's tellin' the truth he ain't no gentleman, and if not, then, by Godlings, he 's a liar."

It would be going too far to say that you could, upon sight, identify the exact province from which each of these picturesque individuals hailed — as Wellesley girls are said to be able to do merely by asking newcomers to that irreproachable institution of culture to say "Dirty Shirt." Yet their language would aid one signally, for the young ladies mentioned cleverly distinguish between "Dŭty Shŭt", "Doity Shoit", "Durrty Shurrt" and other provincialism. The nasal twang, the languorous drawl and the quick "business English" are, doubtless, derived from environment which includes climate, as well as influences of other tongues and native dialects.

What is usual always seems right, even in my own dear New England homeland. I once returned thither and, in conversation with as sainted a lady as was ever loyal to the eccentricities of a cultured generation, I thoughtlessly answered "No" by giving that typical Western double grunt — I cannot spell it — indicative of negation and derived, no doubt, from the coyote. "What did you say?" she snapped, "talk to me, don't grunt." But a little later the same dear woman, when answering a query of mine, gave the Yankee equivalent (nasal) intonation for "Yes." I knew better than to raise an argument as to the relative merits of grunts; but I unconsciously began fingering the railway time-table in my pocket. History shows the influence of provincialisms and provincial philosophy on the world — facts substantiated by all the Leniants and Lintilhacs and their successors.

These dream-children of the novels, mentioned above, would be as unlike as the hay, the cotton, the buffalo and the blue grass from which they came. In olden times the average person traveled very little. No province knew the average man of any other provinces — but, rather, the unusual or exceptional. The wealthy, the unwell or the eccentric were, ordinarily, the chief visitors — as is quite true among nations to-day. No people care to think that foreigners get a correct impression of their nationals from the specimens who travel most and who are criticized, caricatured and cartooned. In olden times our Yankee seems to have traveled more widely than other provincials; and these offsprings of the David Harums and Hester Prynnes could usually read and write. Heaven knows they appeared to be a peculiar people and many of them seemed to feel set apart by the Almighty to record on paper the idiosyncracies, shortcomings and peculiar (and therefore common, if not sinful) habits of all and sundry. Most books were once written by them — and practically all of our histories. Of the dozens who, in the earlier years of the nineteenth century, went down the Ohio and wrote of their tours, not one, to my knowledge, saw through what was superficial in that great provincial valley and reached the real facts. Always and always one bank of the river (the "Yankee", Ohio side) had trim, white houses, nicely painted churches and fences, orderly citizens; and the other side (the Virginia side) exhibited only uncouth homes, unkempt streets, slatternly people who fought terrible duels with naked hands, and he was victor who first popped his adversary's eyeball out of its socket. These annalists, "rancid with philanthropy and ignorance", as Owen Wister once phrased it, did not realize that the life of the plantations lay back from the river; that it centered in the unseen "Big House", hidden from sight; that the system had little place for towns, as such, and that the villages in a plantation country were populated, sometimes in large part, by poor whites.

No doubt such bias played its part to inspire rejoinders from the "Old Southwest", as illustrated by such flashes as the following (equally biased) from the brilliant pen of Henry Watterson: "Of this emanation of commercial prosperity — the New England Idea — the offspring of excessive tariffs and an optimistic educational system — Ohio is the representative, and, as such, is redundant in the cant, catch words and self-conceit of the half-educated, intellectual pioneer; the pride of piety and the misleading ebullitions of a spurious patriotic elation; pompous in moral pretense, ostentatious in esthetic displays, and as totally unconscious of the underflow of depravity and crime as of the touching philosophy of Goldsmith's lines:

> Ill fares the land to hastening ills a prey,
> Where wealth accumulates and men decay."

Thus frontier was likely to be a mystery to frontier. Tom Sawyer would have been at a loss, no doubt, to say whether he had rather play one of his ribald pranks on Peter Stirling or on Specimen Jones. The fierce mien of Old Man Enright would, no doubt, have frightened Hester Prynne; it would, on the other hand, have raised no qualms in My Antonia or Ramona. They would have known that beneath the "horrid" exterior lay a heart as tender as a child's, as winsome, as playful, as affectionate. The dashing Cavalier might easily have been nicknamed "swashbuckler", "bravado", or "sword-eater" north of Mason and Dixon's line as well as south of it.

From another point of view these literary friends of ours, representing so distinctly the striking differences in our provinces, attract attention. Is it not possible that

remain constant, provincialism will exert its beneficent influences — in politics, society, character; in literature, poetry and art. The answer to the exceedingly disheartening conundrum faced by most teachers of American history to young people, how to disassociate the bare facts of history from the exceedingly interesting processes of history, lies here. And while we are founding all associations and clubs that mortal language can define or describe, why not establish one to celebrate and vivify and extol the political, literary, poetic, artistic and commercial influences of American provincialism? Nothing to make a great country great is more necessary than to encourage the love of section — of the country you call "home." "No longer to own the *house* [the italics are mine] where one was born," said that most homeless man who ever owned a palace, Napoleon, "is to be without a *fatherland*." This "sense to place" is deeply imbedded in human nature. It is said to be of less consequence who makes a nation's laws than who makes the songs a people love. And in all time and all places the songs that are beloved are those of local and homey things. It is of Sweet Afton's rivers and Maxwellton's braes and Silv'ry Rio Grandes and Leicester Squares and Alsatian Mountains and Beautiful Ohios and Blue Danubes and Old Kentucky Homes and the Sidewalks of New York that people love to sing throughout the generations. They embody specific places, soils, buildings, climates, winds; they spring out of the very ground. Ramona would not know Hester Prynne's songs, and Uncle Remus or Tillie the Mennonite would not sing those hummed by Specimen Jones or Ruggles of Red Gap. But they would know what they meant at heart.

"This evening," wrote Robert Lyman, a Forty-Niner

en route to California by way of the Horn, "we had 'Dearest Mae', 'Mary Blane' and 'O Susanna.' There was something peculiarly interesting in hearing these old familiar airs sung within sight of the savage and inhospitable coast of Patagonia. . . . Indeed they were truly national airs, and wherever the Stars and Stripes are seen to float there those airs are certain to be heard. Rio harbor rang with them while we were there." Mary Garden, at a reception to Lindbergh, could not sing "Star Spangled Banner" till the words were brought to her from the nearest public library. That is nothing to be proud of; but it is a matter of pride that she doubtless could have sung forty songs carrying the beauty, the individuality and the "imperial integrity" of as many half-known creeks, plains, valleys, hills, mountains, orchards, fields — all of them "racy of the soil", pregnant with democracy. "They made new songs," wrote Sandburg of the migrating Americans, "they changed old songs, they carried songs from place to place, they resurrected and kept alive dying and forgotten old songs."

I have mentioned the significance of section that rings out clearly in athletic parlance, in the clash and clangor of intersectional games. This, too, is reëchoed in college songs, in "On Wisconsin", "When the Green Goes Forth to Battle", "Michigan, My Michigan":

> A song to thee, fair State of mine,
> Michigan, my Michigan;
> But greater song than this is thine,
> Michigan, my Michigan;
> The whisper of the forest tree,
> The thunder of the inland sea,
> Unite in one grand symphony
> Of Michigan, My Michigan.

The students of Colorado College more specifically celebrate the splendor of their world-famous landmark:

Our Colorado, Our Colorado,
Where the Peak, our mighty mascot, towers above;
Our Colorado, Our Colorado,
Here 's to thee our Alma Mater, thee we love.

As far as I am concerned the loudest calamity howler in the country can be president of the United States when Trinity men no longer sing of their elms, when Yale no more loves the violet and when the Tiger no longer stands defender of the orange and the black. Sentiment is the most powerful influence in the world; and love of section, of local tradition, of environment, is a national asset of unmeasured potency; obliterate it and you have civilization's husk only.

True it is, then, and something to which our mourners and ranters should pay more diligent attention, that "our diversification of interests and institutions geographically and socially" is one guaranty of American stability and freedom. How truly this was of vital import in the old days when the Ship was a-building it will be our province to explain in due course. For the moment, however, let us examine a factor of old days and of present days (egregiously neglected) which formed the basis for these many diversified frontiers within our princely domain; one which illustrates perfectly the American flair for both divergence and homogeneity — the lure of the soil.

III

THE SOIL FACTOR IN AMERICAN UNIFICATION

FEW unifying factors of equal importance in American history have been so ignored as the influence of our soils. This is all the more singular because, for two centuries and more, the vast proportion of our people were agriculturists and thought mainly in terms of soils, their products and their location. This prettily illustrates the fact that some things, by common consent, have become "history" and other things, of deep importance, have not been so considered.

We have lately come into a new era in this regard. New handmaidens of history, so to speak, are recognized now as real members of intellectual society. One of these is geography. We have come to know, thanks to Shaler, Mathews, Semple, Brigham and others, that geographical factors have been important in directing the fate of nations. The direction and heights of mountains, the position of lakes and rivers, the presence or absence of great forests, barren deserts and large bayous have dictated to men lines of least resistance to be chosen, policies of agriculture, manufacturing or transportation to be adopted or discarded. If one constantly recognizes these as influences on *men who did the deciding and acting*, the study of geography as a factor (and factor only) is very stimulating and constructive. Economic influences, also, have only lately been properly stressed as factors in nation-building and nation-managing. As long as they are treated as factors, the study of them leads to great clarification of historic trends and tendencies. Climatology has had its influences which were formerly too much ignored. While the laws of this science are exceedingly important in Nature, some difficulty arises in maintaining that they are "laws", in the same sense, when applied to society. This leads enthusiasts to build theoretical edifices with bricks somewhat devoid of straw. But as a factor in history, climatology certainly had, and has, a real influence. The danger lies in letting any one of these factors become more than factors; letting the minuend become the product.[1] With such words of warning as these, let us analyze soil influences, remembering the while that they are only factors.

New England soils, coöperating with a rigid climate, played a part in fashioning Yankee ways of living and

[1] Professor Huntington has ingeniously developed the climatic influences on many phases of world history; to such "frontiersmen" we are indebted — more than the casual critic usually happens to imply. Schlesinger has excellently summed up all such contributions in his "New Viewpoints in American History." It is suggestive of what we may come to find is true (but is now questioned) to have such a man as a director of the United States Weather Bureau say: "I have not the data before me, but I am morally certain that if the mortality statistics of the various hospitals were studied it would be found that more people die under the influence of the east than of the west winds. This may have a marked effect as one of the important environments that have to do with the character of the race that is now coming to be known as 'American.' He has fertility of thought and energy of body. May it not be that the climate has much to do with the development of the indomitable spirit that is now reaching out for the mastery of the world? . . . East winds either hug the earth or have an upward component of motion; they gather humidity, dust, disease; northwest winds come from above with a downward component of motion — from the region where the air is dry, pure and highly electrified, an invigorating air."

thinking. When the giant ice sheets leveled the mountains of Alpine grandeur which dominated that region, they left a land curiously formed. It was dotted with islands, so to speak, of good soil, separated by seas of rocky barren soil. Here and there rivers came into existence; the earth and silt deposited by their waters created long strips of good land of varying dimensions — the river valleys. The rich land of New England was very fertile; no one acre in Iowa has matched in bushels corn grown on one Connecticut acre. It was the paucity of rich land that made New England's agriculture limited.

This fact had to be discovered by experience. It now seems almost humorous that Governor Winthrop should have planned what he thought of as a Virginia plantation on the hills of the present Tufts College campus — little dreaming that his land was composed of many different kinds of soil and, therefore, unfit for any large staple crop, which was the basis of the Southern plantation system. It was no particular antipathy for slavery that explains its slight growth in the North — or made many Yankees become slave traders by sea instead of slave drivers by land. The character, then, of New England soil fixed a principle for that section — the principle of diversified agriculture. Our chief authority of New England, J. T. Adams, has said: "The soil confirmed and strengthened him [the Yankee] in both convictions"; namely, a hesitating belief in the injustice of slavery and a predilection for a town grouped around a church.

Soil played a part, also, in fixing the principles of expansion. The patches — or islands, to keep our former figure — of good lands were, in the main, isolated. The stranger within New England's gates to-day marvels that his train passes through so many wild and forbidding sections in a land which he knows teems with a great population. Men who desired to found new settlements searched out these rich, but isolated, natural meadows, beaver meadows or glades. With good soils as a center, towns were laid out and the incorporators each had a fixed fraction of this soil. It mattered not so much how many acres of pasturage, woodland or swamp these fathers owned; there was plenty of such land; but of the rich soil each man was awarded only a definite and limited fraction — as the western miner, of a later day, had only a certain fraction of a lode or vein of gold or silver. Those Yankees, therefore, held as very precious their fertile land; they drew the lines about it carefully, set corner posts with great accuracy and built their fences along the boundary lines with precision.

Does it not thus become plain that the township system of New England sprang, as it were, right out of the ground? And, if one desired to push the argument, could it not be said that such a system, requiring great accuracy and developing, no doubt, great cunning, helps to explain the cautious, crafty, half-suspicious "nearness" or pure selfishness with which the public has generally endowed the typical Yankee character? The writer, personally, fell heir to a typically Yankee uncle. Raw virtues mingled with raw weaknesses characterize his memory. Intenseness in labor, in charity, in piety described him. Liberal to his church and dozen or so children, he was a maniac for miserliness in other ways. Behind us boys who rode on the hay wagon came Uncle Sam with his two oxen and wooden-wheeled cart; and if he saw so much as one wisp of grass blown by winds into an adjoining bush he would rescue it with the lusty daring of a coast-guard hero saving a life from a foundered ship! He could croon to a baby in tones of gentlest love; but when he took his woes to God down at what he called "Jesus Rock" in the Swamp, folk alleged that they could hear him at "the Creamery" two miles away. He was so like one of the weather-beaten rocks of his pasture, that, if one of them to-day should hail me in his high-pitched, nervous voice, I would hardly consider it more of a miracle than that any frontier, however rough and rocky, or any climate, however bleak and bitter, could produce, in human form, such a weird mixture of Christian graces and barbaric virtues as shown in that Vermonter up close to the Canadian line.

By their soils and other environment those Yankees were molded into a peculiar people — if the good Lord ever had any! The molding unified them. The nasal whine in their voices was not more truly born of the nipping east wind than their attitude to lands, crops, Quakers, Scotch-Irish, slavery, temperance and tariff was determined by the way Fate demanded that they should seek their temporal and everlasting salvation. Probably nowhere, in any region of similar size, did any provincial people ever grow more alike than did the old-time Yankee stock. It is not too much to say that their soils were potent factors in their individual development and in dictating their systems of town and land surveys and local government. Their "life policy and standards," said Sumner, "have become to a very large extent those of the civilized world." Yet the whole history of Atlantic America "is strewn with creeds and institutions which were invaluable at first and deadly afterwards." Roger Williams and the Scotch-Irish in the Valley of Virginia would have assented to that theory. "A Shelley in New

England could hardly have lived," said Bagehot, "and a race of Shelleys would have been impossible."

This becomes plain by comparing the dominant ideas of New England with those of another frontier. There was much that was similar in your typical Yankee and typical Pennsylvania German — background Nordic stock; intense piety; zeal for hard work, tightness of fingers on money and property. If the Yankee outshone the German in general information and in a respect for the three R's, the Pennsylvanian has a very much longer credit mark after his name for religious toleration and eleemosynary progress.

Now the people of each of these two different sections fell heir, shall we say — unless you favor the natural selection theory — to frontiers in our country similar to their respective Old World hives; New England resembled Old England in her varying soil types; and the limestone lands of Pennsylvania were almost a duplication of the soils of the Palatinate. In those wide belts of limestone, swinging down from the Delaware, focusing on the Potomac and following up the Shenandoah to touch the finger tips of similar soil in Tennessee, the great staple wheat country of young America was planted. Long has it maintained its prestige for wheat and diversified agriculture; a century ago Lancaster County, Pennsylvania, was the richest American county in point of agricultural products; it is so to-day, for diversified agriculture. Washington said the winning of the Revolution lay in the hands of the Pennsylvania Dutch and their wheat; and promptly sought their allegiance by appointing a Baker-General for the army from that section. Each of these sections, New England and Pennsylvania too, had a conveniently located port and harbor as a seafaring metropolis; and Pennsylvania, in part, adopted the New England township survey system.

Yet how utterly different was the development of these two frontiers! The great staple crops of those Pennsylvania limestone fields compelled a study of transportation and the solving of its problems not equaled elsewhere in the colonies. Limestone roads were already there — in a state of nature. "Conestoga" wagons appeared in such a country as a matter of course; and, in breeding the English hunter to native stocks, the sturdy Conestoga horse took his place along those wagon tongues. Here, too, Fitch built the first steamboat and Evans ran the first traction engine that snorted along an American highway; here the first toll road was built, as well as the first graded road on which the total ascent was apportioned to the whole distance; here the first canal of real length was planned and begun; here the first successful operation of river locks was inaugurated. Rapid development of all means of transportation led Pennsylvanians to enter fields of speculation also untried elsewhere. Systems of tolls, based on the actual damage done to road surfaces by different-sized wheels or differently shaped hoofs of sheep, hogs or cattle, were here evolved. Here, first in America, toll-road companies were limited in the profits which their directors might divide; and here, as early as 1792, was established the principle that a company's books must be opened for official inspection to determine profits and, automatically, determine a reduction of tolls. Here, too, for the first time in our country, compensation for injured workmen was made compulsory.

Of course all these "things" were done by men; the Pennsylvania soils had remained unchanged for some millions or trillions of years and would never have produced results in ten times as many trillion if men of energy, wit and perseverance had not happened along. But just as sure it is that the same results could not have happened, in the same era, anywhere else on our seaboard. Nor, on the other hand, did Pennsylvania, absorbed in agriculture and lacking fast-running streams, shift as quickly to a tariff-favoring country, in another generation, as did New England, whose rapid streams gave rise to mills and factories.

But look again to the seaboard soils — and this time to the frontier south of the Potomac. Here spread millions of acres, favored by moist, warm airs, fitted for giant staple crops of tobacco and cotton and rice, in a land where white men could not endure happily the taxing grind of outdoor work. What a different society did men develop under such conditions! Its alluring and unhappy features are matters of common knowledge. These far-separated plantations made impossible the compact-building of close communities. Cities were unknown and large towns rare. The profitable crops were those which exhausted the soils most quickly; the plantation had to expand to live. Such expansion could not have advanced profitably by the relatively slow township-system method. On and on the planters moved. Little did some men realize that Lincoln sounded a death cry to slavery, years later, when he proposed, as a mild compromise, that he would not touch slavery where it existed. Slavery could never live if restricted to "where it existed." Biological laws are astonishingly stern laws and soil (not then fertilized as now) could not bear continuous crops of tobacco and cotton.

The lovely white-pillared Southern "Big House" arose from out those tobacco and cotton frontiers as naturally as the big red German barn was a product of the more northerly limestone lands, or as my uncle's tiny cot and the near-by huge hay barn were a product of the rocky soils of Northern Vermont. And, in those Southern homes grew up a society such as never could have appeared on Jake Gantz's or David Harum's farms. With Negro labor almost a drug on the market, men and women had time for self-cultivation, for practicing the fine art of entertainment. It would be a matter of supererogation to expand a theme so simple and so perfectly recognized.

But other soil influences are not equally self-evident. It is remarkable how similar soil types repeated themselves as you glance across our land from east to west. Northern New York, Ohio, Indiana and Illinois are not unlike New England in many respects. Soils are to be judged by growths, and men, once getting acquainted with any soil, become familiar with the growths such soil produces. Lines of temperature and rainfall in our land trend on east-and-west lines in the main. As the pioneer armies in the old French War days fared abroad, men were quick to recognize the soil and forest types with which they were familiar. Agriculturists, more than any men, feel at home in a soil-and-forest land to which they are accustomed. Here they have met and conquered life on the terms such environment imposes. Most of their tools, in the olden day, were made from woods whose characteristics were well understood — as well as a large part of their household and farm furniture. William Spratling, the Southern artist, caught this sense of the thing when he wrote of his Cane River people:

There seemed some sort of curious connection between the lives of these people and the soft white material [cotton] with which their existence had been so closely interwoven — as though their very circumstances had partaken of the same quality. . . . Here was Madame Aubert-Rocque in person, detached from the rush of life and still completely concerned with things of the soil which we have almost forgotten existed.

This is emphasized by all students of the psychology of patriotism — love of one's locality, one's State. As men went abroad they felt this peculiar at-homeness when they entered a frontier of familiar soil and trees, or familiar soil and prairie.

"Everything is better there," moaned the forlorn Napoleon at St. Helena, speaking of his native Corsica; "the very smell of the ground. If my eyes were shut I would recognize it; I have never come across it anywhere else." One would be guilty of gross error to say that a hard-wood's people or a soft-wood's people, when migrating, were wholly ruled by such factors. But they proved, in early days, true lines of least resistance; and while no statistics could be of any inherent value, it is doubtless true that, in the formative days of the Middle West, larger Republican majorities were cast where the predominant forests were of harder wood than anywhere else; and sure it is that your typical Southerner always favored prairie soils to wooded soils.

With interesting regularity the good wheat soils, for instance, are scattered across the longitudes in America. They are found, in isolated "islands", from Maine to New York where their dimensions increase. The large section of wheat land in Pennsylvania, that early "Granary of America", is joined by thin connecting links (like the Valley of Virginia, so important to the Southern Confederacy for its grain) with the stately blue-grass regions of Tennessee and Kentucky. In central Ohio wheatlands widen out as the prairies are reached, and beyond the

Mississippi, stretching into Canada, lie the vast acres made famous by the modern plows and reapers which cultivate and reap whole counties in a single day. Then, as if wonders never cease, frontiers once heralded as "uninhabitable deserts of cactus and sage" were found to bear as high as ninety bushels of grain to the acre — and a Wheatland becomes famous in high uplifted Wyoming, and the lava districts of a Snake River Valley, dreaded by the Oregon pioneers as the forlornest of forlorn countries, bring forth such thriving centers of agriculture as Twin Falls, Burley and Buhl. Again, beyond the Wahsatch, Blue and Sierra Nevada mountains spring up the wheat fields of Utah, Oregon, Washington and California. Where wheat will grow, diversified agriculture is possible. The progress of population and frontier-building was enormously facilitated by the recurring discoveries of large and still larger areas where breadstuffs could be raised. Irrigation and conservation are constantly proving that this process must continue for many years.

Except for occasional rushes into new lands, occasioned by the discovery of rich mineral deposits, American expansion was predicated by the discoveries of rich soils — and the economic development which followed with the building of lines of transportation and great cities. Every prospectus of land companies, even including the propaganda of the early London and Virginia companies and William Penn's circulars distributed by the great Pastorius in the Palatinate, base arguments for migration on soils. Thus William Penn wrote the Committee of the Free Society concerning his forest-empire in the New World:

The country itself, its soil, water, seasons and produce, both natural and artificial, is not to be despised. The land containeth divers sorts of earth, as, sand, yellow and black, poor and rich, both loamy and dusty; and in some places, a fast fat earth, like our best vales in England; especially by inland brooks and rivers; God, in His wisdom, having ordered it so, that the advantages of the country are divided; the back lands being generally three to one richer, having much of another soil; and that is a black *hazel-mould*, upon a strong, or rocky bottom.

The Ohio Company of Associates began its invitation to "adventurers" by the statement that "from personal inspection, together with other incontested evidences, they are fully satisfied that the Lands in that quarter [Ohio] are of a much better quality than any other known to New England people." In after days toll-road companies and, especially, railways pushed the sale of lands by advertising on a large scale the qualities of lands in the sections to which they led. Many of these pieces of literature, as in the case of an early Illinois Central booklet, give detailed statistics of soil composition:

In many parts of the world [reads this *Guide to the Illinois Central Railway Lands*, written seventy years ago] it is found necessary to improve the soil by mixing and combining different earths; and also by adding to the organic matter. But Nature, so far as relates to the soils of Illinois, has kindly performed these offices for man. Experience has shown that a soil, composed of one earth alone, whether it be sand, clay or lime, is unproductive; but that the best soil consists of a due admixture of all these earths. In examining . . . the soils of Illinois, we find that the proportion of clay varies from 18 to 64 per cent.; of sand, from 25 to 75 per cent.; and of lime, from 1.3 to 3.3 per cent.; but what is most noteworthy with regard to them, is the remarkably fine state of subdivision in the particles. The soil, when dried and crushed, crumbles into an almost impalpable powder, and hence is in the best condition to afford nutriment to plants. . . . In England and in the

Atlantic States, the annual application of manures often costs more, per acre, than the fee [cost] of the Illinois lands. The mechanical analysis of these soils shows that there is present from 5 to 10 per cent. of organic matter; while the chemical analysis indicates from .18 to .33 per cent. of nitrogen. It would take half a century of cropping to exhaust this accumulation of organic matter.

Such propaganda was, of course, also made use of by tricksters to dupe the unsuspecting. Men had learned that certain growths usually indicate certain types of good land; and especially alluring were reports of trees of great size. Under given conditions such deductions were trustworthy. Washington, for instance, measured, with no little enthusiasm, a giant sycamore on his lands on the Ohio which was found to have a circumference of near forty-five feet at a point on the trunk three feet above the ground. A reputation for truth-telling in connection with trees now served him in good stead — and the soil of his lands was as rich as the measurements of that sycamore suggested. But the mere name of a tree might prove deceptive. Similar trees, under different drainage conditions, developed into utterly different growths. The sturdy oak of England and New England might betoken excellent soil; descriptions of "oak openings" in the West might create in the minds of sanguine people a ravishing prospect of agricultural competency, but the cultivation of such soils "on location" was usually more productive of blisters than bliss. Yet, whether advocated by honest men or by leeches in human guise, the rule mentioned was universal, soils dominated migration in all the formative years of the Republic.

While these richer soil provinces were widely scattered, yet the unifying influence on nation-building exerted by them is almost self-evident. You catch, even to-day, this sense of the thing if you become a gypsy and join the motley caravans of those who travel by automobile and congregate by camp fires in the public camp grounds along America's modern highways. Let your eyes be shut to automobile, gasoline stove and such modern devices, and listen to the gossip and you can well believe you are a pioneer on old Braddock's Road or on the old Oregon or Santa Fé Trail. Men discuss with energy the countries from which they hail and answer questions concerning home crops and lands; they inquire with avid interest of the lands toward which they are faring to learn what is to be expected in the way of opportunities and difficulties. The toils and the accidents and humorous incidents of wayfaring are matters of consolation or jest. A feeling of companionship and fraternity springs up overnight; whole life plans are often changed — just as a week's ocean voyage brings people of other levels of society together in friendships which are frequently lifelong.

Thus it was on the old frontiers. A nation was moving west and, in general, with similar interests, hopes, fears and expectations. The problem was to find good homes; ambitions were set to the same tunes; alliances of wills to conquer were made. And as a result the human atoms, though far dispersed it may be, were linked in bonds of a common outlook and purpose. Intellectual horizons were broadened; sectional antipathies were allayed. The Oregonian learned that California's heat was a "dry" heat; that Montana's cold was a "dry" cold; and was immediately inspired to prove to any one that Oregon's rain was, after all, only a "dry" rain or, at worst, but a "high fog."

The recurrence of soils of established reputations helped

to banish the bugaboo of Distance. It greatly lessened the hardship of breaking away from home acres to know that, in "far-off" New York, Kansas, Texas or Oregon, soils of known characteristics were to be found; soils that would respond systematically to known methods of agriculture; soils that reacted to changing weather, to heat and frost, snow and rain, just as did the home acres. This seemed to shorten the distance; it alleviated the dread of migration and gave promise of success and a future reunion with loved ones in the frontiers toward the Pacific Ocean. These marching agriculturists breathed that very "aroma of nationality" some one has mentioned. Said James Bryce: "The growing strength of the national government in the United States is largely due to sentimental forces." The common cause of frontier occupation and home-building welded Americans into one people, no matter how far separated they were from each other or from "home." They became American in an intense sense. They were unified into men of broader mold, of wider concepts. This shows on every page of their political history. To the pride and spirit of independence bred on the old frontiers of Pennsylvania, Virginia, Kentucky and Tennessee was added a new sense of political power which united this later West in many fashions at many times — for better or worse.

The invariably interesting, if erratic, Ingalls of Kansas — who was never more spicy than when most erratic — was hitting at the mark when he preached his economic sermon on "Blue Grass", and advanced the proposition that this grass was "the salutary panacea", "the healing Catholicon", "the verdant cataplasm" for a backward civilization. He did not know how this grass acquired (through its seed) its name, and he attributed to it an effect only to be obtained by man's cultivation of it; but, overlooking these fundamentals, his words sparkle with novelty and make toward a truth:

There is a portion of Kentucky known as the "Blue Grass Region", and it is safe to say that it has been the arena of the most magnificent intellectual and physical development that has been witnessed among men or animals upon the American continent, or perhaps upon the whole face of the world. . . . All these marvels are attributable as directly to the potential influence of blue grass as day and night to the revolution of the earth. Eradicate it, substitute for it the scrawny herbage of impoverished barrens, and in a single generation man and beast would alike degenerate into a common decay. . . . Our Kansas politics have been exceptional, violent, personal, convulsive. The appetite of the community demands the stimulus of revolution. It is not content with average results in morals. It hungers for excitement. Its favorite apostles and prophets have been the howling dervishes of statesmanship and religion. Every new theory seeks Kansas as its tentative point, sure of partisans and disciples. Our life is intense in every expression. We pass instantaneously from tremendous energy to the most inert and sluggish torpor. There is no golden mean. We act first and think afterwards. These idiosyncrasies are rapidly becoming typical, and unless modified by the general introduction of blue grass, may be rendered permanent. . . . Under these benign influences, prairie grass is disappearing. The various breeds of cattle, hogs, and horses are improving. The culture of orchards and vineyards yields more certain returns. A richer, healthier, and more varied diet is replacing the side-meat and corn-pones of antiquity. Blue grass is marching into the bowels of the land without impediment. Its perennial verdure already clothes the bluffs and uplands along the streams, its spongy sward retaining the moisture of the earth, preventing the annual scarifications by fire, promoting the growth of forests, and elevating the nature of man. Supplementing this material improvement is an evident advance in manners and morals. The little log schoolhouse is replaced by magnificent structures furnished with every educational appliance. Churches multiply. The commercial element has disappeared from politics. The intellectual standard of the press has advanced, and with the general diffusion of blue grass, we may reasonably anticipate a career of unexampled and enduring prosperity.

But by what miracle of migration were the dry, uplifted plains beyond the Mississippi, where the "salutary panacea" of blue grass could not go, to be made the luxuriant home of millions? Blue-grass empires had meant wheat empires, but "soft" Eastern wheat could not withstand the alternating scorching droughts and chilling blasts of those highland plains, in the "Land that God Forgot." Insidious proverb! How well God did remember it is shown in that mighty hard-wheat empire of to-day! Curious enough is the story of how the seed, which should make that well-remembered "desert" bloom, came to it from six thousand miles away.

When Russia took Crimea from Turkey in the eighteenth century Catharine the Great sought in Western Prussia for sturdy Mennonite colonists who would develop the land as the shiftless, native population never had. Land to the amount of one hundred and sixty acres was granted to each family, together with special privileges and immunities, to hold good for a hundred years. As time went on the prosperity of these enterprising foreigners on the Molotschna (Milk River) proved as aggravating to the native Russians as the prosperity of Stephen Austin's emigrants to Texas proved to the Mexicans in 1825–1830. At the outbreak of the Franco-Prussian War, Russia, as the price of neutrality, was allowed to annul the promises made to the Molotschna

Germans on the condition that they be allowed ten years in which to migrate again if they so desired.

Enterprising men of this doomed colony which had won a memorable fight to acclimate "soft" Prussian wheat to the high steppes of Crimea came to America just when the Atchison, Topeka and Santa Fé Railroad was looking anxiously for emigrants who should occupy its Great Plains frontier. The fight to grow soft wheat there had failed. But the Molotschna pioneers had the identical "healing catholicon" for those "barren wastes." One hundred thousand acres were now purchased by their agents from the newly built railway. With the emigration from across the sea came twenty or thirty bushels of Russian or "Turkey Red" hard wheat, a gift of the Old World to the New, more valuable than many shipments of jewels, paintings and tapestries. It planted our whole hard-wheat empire. This "discovery", so to speak, of the Great Plains frontier as the fruitful home of wheat made Kansas and all her sister commonwealths the goal of millions of "giants" in strength, in property, in patriotism. By means of such seed the Plains' soils may be said to have drawn a great population westward.

The discovery of gold, silver and other metals also brought westward great inroads of all classes of men. This might have proven disastrous to society, for the lustful greed of many, bringing at times near-anarchy, bade fair to wreck all that had been built up. Very fortunate it was that the first stroke of this kind fell upon the one western frontier best prepared of all to withstand the blow. In olden times, when the Spaniard had felt his way northward from Mexico, so little was known of the geography of our Pacific coast that men conceived the present Gulf of California to be an arm of the sea which, connecting with Behring Straits, cut off from the continent a beautiful island of palms, flowers and fruits known as California. In later days the enterprising Father Kino corrected all this misinformation by more accurate mapping. Yet so utterly different was the discovery, occupation and development of California from all the rest of the West that it seems as though it really might have been a vast island separated from our coast by many leagues of sea.

About the time of our Revolutionary War, when Western Pennsylvania and Kentucky were the "far frontier", the *padres* of sainted memory came northward from Mexico to plant their beloved missions along the Pacific Coast from San Diego to San Francisco. The necessity of giving work to the native Indians whom the missionaries came to save, as well as to sustain the missions, led to the development of agriculture and cattle raising. By leaps and bounds the stock-raising industry grew. Its prosperity made possible the building of that chain of shrines, mission houses, along *El Camino Real* — the *padres'* pathway from south to north.

So great became the output and surplus of products of the cattle industry that keen skippers, whose noses seemed to scent bargains and profits across every sea, began to come to California harbors. This trade brought speculators and investors to a frontier heralded as rich beyond description. These came from many shores, but Americans sufficiently predominated to coöperate with the home country to effect later the almost bloodless conquest of the land for the Stars and Stripes during the Mexican War. Those unfavorable to the Hand-of-God theory in history see nothing remarkable in the astounding coincidence of the treaty which gave the United States California and the discovery of gold on the American River. Only nine days elapsed between these events! Had that discovery been made long enough before the Mexican War so that the enormous mineral wealth of the land could have been known by the world, one's imagination is taxed to picture the complications — intrigues — alliances — wars — which might have ensued.

Fortunately, however, the soils of California had already summoned to the land a population and had given to that frontier a stability and resiliency that could withstand the shock of the advent, in one year, of nearly a hundred thousand men — good men, adventurers, murderers, cutthroats and thieves. Royce has described vividly the descent upon California by trail and ship of this horde of excited treasure seekers; and well does he say that no young commonwealth was ever subjected to such an invasion by such a frantic host of men.

That the newly fledged State of California could have stood the test, maintained fair semblance of law and order and provided for the sustenance of so many thousands of hungry men, is attributable to her soils which, said her first governor, in the very midst of the rush of the Forty-Niners, contained a treasure for the State beyond the value of any mineral deposits. "The future of the State," said Doctor Pond, a pioneer of '52, "as founded on its agricultural possibilities . . . brightened our sky and led on towards a settled population and a substantial growth." Moreover, Californians wrought out from Spanish precedents new laws for the control of lawless men, statutes covering water rights and placer-mining rights, and enforced them with notable success. This becomes important to us from the frontier-cell viewpoint stressed in these pages. In fast succession rich mineral deposits were discovered in all parts of the West, from the Canadian line to Bisbee and Douglas. In many cases Californians were pioneers in these adventures; if not first-comers in every case, they soon appeared. They brought the lessons learned on the American, Yuba and Feather rivers; they also brought and established known and tested laws to operate in these newer frontiers; thus regularity, stability and unity were the heritage to all the West from an older and established frontier which had previously experienced a similar type of sudden pioneering by many men, some of whom were unprincipled and vicious. And, to an extent rarely recognized, the productive fields of California provided the foodstuffs necessary to make possible the successful exploitation of mineral lands to the eastward, in the Rocky Mountain frontier.

The philosophy of history, a common phrase with the expert, but very vague to the man in the street (especially when the scientist uses as synonymous the expression, "the chaos of history — and its madness") is said to have been "upset" by such a discovery as that of gold in California. In simple language the philosophy of history is man's method of explaining the emergence of the "hidden forces" which Christians (and express companies) call "Acts of God"; it is the story of processes; certain causes acting through the years produce certain results. Not infrequently "decisive" battles are said to have "upset" the logical trend of events, although, long ago, Montesquieu pointed out that "if the fortune of a battle . . . has ruined a State, there was a *general cause* which brought it about that that State had to perish by a single battle." The sudden introduction of any new and extraneous influence seems to overthrow existing processes. Such influences are very often exerted by a material force; the opening of an ocean pathway around Africa to India;

the discovery of a new continent like America; the finding of a great limestone belt in Pennsylvania or a blue-grass region in Kentucky; the discovery of gold in California or of silver in Nevada.

Perhaps the most interesting part of the story of the world is the sudden introduction of such "upsets." Taking California gold as an illustration, how often in our history have minor upsets of a similar character exerted a like influence! Is this not the very subject of this chapter? The finding of the rich Wabash, Marshall and Miami soils of the Ohio Basin challenged the "philosophy of history"; the discovery that the American desert frontier would "blossom as the rose" was an "upsetting" influence; the knowledge that the seemingly sun-dried grasses of the plains were cured "on the hoof", so to speak, was another innovation — and so was the discovery that Oregon was one of the finest grazing grounds on the continent.

One wonders, then, if, after all, the real "philosophy of history" does not also concern man's reaction to these "upsetting" influences; his ability to cope with the unforeseen, the unexpected; his sagacity in turning to account suddenly uncovered frontiers — of mine, soil or economic opportunity. And here, too, processes operate fundamentally. The Californian found, in Spanish precedent, his laws to fit a new era of mining; the Yankee in New York and Ohio put into practice the rules of the agricultural game learned in New England; the Palatine German practiced in Pennsylvania arts bred in Palatine blood. The "upsets", then, really prove the philosophy of history rather than undermine its fundamental theory. Are they not what Ferrero always had in mind when he used the word "Destiny"?

The discovery of an unparalleled series of unexpected economic opportunities as our frontiers were occupied tended to produce a psychic unity in our people. A common thrill of adventure possessed them; a common feeling of admiration was prevalent at the knowledge that the Californian had mastered his perplexing food problem; that Captain Lauchlan McKay had rerigged more than half the spread of sails of his gallant *Sovereign of the Seas* (after a Pacific storm) without going to port and made San Francisco from New York in one hundred and three days, a record never beaten but once up to that time; that John Cowan had found "Last Chance Gulch", the fourth great Montana gold region; that at the sight of his compass needle old man Burt had cried out in a panic "Look around here, boys", and discovered the great Marquette ore beds; that the dry farmer had brought forth a good crop; that an irrigation ditch had won ninety bushels of wheat to an acre from soil which "God forgot"; that Johnny Appleseed had planted 100,000 square miles of fruit. The sensing of the conquest over Nature begot a new brotherhood and created a new Americanism.

I honor such of those fragmentary papers as remain, dim with age, which represent to me anew the vital experience which compelled men, in Sumner's words, to get a "new outfit . . . of use and wont" on all those frontiers — the contract for the first drove of cattle driven north from Texas; the permission of the Spanish governor of California to let Ewing Young drive cattle northward to Oregon; the agreement between Captain Sutter and Marshall for the mill by the stream where the latter found California gold; the order for the first far-western printing press brought from Honolulu to Oregon; the agreement to bring from the far Crimea "missionaries" of hard wheat; the first car of beef shipped to an eastern slaughterhouse; the contract for the Overland Mail or the Pony Express. How little men dreamed that their faith in making such rash promises to sell or buy, dig or print, ship or drive, would break down mountains of "going-to-the-devil" pessimism! For everywhere and always there were clashing interests, divergent aims and ambitions — centrifugal and centripetal forces building up or tearing down. We must now see that this has always been the political process — even in those background days when dim blue prints of a future nation began to challenge the imagination of the patriots of our first colonial frontiers.

IV

A VISION OF OPPORTUNITY AND POWER

How regrettable it is that the old methods of teaching American colonial history so deluged the pupil with facts and so ignored the splendid processes which were always at work that, when Carl Becker brilliantly elaborated them, a moribund critic said his book was not a "history" but only an "essay"!

For example, the pupil of old was ragged about the differences between proprietary, royal and charter colonies; whereas the all-important thing was their similarity — the fact that in all of them the strange tearing-down, building-up process was always at work to fashion a nation-that-was-to-be; and with strong men working confidently on their "small improvements" in "their night", and calamity howlers crying that everything was going to the Devil. We miss the whole point of the thing if we do not see these centrifugal and centripetal forces in conflict in all those formatory years, and see that out of stress and storm, patience and violence, sacred faith and hopeless resignation, ranting pessimism and sparkling optimism a nation was born by *overcoming*. For then we are inspired to believe that by overcoming can that Republic be projected into the future to play the part intended for it in the world. By that knowledge are we "dedicated to the great task" lying before us.

The fact came out in an Ohio murder trial not long ago that there was no county in that State in which some one had not been killed with the rail of a fence in a quarrel over boundary lines. One of the many causes of jealousy and wrangling between those old American frontiers was the position of the boundary lines between them. What a waving of "fence rails" and spilling of brains resulted! No wonder Ben Franklin said that no one of the colonies but loved England more than it did any neighbor. Take Franklin's own colony as an example — for all its sturdy peace-loving Quakers. On the east there were the disputes in the Jerseys. On the south, Mason and Dixon had to be brought from England to settle the quarrel with Delaware and Maryland; interestingly enough, it was now found that Philadelphia was not in the colony of which it was the capital; that circular northern boundary line of Delaware to-day is a standing reminder of the time when Philadelphia was, so to speak, pushed back into Pennsylvania! On the north, Connecticut men claimed that the Nutmeg State went underground through New York but, with Yankee cunning, came to the surface again in "Penn's" country. Here a veritable war ensued, the Pennamite War, and noses were broken and heads cracked ere Connecticut's claim was disallowed. On the west, a more portentous war between Pennsylvanians and Virginians over the boundary line was only averted by the coming of the Revolutionary War. Pennsylvania by charter extended five degrees west from the Delaware River. Did that line curve in the west as the river curved in the east? If so Pittsburgh lay in "Virginia"!

These illustrations suffice to show how, almost everywhere, boundary lines bred trouble. Cases differed in various provinces, but the result was as fraught with difficulties as the episode of the Mississippi River islander who refused to pay taxes on his island, to anybody. The Commonwealth on one side of him reached to the "steamboat channel", and that on the other side extended to the "middle of the river"; this pugnacious citizen's island lay between those lines of demarcation; he was in neither State, — not even in the United States! Colonies which were not neighbors (except on paper) were at loggerheads over boundary lines; New York, Massachusetts and Connecticut disputed Virginia's "arrogant" claim to a vast Ohio Valley region in which Pittsburgh lay.

Such disputing over metes and bounds seems to have made it easy for the colonies to bicker over other topics — if not, indeed, to enjoy finding questions for disagreement. Offhand, it would seem impossible to quarrel over the matter of taking a census of colonial populations. Yet great wrath, accompanying accusations of treachery and deceit, arose in this connection. In early days, when money and men had to be raised for defense against French or Indians, each colony's quota was determined by population. The moment one colony believed that another was not counting noses correctly, in order to escape raising its rightful quota of money and "warlike Christian men", a storm of protests arose. This grew so violent, that, in one case at least, a colony voted that no census of its population should be made at all! This phase of early American history quite faithfully represents its old European background, as did all boundary-line quarreling; no end of disputes among rival States in Europe had arisen over the unwillingness of allies to furnish proper quotas of men and money in offensive or defensive alliances.

Again, each colony retained the right to make its own money. Standards of value differed. It was not long before the money of one colony was not deemed valuable on an even ratio of exchange in another. William Dean Howells in later days wrote an amusing description of his working hard to earn some Ohio money and, with a quantity of this medium of exchange jingling in his pockets, treating himself to a visit to Niagara Falls. At the very outset his pleasure was blighted by the refusal of the owner of a marvelous two-headed calf to admit the boy to the tent containing the wonder since he could offer as payment only "despised" Ohio money! Such insults burned. In colonial days boycotting resulted — with all the accompanying rancor usual in such cases. So, also, each colony had the right to fix the tariffs to be charged on goods coming into it. This instantly led to increased enmity. Goods were shipped to colonies charging the lowest rates and were then smuggled into those charging higher. Some colonies had no important ports; these colonies were held in a sort of commercial vassalage by neighboring colonies which had excellent ports. New Jersey, for instance, felt herself thus held in vassalage by New York. Curiously enough, it was the bitter rivalry over tariffs between Virginia and Maryland, both fronting the Potomac River, which led to the succession of conventions which developed into a convention which took up all the knotty problems of colonial rivalries and at last evolved our Constitution.

Such difficulties as these over money and tariffs again illustrate the likeness of America in colonial days to Europe. The same results had followed the same provincial restrictions and boycotts in Europe for hundreds of years. The New Jerseys and New Yorks of Europe, its Virginias and Marylands, had suffered from these same trade conflicts almost since the beginning of history.

Human nature, the knack of self-preservation, the insistence for individual success and profit, remains the same in all climes and ages. The willingness to curtail for the common good; the ability to sacrifice and search eagerly for the compensations which may lie elsewhere; the surrender of rights, privileges and prerogatives in order to make what you still have left of much greater value than before — all these ideals had to be manufactured out of whole cloth by men who had the faith to travel rough roads.

Better known to the average American, no doubt, are the political and religious antipathies and disputes which played their part as disruptive factors in colonial days. The exile of Roger Williams to Rhode Island; the fate of the Quakers on Boston Common; the almost as inhuman treatment of Scotch-Irish pioneers in Worcester (whose half-built church was burned to the ground with the best people of the town looking on "with folded hands"); the sparks which flew when Quaker, Huguenot, Scot, Yankee, Swede, Irish and German occupied the limestone region of Pennsylvania; the pious sacrilege of the western Pennsylvanian who accosted the itinerant preacher: "I want you to know, Sir, that I have made a promise to kick out of my house every man that comes in it that has graduated at [Washington and] Jefferson College and studied theology at the Western [Allegheny] Seminary"; the quiet wrath of stolid Presbyterian elders who were forced to form a hated "vestry" in order to establish local government in the high-flung Valley of Virginia; the detestation of Established churchmen of the Atlantic lowlands for the lesser breeds of circuit riders who planted their wild flocks in the mountain frontiers of the Southern Alleghenies — all represent phases of disquieting social elements of centrifugal influence. Asked by a circuit rider whether there were any Presbyterians in her part of the mountains, a gaunt woman, with the flash of an eye toward the rafters, replied: "Oh, I dunno; John 's got the skin of a lot o' varmint up in the loft." And at least one bristling Calvinist, describing the Established lowland clergy of tide-water Virginia, said that they preached three times a year against card-playing, cock-fighting and horse-racing and spent the rest of their time enjoying those same bedeviled sports. And even the saintly Hooker of the Connecticut Valley called down the wrath of God upon the lying churchman of Boston for telling newly arrived emigrants that everything had gone "to the Devil" in the valley, and that Hooker's nine cattle had all died the preceding winter; whereas he never had but eight and they all thrived famously.

In colonial days this form of rivalry was expressed, not so much in policies (in which, as we shall see, there were seeds of unity and amalgamation) as in the jealousy of States of small domain toward States of larger size. This overbearing attitude appeared in a score of ways and, at times, was perfectly justified; that it was sometimes justifiable, however, seldom made it less irritable. In the first attempted union of the colonies, the New England Confederation (to be emphasized for some admirable characteristics elsewhere), each party to the agreement was to have equal vote in important matters. But when it came to a genuine crisis, Massachusetts Bay assumed the prerogative of outvoting her allies and having her own way. Such instances of domination, exceedingly common and the cause of many upsets in European history, were frequent in our colonial history.

For long years those who hoped for a dimly seen ideal of unity were in the hopeless minority. But mighty processes were at work to accomplish the miracle of American unity. To see that this was true must hearten all who are weak-hearted to-day. What were they? In the first place, although our English forefathers essayed a task fraught with enormous difficulties when they began the physical conquest of our continent, and one for which they had little training and no experience, their very "weaknesses", at which their French rivals smiled so condescendingly, proved to be their strength. In their slow, methodical way, the English laid solid foundations along their coast-wise empire and built westward by means of compact settlements. The Dutch and German frontiers in the middle colonies (themselves honeycombed, however, with English stock) built after the same pattern, found protection in well-grounded English law and, with increasing uniformity, began to use the English language in counting-house and market. With reservations, we think of the Atlantic coast colonies as using the English language and bound together by it; automatically, then, the psychologist's dictum was adhered to — New World Englishmen worshipped as they pleased but, in general, spoke one tongue. Again, the heroes of England were their heroes; and legend and tradition of race played their part, along with language, to mold colonies which had many difficulties and differences into one colonial empire. The songs of England were their songs — and, if so, what mattered the laws? The universality of the English language gave to all colonies alike the great heritage of English literature. Under pine or palmetto the same great books were read, the same aspirations aroused, the same ideals fostered.

Again, the colonies drew common inspiration from the Book of Books — and this was as true of the German and

Dutch settlements as of the predominant English settlements. The Bible — as a builder of the Ship — has never been properly emphasized; it was a factor in welding quarrelsome neighbors together into a psychic unity, long before they became politically one. In its pages was found every evidence necessary to prove the impotence of disunion and the effectual power of the States which sank common differences in order to form close associations. The history of Israel was a continuous story of alternate provincial alienation and national unification. Not one cause for colonial antipathy, perhaps, but may be found there; and scores of illustrations in Israel's checkered history proved that only in unity was there strength.

These amalgamating influences were, of course, reinforced by the close trade relations which bound Mother-Country to the colonies. The habits of Boston and Philadelphia were those of Mayfair; the modes of Whitehall were those of Williamsburg. What was "stylish" in England became fashionable in the colonies; when ordering hats or gloves or shoes, George Washington merely told his agent to follow the vogue prevalent at the moment in London. To a considerable extent young men, like Washington's father and his two half brothers, were educated in English universities. These contacts, often described, were very close and common; they need, on our part, only to be mentioned to be recognized.

All these factors were abetted by geographical position and relationships. No mountain walls, such as the Alps or Pyrenees, separated these colonies; no arid deserts lay between them. Rivers, like the Hudson, Connecticut and James, served as highways into the land. The Atlantic was a common pathway between them. All this aided mutual acquaintance and the interchange of commodities.

It was thus easy and natural for the colonies to unite, formally and informally, to oppose enemies from without. It doubtless seemed ominous indeed at the outset, when so many rival European powers seized at one and the same time "spheres of influence" in this New World. We now see this to have been propitious for the cause of the United-States-to-be. For example, the occupation of that strategic New York-Maryland frontier of the Atlantic seaboard by Holland and Sweden was fortunate, since it forestalled the entrance at that point of England's more formidable rivals, France and Spain. This made the later English assimilation of that section possible without unbalancing the European scales; the consolidation of all the English-American seacoast cost scarcely a single life; it might have cost thousands of lives and millions of treasure. In the second place, the colonial wars between the enemies, France and Spain, which lay on either flank of the English colonies, did far more than is generally realized to unify the latter — to fit them for the final struggle for independence itself.

These hostile neighbors (and this of course includes the Indian tribes) forced the colonies into various coöperative associations or leagues for mutual protection. When threatened from without, men stop quarreling over boundary lines, lest an enemy seize the lands to be bounded. When menaced from without, men stop bickering about census-taking lest an enemy destroy the existing population and lift the polls to be counted! The New England Confederation of 1643 is a type of the kind of associations which were formed by the English colonies in these years. Its good points and its faults are worthy of a moment's notice.

The articles of agreement of this Confederation described the causes (mainly "sundrie insolencies and outrages" of the Indians) which led to the creation of "The United Colonies of New England"; this embraced Massachusetts, Plymouth, Connecticut and New Haven. It did not include Rhode Island, which, because of its "heresies", could be eaten alive by savages for all its neighbors seemed to care. The object was to form a "firme and perpetual league — for offence and defence, mutual advice and succore upon all just occasions both for preserving and propagating the truth of the Gospell and for mutual safety and wellfare." For forty-one years this loose confederation exerted some power, coming automatically to an end with the recall of the Massachusetts charter in 1684.

While this first "United States" was not of large importance, it served some ends for which it was formed and was of consequence in international relations; in that aspect it promoted "the peace of God's people with the Swedes on the Delaware — with the French of Canada, with the Dutch of New Netherland — and with the Indians." That any such organization, weak or strong, should have existed is important from our standpoint. Whatever its faults, it forever formed a basis of comparison, an ideal to think about — a mental blue print of what some day might be! What the Confederacy did accomplish was remembered. It sounded the first call "Be a Nation." Wherein it failed, the reason for that failure was remembered. Its every act — and all the reactions — formed precedents. Herein, whether man foresaw it or not, lay the gist of the whole question of establishing any kind of coöperation between the English colonies; and herein lay the crux of the matter when a final American Union was fashioned. The development of representative government on our shores was almost automatic; all the seeds had long ago been planted in the hearts of Englishmen. But the art, the judgment, the good sense required to recognize a true from a spurious "independence" was not automatic; they had to be acquired; and all of our colonial history proves the psychologist's modern dictum that acquired characteristics are not passed on by inheritance! The New England Confederation, and its many successors, proved incontestably that nothing so much as a spurious idea of independence blocked the path toward genuine cohesion and unity. For, from another standpoint, it was, also, a precedent. It was wholly extra-legal; it had no standing in the eyes of the Mother Country; it was a creation of the colonies themselves, spontaneous, unauthorized. It was a feeble gesture — but the hands that made it were reaching toward the light, "in witness of the Dawn."

V

"GROWING UP IN WAR"

It is pointed out elsewhere that the English colonists showed no adeptness for exploring the interior of our continent; but that, in no half-hearted way, they came "to have and to hold" through compact building the sections in which they settled. But the war with France changed all this, and the stories of Washington, Braddock, Amherst and Wolfe occupy their well-known pages of our national annals. But look closer for what lies between the lines. Whole chapters of activities, preliminary and supplementary to these major events, are overlooked because of their seeming minor consequence. Yet, for our purpose, they must be regarded carefully. In every campaign there were outriders; scouts, spies, pioneers and engineers always went in advance to search out the land, to ascertain where grapes (provisions and fodder) were located and where the giants (enemy) lay. Many proposed campaigns were thus prospected, so to speak. To many points of the compass were those above-mentioned advance agents sent. Scores of reconnoiters were launched, districts strategically examined, rivers and mountain valleys explored.

The result was that these military operations, whether of major or minor consequence in the end, opened up whole leagues of territory in every direction to the colonists' eyes. Scarce an important valley, from the original "thin red" frontier of 1740 to the Great Lakes and Ohio, but came under the observation of some keen-eyed scout, some party, some regiment or army in this period. These men, in general, were agriculturists; they had met life in terms of soil, trees, swamps, arable land. They were connoisseurs of ability. As such, they formed armies of exploration as well as armies of conquest or occupation. The French supplied, so to speak, the very initiative which they said the English lacked. In fighting the French and their Indian allies, the English colonists acquired an entirely new and accurate idea of the regions beyond their borders. About the blazing fires in their homes after the war was over, these soldiers talked of "America" in terms never dreamed of a decade before. The rich soils of New York, the orchard country of lakes George and Champlain, the fertile valleys of Vermont, western Pennsylvania and Virginia, the shores of the Great Lakes were the themes of the D'Artagnans of the colonies. It mattered not at all whether those "Promised Lands" had been first sighted by a whole army, by one scouting party, by one reliable courier or by one escaping prisoner who hid by day and traveled by night — as the rich Missisquoi Valley in Vermont actually was — such memories invoked an alluring refrain, "Be a Nation", and kindled two virile ideas.

One idea was that of opportunity. These men invariably compared the lands seen or heard of with their own. Very often this meant comparing a poor with a rich country. While love of home was a sterling English characteristic, the betterment of condition and the need of an outlet for increasing population were things not to be overlooked. By the hundreds men said, "That is the country for me"; and by the thousands they said, "Son, that country I saw is the country for you." After the Old French War, which brought under the king's flag all the continent to the Mississippi River, a stirring, a restlessness, a longing began to echo in all the colonies. New Englanders, blocked in the north by Canada and on the west by their firm league of friendship with the Iroquois, turned in other directions. Some moved southwest, like the Lincoln family, into New Jersey and Pennsylvania; some looked to the south and enlisted in the Lyman Colony in the Lower Mississippi country. From the limestone Pennsylvania region strode forth the Hites, the Boones, the Lincolns, the Lewises and the Finlays to occupy the Valley of Virginia and pierce even to the rich blue-grass regions of Tennessee and Kentucky. While the king's Proclamation of 1763 prohibited the building of cabins westward of the crest of the Alleghenies, staunch friends of the self-same king, such as George Washington, recognized the decree as a temporary measure to allay the Indians; despite the decree Washington, for instance, kept his agent, William Crawford, steadily threading the glades of the Ohio Basin in search of good lands. Even in royal circles Englishmen of vision planned new kingdoms beyond the Alleghenies, such as the Walpole Grant.

Pennsylvanians quickly seized the site of Fort Duquesne — whereon Fort Pitt had been built — and laid in 1765 the foundations of Pittsburgh. By 1770 Washington himself was far down the Ohio River, surveying bounty lands along the rich Great Kanawha River. The Henderson Company of North Carolinians purchased "Kentucky" from the Cherokees and sent Boone striding forward to lay the foundations of Boonesboro and also Louisville at the "Falls of the Ohio." These experiences in the old French War, which made a Great West known to these colonists, suggested the idea of opportunity — the vision of growth, migration, new settlements, enlarged horizons and all the allurements of a rich Promised Land at their very doors.

The value of this for us, here, lies in the fact that this inspiration was not felt in one colony alone but in them all; not only by men of New England but by men of New York and Pennsylvania and Virginia. It was a universal inspiration; it spread like a contagious disease down the whole nine-hundred-mile frontier. Men caught the vision of a new blue print of what the colonies could become, of a great people going into a new inheritance. The detail of how a genuine conquest could be made of the vast West was still a mystery — but a consciousness of a Promised Land had arrived. In God's time a great leader would, as we shall see, propose a plan of systematic conquest.

This idea of opportunity was, of itself, an inspiration toward unity. Nothing so unifies a nation as a common vision of new possibilities — of lands to be won, of rivers to be mastered, of mountains to be scaled, of wide fields to be plowed and harrowed. Despite all the rivalries and quarrels and bickerings of that day, there came to these American colonists the solemn, inescapable pride which comes from the inheritance of "castles of Spain" possible of indefinite development. It started the ringing of the rising bells in the dormitory of men's souls; bells which repeated, in every alluring cadence, the challenge: "Be a Nation." The vision of a great west to be occupied psychically unified the colonists.[1]

[1] The writer, formerly a pupil of Professor Frederick Jackson Turner, has been often indebted to the works of that pioneer who first correctly emphasized the importance of the frontier influence on American history. What is said on

This sense of opportunity in its complex relationship to the frontier has many ramifications. One of these, the automatic, even if unconscious, sense of renunciation of the past which possessed our pioneers, is graphically depicted by James T. Adams:

> When the leaves of the forest path closed behind them it was as though a green curtain had fallen, which was to separate them from the busy half-mercantile life of seaboard town and farm. Their eyes and thoughts no longer turned eastward to follow the wake of seaborne ventures, but westward to vast tracks of untilled soil and endless forest . . . where an American life divorced from the old world was to be born. It was as though men had to some extent been walking backwards, still looking overseas so long as they did not pass beyond the limits of tide-water bay or river stretches. It was when they definitely abandoned these, and the long line of pioneers plunged into the wilderness beyond, that the great renunciation took place, not less dramatic in retrospect because then only partially realized.

The other idea suggested by the old French War was that of the potential, latent power of the colonies. In a broad view one cannot say that the colonial troops, of themselves, and under their own leadership, won any series of astonishing victories. The capture of Louisburg, Crown Point, Ticonderoga, Niagara and Duquesne exhibited genuine bravery. The conspicuous defeat of

this page, and those immediately succeeding, would be reinforced by such quotations from Professor Turner as: "Whatever region was most recently reclaimed from the wilderness, was most characteristically Western. In other words, the distinctive thing about the West is its relation to free lands; and it is the influence of her free lands that has determined the larger lines of American development. In adjustment of themselves to completely new conditions, the settlers underwent a process of Americanization. Men who had lived under developed institutions were transplanted into the wilderness with the opportunity and the necessity of adapting their old institutions to their new environment, or of creating new ones capable of meeting the changed conditions."

Braddock has been the most miswritten event of the struggle; in effect, that soldier's campaign was a success.[1]

As a recent historian, Professor Paxson, quoting the present writer, has pointed out, Braddock was essentially a victor for being *there* — across the mountain wall with a force of twenty-two hundred men intact, despite the almost insuperable handicaps with which he had to contend. The Alleghenies had been conquered; they were the chief foe; they were the main defense of the French. And when Forbes came, three years later, the French fled without a struggle — as they were preparing to do when they found Braddock had overcome that mountain wall. By making such campaigns, by holding Indian-infested frontiers, by winning some notable victories and numerous minor forays, by coöperating in some instances with alacrity to do and dare, the war was won.

England never found those colonies the same in the years after that struggle. She learned that, unaccountably, their love for the empire, so gloriously raised up on swords of Wolfe and Clive, and by the statesmanship of

[1] Braddock's army was not ambushed in a hollow, as so many accounts state; and, beginning with this false premise, most details of the combat are given an untrue explanation. No reputable colleague, as Washington, Gage or Orme, left records which impugn Braddock's conduct of the campaign; the stories of terror-stricken refugees from that curious accident of slaughter on the Monongahela naturally laid the blame on the army's dead leader. You do not find such blame expressed by the responsible colonial comrades of Braddock's. By sheer accident, due, not to the cleverness of the enemy, but, rather, to their dilatory arrival on the battle-field, Braddock's army was caught on the summit of a ridge; no tactics, either of the European or frontier school of war, could have won the battle for Braddock there; escape was possible only by going forward or by an outright withdrawal. Such radical movements were forestalled by the suddenness of a torrent of fire poured from unseen muskets from the upward-sloping sides of the hill by an unseen foe — concealed by dense undergrowth but having the English clearly silhouetted against the sky. This awful sense of being slaughtered, so to speak, by a death-ray, by unseen enemies, created a panic and put an army to rout.

Pitt, had suddenly gotten "off center." A devotion to their part of the empire now outshone their love for the whole empire. A mesmeric love of country had been born. Over the noise of local bickering and the babel of intercolonial strife sounded a new note, instinct with a kind of crude, coöperative zeal. The new British Empire, now so splendidly enlarged, failed to elicit the old affection. America had gone ahead fast. Perhaps, as Bosanquet lately said of Germany, a lack of political liberty had bred in the colonies a morbid self-consciousness. Its peoples showed a readiness, quite un-English, to ignore precedents, flaunt convention, override custom, try novelties, seek "new things."

Singularly enough, this was not true of any one section; the ailment broke out simultaneously all up and down the line. Whatever the change was, it was expressed with alarming uniformity. It was, in fact, born of a new sense of entity; a new feeling of physical unity; a new conception of man power — and the dignity which comes from such inspirations. "The American is a new man," wrote J. Hector St. John Crévecœur, "who acts upon new principles; he must therefore entertain new ideas and form new opinions." Every man and woman who felt thus was an American, not an Englishman or Englishwoman. A new race had evolved, with a new psychology of patriotism. The land was new and, like the land, these people-in-the-making were traveling new roads, physically, morally, mentally, to new goals. In the words of Partridge, they became possessed with the "mood of intoxication"; and the aspect of that mood which dominated them was "the inpulse to seek an abundant life." Readily the people conceived a liking for new machinery for making laws, social customs, political affiliations. And in this new sense of latent power there was unity, just as there was unity in the new sense of opportunity. In fact, one idea supplemented the other; for power was necessary to develop the opportunity; the opportunity was enticing only as a sense of the ability to improve it was present. Moreover, as De Tocqueville pointed out, there was an ominous synchronism in both American material and psychical advance; one colony did not far outstrip another in "civilization", as that writer used the word. "Maine and Georgia," said De Tocqueville, "which are placed at the opposite extremities of a great empire, have more real inducements to form a confederation than Normandy and Brittany, which are separated only by a brook."

Herein lies the fundamental explanation of the events which led to the struggle for, and ultimate creation of, American independence. The incidents in the story, the occasions of the conflict, go but a short way to explain it. Stamp acts, navigation laws, Boston massacres, parsons' causes, Boston port bills and Quebec acts were only marks on the physician's chart which showed the progress of the fever; they in no wise accounted for the disease. For it must be recognized that while the colonies developed new blood, and lusty channels for its transmission, England was suffering, politically, from a hardening of the arteries. With the birth of the empire, there came no corresponding enlargement of the concepts of government. A score of customs, habits, formulas, prerogatives, systems and what-not had come to have the approval of honorable usage and had led to the present successes. Time-honored committees kept on meeting in time-honored places in time-honored ways. They followed time-honored theories with time-honored paraphernalia, deliciously obstinate to recognize that "to-morrow will not be like to-day; new forces will impinge upon us, new wind, new rain and the light of another sun; and we must alter to meet them." And if circumstances did wrest from them the shadow of an iota's compromise, how perfectly did they follow the dictum: "[Men desire that] the new thing shall be in the fashion of the old; it must be an alteration, but it shall contain as little of variety as possible . . . in unavoidable changes men like the new doctrine which is most of a 'preservative addition' to their old doctrine. . . . [The great difficulty] is not of making the first preservative habit but of breaking through it, and reaching something better." Men of great name and influence, in the most approved of ways, attempted to hitch England's car "to a Star", using the same harness formerly employed on sturdy horses. Old routines were followed; old shibboleths devoutly worshiped. New wine was poured with great ceremony into old bottles; and the bottles broke. The breaking was called "revolution"; Washington, Adams, Hancock, Henry *et al.* were called rebels. If so, the bursting of the chestnut burr is "rebellion", and each winged maple seedling is a "rebel."

The "insulting arrogance" of the Americans as, one after another, they defied the British ministry's efforts to bring them to terms, fed the flames of independence and brought a spirit of unity never known previously among them. Such overt acts as the creation of committees of correspondence, which cemented the colonies together in uniform schemes of "treachery", aroused anathema in Whitehall; and the sound logic of Burke and Chatham in Parliament prodded the British ministry to even yet more headlong measures provocative of war. Incident followed incident until, at last, a people's fighting blood was aroused to action and, to consummate a long story of unifying influences, a confederation was fashioned and the United States became a tentative nation.

This latest Union bore numerous likenesses to the many which had preceded it. No one of them had ever infringed in the least upon the right of the colonies to decide, each in its own way, questions of internal government. This was the kernel of the discussion with the Mother Country. She had set up claim to the right to fix taxes without consent of the colonies. One of the most flagrantly "rebellious" acts of any colony was committed by that "most loyal colony of Virginia" by passing the noted Virginia Resolves; "every attempt," read this document, "to vest such power [to lay taxes] in any other person or persons whatever than the General Assembly is illegal, unconstitutional and unjust, and have a manifest tendency to destroy British as well as American liberty." It is a far cry, in years, from the New England Confederation to the Articles of Confederation; but an ideal outlined dimly in that far-off day had persisted steadily and became triumphant when colonial days drifted to a close and the United States of America was created.

How excellently did these Fathers, feeling dimly in "their night" toward a now-famous goal, illustrate the soundness of Emerson's compelling words: "Far the best part of every mind is not that which he knows, but that which hovers in gleams, suggestions, tantalizing, unpossessed, before him. His firm recorded knowledge soon loses all interest for him. But this dancing chorus of thoughts and hopes is the quarry of his future, is his possibility." Bagehot strikes the same note when he says that life is not a set campaign but an irregular work, "and the main forces in it are not overt resolutions but latent and half involuntary promptings." It was "half involuntary promptings", this "dancing chorus of thoughts" in England's erstwhile loyal colonies, those

> "fancies that break through language and escape",

which made havoc in Whitehall — but particularly because it was a *chorus*, not a solo by one fanatical Henry or Adams or Hancock. The people of a whole land were singing of a liberty that once had only "hovered in dreams, suggestions, tantalizing, unpossessed", but which was now echoed concretely to all the world in a Declaration of Independence.

The best proof that a genuine spirit of unity prevailed among the States of the newly formed nation is that the War of Independence was fought and won by a people which had no government; by a people which, so to speak, grew up in war. The statement is literally true. Under committees (of Congress), with very limited powers, the nation operated steadily until a substantial government was established. Frothingham well says, "This power . . . was strictly influence, not government. Not one of the popular leaders, perhaps, had a just conception of the political machinery which the public needs required." The great handicaps under which Congress labored and the great difficulty to make the "Sovereign" States coöperate prove most conclusively that the war could not have been won had not a very genuine spirit of unity and loyalty been present. The more plainly you depict the roughness of the road, the weakness of the machinery which was employed, the more you must emphasize the spirit which lay behind the machinery — for *something* won the war! "The spirit of the people," says Bancroft, "supplied the place of efficient political machinery." That made the

Ship strong. And it is always so intangible a thing — this "spirit of the people" — that men then, and men now, misjudge its power. It was Macaulay's ignoring of this factor which led to his misjudgment of the American experiment in popular government — the emergence of salutary "hidden forces" which "no man can understand."

One might almost say of the Fathers, there had to be their darkness — "their night." There had to be a period of inefficiency in operation if no one of the leaders had a "conception of the political machinery." If you cannot "mount up with wings of angels" or "run and not be weary" perhaps you can do the humdrum thing, "walk and not faint." Our nation had to learn to walk first; true, it nearly did "faint" over and over again, with the calamity howlers and Going-to-the-Devilers shouting "I told you so." Yet probably nothing except that very experience, and the dangers which accompanied it, made possible the firm union which came with the Constitution. A great law was being adhered to; the law of natural growth. The fact that the colonies submitted in these years to any restraint, that they would assent to any advice, that they would take any orders from without, was, under the circumstances, an event of promise and hope. Hard experiences were endured ere the lesson of government was learned and the sacrifice of a spurious "independence" was found to be indispensable. But let us not so misjudge the time of trial as not to see that any obedience to Congress now was a step forward from "their night."

Doubtless nothing so strengthened the Ship in these days as the organization of strong local governments. Aiding in this work, Congress laid the only foundation on which the colonies could successfully make war. What did any of the plans of union of those earliest colonial days do toward strengthening the political and social order of the associated members? Nothing, except by offering safety from enemies. We thus see that a great change had come, then, when the central clearing house of sympathies and influences, the Continental Congress, now helped to form strong State governments. In a revolution what revolves? "Hearts," answers the idealist; "Constitutions," replies the statesman. The real American Revolution was effected when the "Old Thirteen" adopted State constitutions and began to function under them.

The rapidity and especially the uniformity with which this was done was notable. The work was practically completed in every State within a space of eighteen months. As a factor making for unity this spontaneity is an item. Of still greater interest was the uniformity of ideals which lay beneath these constitutions. True, a basis had been fashioned for them in the colonial charters; some colonies only altered a few words to change a colonial charter into a State constitution. But what a chance was here presented for radicals and extremists to propose impossible tenets! What an opportunity for those "forest-bred statesmen" (as some Englishmen scornfully dubbed them) to set up Bolshevistic ideals! The spirit of the people, working out their own salvation, is shown handsomely in the sanity, conservatism and enduring qualities of the constitutions then formed in those "red-hot" Revolutionary days. Many of them were not changed in the least for fifty years or more. Their likenesses were more important than their differences; in them all three branches of government were established — Executive, Legislative and Judicial. To them was that dreaded thing — power — bequeathed. What the people now denied to a central authority, they did uniformly give to their local authorities, for they knew this was indispensable to local integrity. This was to teach them that it must be, likewise, indispensable to national integrity. A hidden force thus slowly began to emerge.

Again, the value of this school in educating "politicians" to become statesmen cannot be overestimated. In fashioning the political machinery to operate a local unit successfully, men became more proficient in the art of government; they took genuine lessons in idealism, in efficiency, in the practical handling of public opinion. If it was true that our fathers had "no conception of political machinery" before they undertook this building of local governments, they cannot be said to have failed in that effort nor to have missed invaluable experience by performing their work. Fortunately the distance of America from England, and the wide-flung extent of the colonies, made it necessary for the enemy to localize the war; major operations were never going forward in many States at once. The consolidation of the States under constitutions made defensive operations more effective; in fact, they gave an intensity to unification that could hardly have been rallied otherwise. "America is growing up in war," said a contemporaneous writer, "into greatness and consequence among the nations."

In idealism no people, perhaps, were ever more united than were Americans when the Declaration of Independence was declared. It was a notable document because of what it said — and even more interesting, from our standpoint, for what it left unsaid. It could have been ruined by the addition of one paragraph. It left unmentioned the topic of *how* independence and unity were to be effected. It offered no plan for exerting the much-dreaded *power*. The election of a Congress followed, and the appointment of committees; these committees fought and won the war. To form "a more perfect union" wise men later proposed the adoption of "Articles of Confederation" which offered, in plainer language than had been used previously, a set of rules which should govern the action of Congress; they stated the exact powers of Congress and very specifically declared that each State retained its sovereignty, freedom and independence; they declared that every right, privilege and prerogative not accorded to Congress remained with the States. These Articles, because they did not create an organization which could exert the necessary functions of an able-bodied government (leading, in the end, to near-anarchy) were rabidly denounced by many, yet government under the Articles was a very distinct step in advance over government by committees of Congress. It was exceedingly important that, in some way, by some scheme, the nation should learn to classify powers; should come to realize that, if we were to be a nation, some powers must rest with a central government and some with the confederated States. It did not matter so much at this moment how the classification was made, or what measure of success was attained. What was absolutely vital to eventual success was that the *making of the classification* should "emerge." In the years 1776 to 1781 all the States ratified the Articles of Confederation. But, in the struggle to bring this about, an important and interesting debate arose which must attract our attention.

We have touched upon the topic in the large when the rivalries between the colonies with reference to boundaries were described, as well as the prejudice of the colonies of small dimensions for those of indeterminate size. This question became acute now, as plans were being made for a nation of States. But the problem in this new guise was correlated with fresh topics of concern. As the end of the Revolutionary War approached, it was confidently believed that the United States would come into possession of a great western territory — that region beyond the Alleghenies which was claimed, paradoxically, in part or in whole by at least six States. Also, be it noted, that Congress at the outset of the war, and again in 1780, had offered bounty lands to all who would enlist in the war for freedom. Where did Congress own any land with which to fulfill such promises? Nowhere. It was little Maryland, so jealous of an unlimited Virginia on the one side and of a gigantic Pennsylvania on the other, which now took the firm stand that all of the vainglorious boasts of "sea-to-sea" dominion, or other indefinite claims, should be abandoned by every State if an harmonious union was to be formed. In fact, she laid down a barrier to any real Union by refusing to sign the Articles of Confederation until all bombastic land claims should be discarded. "If new territory is to be secured by victory over England," said Maryland and her allies, "it must be national territory."

Acquiescence in any such plan by States which had long enjoyed the imperial prize of vast domain is an item in our story of unification not lightly to be passed over. It was the first outstanding illustration of the surrender for common good of (so-called) rights of a material character. Such surrender certainly paved the way for giving up other rights of dearer value — of an ethical and spiritual character. This was a genuine step toward unity. Beginning with the State whose claim was the flimsiest, New York, and coming down the line, each State boasting possession of the trans-Allegheny frontier (with fair reservations) made the surrender, and the Articles of Confederation were announced to have been adopted by the entire roll of States, March 1, 1781.

But surrendered to whom? The pessimists who decried the Congress of Confederation, its powerlessness and inefficiency, had no inkling of the strength which the Faith of the Fathers was now to exemplify when it resolved to issue its famous Promise of Statehood. Revolutions had been precipitated often before; Declarations of Independence had been promulgated on many occasions. But here was something absolutely new. It was doubtless the most "American" thing that any legislative body in the world had ever contemplated up to that hour.

VI

THE PROMISE OF STATEHOOD

An inestimable asset for unity lay in the knowledge that a great, rich frontier kingdom west of the Alleghenies had now come into the possession of the struggling young Republic with the close of the Revolutionary War. The narrow seaboard occupied by the Thirteen Colonies was not only of limited size; it was watered by an ocean on which enemies might come any day for purposes of conquest; a large proportion of the Atlantic coast soil was sand, slate or shale — poor land. While some men were quick to point out that the forbidding ranges of the Alleghenies were difficult to cross even with pack horses on Indian trails, others repeated with eagerness the stories brought back by hundreds of old French War veterans that the soils of the Ohio Basin were inestimably rich; they also said that if the Alleghenies were a formidable barrier for friends they would be an impossible barrier for foes, since they could so easily be defended. The legend that Washington had more than once reminded his men that if the Revolutionary War could not be won along the seacoast he would retire with his faithful to the country behind that mountain wall where the British could never triumph over them was oft repeated. "Washington knows," they said; "he has been there." In many other ways this "Great West" piqued the imagination of men;

a physically growing country offers, in numerous ways, a continuous prospect of new things, new ideas, new inspirations. The growing nation is the one which is always reaching out for objectives — territorial, economic or physical.

This fact became very evident with us when the men and officers of the Continental Army began to think over the bounty-land promises which Congress had made in 1776 and repeated in 1780. The surrender by the claimant States of this western country to the nation put Congress in possession of land with which to fulfill those promises. Thousands of men immediately let their imagination drift over that mountain wall — to their "Castles in Spain" beside the fertile frontiers of the Allegheny, Monongahela, Muskingum, Scioto, Miami and Wabash rivers. By campfire and blazing home-hearth they talked of the "Promised Land", of what Washington and Daniel Boone and George Rogers Clark had seen there. "The United States is going to be a great nation," they said. Pessimists who saw everything "going to the devil" were quick to point out that the barriers of mountain ranges, never less than sixty miles in width, were imperative boundaries of empire and commerce and sympathy; that the flanks of the new territory were guarded by England and Spain; that the Indians were fierce and unconquerable. But the ardent men who now owned "Castles" there were not to be denied even their dream; they had the faith that overcomes mountains.

This view of the case now received remarkable support from the very Congress of which, because of its legal weakness, many men had come to despair. From being only an impotent committee, so to speak, drifting in any direction which its majority willed, and powerless to enforce any decision, this Congress suddenly found itself a landed proprietor, an absolute master over something! It now was owner of a Great West; it could legislate regarding that empire without fear of any veto. Too much has that Congress been judged by its acts in matters over which it had no real control and not enough by its acts in matters like this western frontier, over which it had final authority. In the broad view (unless you are obsessed by the "hind-sight" complex) the handling of this problem by this much-discounted Congress must always stand high in the annals of original legislation. Only a little knowledge of the case will prove how many serious errors and grave mistakes of far-reaching consequence could have been now made by it. It escaped all such errors and laid down a program which has been sincerely admired by all men without exception to this day. It was a showing of nerve, bravery and sound judgment.

You must realize the deep meaning of any act which might now be passed concerning this *first* "Great West." Such legislation formed a precedent of solemn importance. Nothing could now more fundamentally work for unity, coöperation and consolidation as wise and successful legislation on this subject; and surely nothing Congress could do would prove so centrifugal, so disintegrating or so disastrous as to make a mistake in laying down the principles of American expansion. The success of most enterprises depends upon the formation of correct principles of growth and development. In business this is of superlative importance — spelling success or failure.

The first act of this Congress with reference to this national inheritance was wholly novel — as daring as history records. Congress was induced to vote that this new empire, over a quarter of a million square miles in extent, should eventually be divided into States which would (on securing the necessary population) enter the Union as sovereign States on the same terms as the original Old Thirteen. At no point, I believe, in American history, does what we know has happened becloud our vision more than just here. It is necessary, if we would see the splendor of this conception, to take our place in the midst of those men and view the prospect with their limitations. Only so can we appreciate how almost fanatical was their giant faith. Five or six States might thus be created from this new territory. Who would be their citizens? Spaniards? English? French? How could their true allegiance be relied on? Would the great Indian nations remain, be ousted or be assimilated? What expensive wars would not be fought with them? What powerful alliances would they not make with France, England or Spain? It would be a frontier country. How could its twenty-four-hundred-mile border line be securely defended? Its rivers ran in an opposite direction from the parent body, the Old Thirteen. Commerce, since the dawn of history, had followed drainage lines; goods move downstream cheapest. Would not the commerce of the region play straight into the hands of Spain? Who would settle a land thus jeopardized by situation, by hostile neighboring nations, by a commercial future that seemed to drift the wrong way? How could such citizens expect to be nurtured, be succored and defended, from enemies in close proximity, by weak parent States located far across rough mountain ranges?

These, and a score of other nettlesome questions, were suggested by men of faint heart. And if you let Ohio, Indiana, Illinois, Michigan and Wisconsin sink out of sight and mind, and forget all that did happen, it must be admitted that the most those thoughtful Fathers could have done would have been to make it possible for future States to apply to the Union, show their credentials, proofs of loyalty and true Americanism, and request the favor of admission on probation. So all the world had done before them.

But no. The promise was given outright, in "their dark", "In Witness of the Dawn." It bore significant results and created an epoch-making precedent. The immediate result was to force this same Congress into other decisions necessitated by this promise. All this influenced the people, especially all bounty-land holders in the army. Imagination was quickened; high and low were moved to plot and plat and prophesy; in soldiers' tents at Newburgh on the Hudson, in humble cottages in New England and New Jersey, in stately Monticello and Mount Vernon, men drew designs of commonwealths in far-off "Ohio" or "Illinois." This signal act of courage inspired plans for migration; made breaking home ties seem easier; rendered the bugbear, Distance, less formidable; lowered the mountain barrier and smoothed the road. The Flag was going westward! All the protection it could guarantee was to be the emigrant's heritage. He would some day belong to a State with the very same rights as the Old Bay State or the Old Dominion.

These beliefs, called by some "weird hallucinations", were strengthened by the activity of Congress along the line to which it had now committed itself. If new States were in the offing, beyond the mountains, serious business must be transacted. Schemes of government were necessary. The emigrants would be agriculturists and a land system had to be established. Some plan to bridge the mountain barriers was necessary (here the "going-to-the-devil" pessimists laughed loudest) so that commerce would enfold the new with the old States, and link them in the great brotherhood of business. Pens and quills got busy over the interesting speculation of what form government should take in the new country to which men now applied the novel name, "territory."

The coteries into which these State builders fell were two in number, those in one being (so to speak) idealists and those in the other being materialists. The one thought mainly of the political phases of the question; the other of the financial. Long ago Silas Deane in Paris in 1776 pictured that trans-Allegheny country as an Alsace-Lorraine, the capture of which in the Revolutionary War might, by the future sale of its land, recompense the nation for the whole cost of the war. Thomas Paine in 1780 likewise planned a twenty-to-thirty-million-acre State beyond the mountains to be sold for a similar purpose. Most interestingly, this undoubted genius caught one vital phase of the question when, in outlining the commercial development of such a State, he suggested that its produce must move downstream — toward Spain; but he pointed out that, on the other hand, the Mississippi currents forbade manufactured goods from coming up from New Spain; they must therefore come overland from the Atlantic seaboard. By what means this shipment of freight across the mountains was to be effected Paine did not state.

On the other hand, such stalwarts as Pelatiah Webster decried mass sales of land for temporary profit, a short-sighted policy which he compared to killing the goose to get the golden egg; he strongly urged the establishment of the old and tried New England step-by-step system of occupation of the new frontiers by the orderly township system of surveys.

Meanwhile the officers and men in the army camps formed associations to accelerate the progress of Congress in the work of fulfilling its bounty-land promises to them.

In resourcefulness these men were typically Yankee. Who in American history had ever proved this more clearly than their leader, General Rufus Putnam? When the colonists were at their wits' end to oust the British from Boston, Putnam's active mind, tutored by a British manual of engineering, gave his countrymen the solution of the riddle. Entrenchments were to be *built*, not *dug*, on frozen Dorchester Heights! How many volumes tell of the amazement of the enemy at finding the Americans securely fortified over night on that hilltop; but do any of them tell the secret of the maneuver — the adoption of Putnam's plan; of the felling of the Roxbury orchards for the making of the modern crates ("chandeliers") which, merely placed in position and filled with wood, rocks and hay, formed the "entrenchments" which overawed the Redcoats and led to the abandonment of the capital of New England?

The largest of these groups of soldiers, under the leadership of this resourceful Putnam, now urged that a State be created outright for them in "Ohio"; if their bounty lands were to be contiguous, and they could move in a body to occupy them, it was pointed out that numerous difficulties would be immediately settled safely; a patriotic army of soldiers would allay all fears concerning the Americanization of that region; and with these patriots, tried and true, would move reverence for American institutions and traditions — love of religion and education.

We have faithfully performed our duty [ran Putnam's memorial to Congress] as history will record. We come to you now and ask that, in redemption of your promise, you give us homes in that Western wilderness. . . . All we ask is that it be consecrated to us and our children forever with the blessing of that Declaration which, proclaimed to the world and sustained by our arms, established as self-evident that all men are created equal. . . . We will hew down the forests, and therein erect temples to the living God, raise and educate our children to serve and love and honor the nation for which their fathers fought, cultivate farms, build towns and cities, and make that wilderness the pride and glory of the nation.

I know of no prettier illustration than this in American history of that knowledge which was a "dancing chorus of thoughts" and a "quarry of the future" to lead men of faith to fashion a new frontier. The so-called "weakling", "resourceless", "impotent" Congress therefore faced a knotty problem having many sides and aspects. Its decisions would have an immediate effect for a great good or evil; and here, too, it would establish a precedent of vital concern perhaps for generations. But the daring of its first notable decision was now to be supplanted by development of details on an ethical and political par with that initial decision. The first was the decision as to what land system should be adopted; the second was to enforce the method chosen; the third was to settle a frame of government for the territory and put it into action on the ground.

Two systems of handling public lands were prevalent in our country. In the North the New England township system prevailed. It provided for the survey of land into townships and their subdivisions. This preceded sale. The purchaser of land received a title to a distinct area;

its metes and bounds were fixed and known; and he received a title as against both State and neighbor. This system begot regularity, conformity, security to title. In the South the squatter system prevailed under various guises. If Washington's western agent, elsewhere mentioned, found an attractive glade for his employer, he blazed its outline on trees and made a survey of it; Washington filed that survey and got from the governor a patent to it; it gave him title as against the colony or State — but not as against his neighbor. This system had its weak and strong sides. It led to confusion in overlapping titles, neighbor disputing with neighbor, each having a claim to the same land from the State. Courthouses, in Kentucky for instance, were filled with equity suits; Collins, the historian, found seventy thousand of these filed in six courthouses! It was, on the other hand, a good system in colonial days because it inspired initiative — hastening the advance of population in critical days when so many influences retarded it. It begot the first "Go West, Young Man" slogan. It peopled a wild frontier in days when a frontier population was a vital desideratum.

The choice of Congress lay between these two systems. One meant regularity and security — qualities necessary for national harmony and prosperity. The other meant, no doubt, faster expansion, more alacrity in occupying a vast *hinterland*. And beyond the Mississippi lay ever vaster frontiers. Might not this Southern system greatly further the extension of national domain? Whether by accident or planning, the committee of Congress now appointed to propose a national land policy contained a majority of Southern men. It might be supposed the committee would favor the system employed in the South.

But its decision and report to Congress was in favor of the Northern system. The Southern system would have made things easy for Congress. The adoption of the Northern system entailed great burdens. Yet Congress adopted the committee report.

Nothing for the essential unity of jealous, bickering States, now suffering an ominous relapse from the heights to which warlike patriotism had raised them, could have been more salutary than these decisions. If we could weigh measures by Troy weight it would perhaps appear that this new, inspiring western program really did save the day and make unity under a Constitution possible in 1788. Those who believe in the Hand of God in history (and in black crises our Washingtons and Lincolns have universally acknowledged in prayer such a belief, to the dismay of your typical hard-boiled materialist) might well point to the coincidence of the prospect of the dismemberment of the tottering confederacy (when hundreds said we were "going to the devil") and the formation of sane plans for the expansion of the Republic (when hundreds said they were going west) as a signal intervention of Providence.

Two circumstances, one of personal initiative and the other of coöperative action, now played a conspicuous part in these troublesome days to reassure the nation that the boldness of Congress was soundly based.

VII

WHEN FAITH REMOVED MOUNTAINS

THE circumstance of personal initiative just mentioned was the powerful voice of George Washington, who now prophesied a splendid future for the western States-to-be. How much it is to be desired that authors who wish to keep Washington human would study his life with a sense of relative values. Their system of psychology seems to imply that only sordid, sensuous, gluttonous or parsimonious characteristics prove that a man is human. By such a code the important fact about Phidias would be "Did he brush his teeth every morning?" and not "What inspired the dream of the Parthenon?" — and about Lincoln, "Did he have on clean cuffs when he gave the Gettysburg address?" Such gross sensationalism should give way to the abundant facts of constructive nature such as depict, for instance, the Washington of 1784.

He had just refused Lafayette's urgent invitation to cross the seas and visit France. What deep satisfaction would not have come to this Virginia planter, now "the best-known man in the world", could he have received the plaudits of Europe? But his answer was "No" and, instead, he mounted his horse for a last ride into that West where his boyhood battles had been fought. To the youthful heart of thirty years ago (and oh, that some of his biographers could see something human in this!) every glade and mountain had been flecked with romance; he then wrote his mother that one meadow offered a "charming" field for a conflict; that whistling bullets had a "charming" sound. He wrote Braddock begging him not to attack Fort Duquesne until he (Washington) could catch up with the army, as he would not miss the experience for "five hundred pounds!"

With what different eyes did the Victor of Yorktown now look across the same landscape, thirty years later. The storms and stress of war, and the thousand difficulties under which his work had been done, had sobered the gay spirit which once made the lad Washington the humanest of humans. In its place, however, we find a surprising ardor, an enthusiasm, hardly to be expected of him and quite unmatched in any man of his time. He saw the future in terms which few, if any, of his contemporaries understood. His spirit had completely broken its chrysalis-shell of provincialism (and, mind you, he had been so ardent a Virginian in 1758 that General Forbes had written to England in disgust that Washington was "no gentleman") and had now become a nationalist without a peer. During the last year of the Revolutionary War, while in camp at Newburgh, his eagerness to get, at first hand, a glimpse of the wonderful new nation-in-making which he had fought to free, impelled Washington to journey up the beautiful Mohawk Valley. On this tour he was inspired with the splendid prospect of New York's imperial future.

"I could not help," he now wrote, "taking a more extensive view of the vast inland navigation of these United States and could not but be struck by the immense extent and importance of it, and of the goodness of that

Providence which has dealt its favors to us with so profuse a hand. Would to God we may have wisdom enough to improve them."

Such words from such a leader could not but challenge all men of small courage who saw everything going to the devil. The impression of his northern tour determined Washington (whose private interests in the West also needed his attention) to make the journey we have mentioned. But now his eyes rested with intense interest on the western rivers; he saw in them the prospect of accomplishing the impossible; he acquired that faith which, literally, was to remove mountains. It taught him some mighty fundamentals: that a strong nation must be a growing nation; that the surest national unity (in actual practice) was commercial unity; that the people of the narrow seaboard Republic, with its comparatively sterile soil, must be fed by the rich lands of the West; that the ardor of the western peoples for the Republic would "die a-borning" unless lines of trade and commerce bound them closer to the parent States than their natural highways (the Ohio River system) could bind them to Spanish markets on the Mississippi. In imagination he saw water thoroughfares of thriving commerce unite New York's rivers with Lakes Ontario and Erie, and the Pennsylvania and Virginia rivers linked with the finger tips of the Ohio. He saw on these streams the "argosies of magic sails" which should weld our East and West into one homogeneous, prosperous nation.

The Western Settlers [he wrote] — from my own observation — stand as it were on a pivot — the touch of a feather would almost incline them any way — they looked down the Mississippi — because they have no other means of coming to us but by unimproved roads — The way is plain and the expense deserves not a thought, so great would be the prize — It is to open a wide door and make a smooth way for the Produce of that Country to pass to our Markets before the trade may get into another channel — The Western Inhabitants would do their part — weak as they are — rather than be *driven* into the arms of foreigners; the consequence of which would be a separation, or a War —.

In his methodical way, Washington went to the roots of the matter. Like a Roosevelt he hobnobbed with rough denizens of the mountain valleys and coves to learn their lore of the little-known tributaries of the Potomac, James and Susquehanna on the east, which reached out to the Great Divide toward those of the Monongahela, Youghiogheny, Allegheny and Great Kanawha on the west. He followed the buffalo trails of the Mountain Lake Park and Deer Park regions, sleeping in the snow with no covering but his great coat. He plotted the paths of empire in terms of streams unknown to any other man in his homeland. Naturally, he could think in no other terms except those of his era and, therefore, talked of canals, canalized waterways and portage roads. But the later railways were to follow those same lines of least resistance and elevation; and many of the very station names in the time-tables of the Pennsylvania, Erie, New York Central, Baltimore and Ohio and Chesapeake and Ohio railways would be intelligible to George Washington could he rise from his tomb to-day and read them.[1]

[1] Going westward on the Baltimore and Ohio from Washington, D. C., to Pittsburgh, Washington would recognize as familiar such station names as Point of Rocks, Catoctin, Cherry Run, Sir John's Run, Patterson Creek, Cumberland, Cassellman, Ohio Pyle, Jacobs Creek, McKeesport, Braddock and Pittsburgh. He made the first description, from the pen of an Anglo-American, of the present Deer Park and Mountain Lake Park resorts on this railway on the summit of the Alleghenies. On the Pennsylvania Lines west of Harrisburg

Had Washington been an adventurer, an eccentric or even a pure idealist, the great appeal he now made to the nation through Governor Harrison of Virginia could not have had the weight it did. The well-known character of the man made the document timely in its appearance and compelling in its appeal for national unity and cohesion.

"No well-informed mind," he now wrote Harrison, "need be told that the flanks and rear of the western territory are possessed by other powers, and formidable ones too — nor how necessary it is to bind all parts of it together, by one indissoluble bond — particularly the middle [Atlantic] States with the country immediately back of them — for what ties let me ask, should we have upon those people; and how entirely unconnected should we be with them, if the Spaniards on their right or Great Britain on their left . . . should invite their trade and seek alliances with them?" "Open *all* the communications which nature has afforded," he wrote Henry Lee, "between the Atlantic States and the Western territory . . . and sure I am there is no other tie by which they will long form a link in the chain of Federal Union."

Not only was this influential leader sound in his theory that development of transportation was a prime essential to national growth; he was equally certain about other

he would recognize Mifflin, Tyrone, Kittanning Point, Conemaugh, Latrobe; and on the various lines west of Pittsburgh he would know the historical associations of such station-names as Beaver Junction, Yellow Creek, Mingo Junction, Salineville, Cuyahoga, Upper Sandusky, Fort Wayne, Steubenville, Pipe Creek, Mahoningtown, Shenango, Killbuck, Coshocton and scores of others. On the New York Central Lines he would recognize every old-time station-name in the Hudson and Mohawk valleys, as Schenectady, Johnson, Little Falls, Canajoharie, Wyoming, etc., etc. In many cases, were he to leave a modern train at towns newly named, as Franklin, Erie, Grafton, Terra Alta, Wheeling, Greensburg, Bedford, Parkersburg, Point Pleasant, Utica, he would know his way about as soon as he could get a bird's-eye view of his surroundings.

things concerning which some men had lively doubts. For instance, he was confident that the new West would soon acquire a great population. "There are," Washington pointed out, "at least 100,000 Souls West of Laurel hill [the most westerly range of the Alleghenies in Pennsylvania]; . . . the spirit of emigration is great. People have got impatient, and, though you cannot stop the road, it is yet in your power to make the way; a little while and you will not be able to do either." [1]

Also he was equally confident of its immense agricultural wealth. In imagination he took his stand at Detroit, Michigan, and pointed out the routes by which splendid cargoes of western grain could reach the Atlantic seaboard. This was done so minutely that the actual mileages Washington gave need little altering to-day to be made somewhat correct.[2] He also saw an era of growth

[1] A. B. Hulbert, "Washington and the West", 104, 189.

[2] The following is Washington's outline of inland water route from Detroit to New York City in 1784:

From Detroit to Albany
is

To Fort Erie, at the N end of Lake Erie	350	
Fort Niagara — 18 miles of wch is Land transpn	30	380
Oswego		175
Fall of Onondaga River	12	
Portage	1	
Oneida Lake by Water	40	
Length of D° to Wood Ck	18	
Wood Ck very small and crooked	25	
Portage to Mohawk	1	97
Down it to the Portage	60	
Portage	1	
Schenectady	55	
Portage to Albany	15	131
In all		783
To the City of New York		160
Total		943

of the Ohio River commerce which probably no other Atlantic American of his day visioned. He stated now, in 1784, that ocean-rigged vessels would be passing down the two thousand-mile track of the Ohio and Mississippi to the Atlantic, carrying the produce of that great rich section to all ports of the world; such ocean-rigged vessels were built on the Ohio and crossed the Atlantic within eighteen years, as we shall see.

Washington's firm optimism was a factor [1] for unity in these troublesome days which spread a healthful influence

[1] Friends of the present writer have frequently suggested that he make some formal reply to criticisms passed on his writings on Washington by Rupert Hughes in the latter's much-discussed "George Washington." I have not done so for two reasons: nothing is gained by answering criticisms; and, again, the reply I would make would not meet the expectations of friends. A generation ago McMaster said we were by way of keeping the President and the General but that George Washington "is or soon will be an unknown man." It is only an asset to history that one of Mr. Hughes' literary skill and great audience should aid us in keeping the man Washington. Doubtless when his book is a generation old (as are mine which he criticizes) he would be glad to alter some words and phrases, especially if he wrote in days when, to him, everything was "charming." Only in one instance in particular would I object to his perfectly honest strictures. I refer to his minimizing the significance of the *Journal* which Washington wrote out overnight, after his return from the French forts in northwestern Pennsylvania. I still believe that very few college-trained boys to-day could, from rough notes, in a very few hours, and while physically and mentally unfit for literary composition, prepare so well-poised and clearly expressed a document of ten thousand words in length. It is a little beside the point for Mr. Hughes to say, in minimizing the performance, that the facts related were not new — *although they were novel enough to justify publishing at once both in England and in France.* I deem the feat, under those circumstances, performed by a young man who had had almost no educational training (so called) to be the most significant fact of his life up to that time. So much by way of a reply to a specific criticism. As to Mr. Hughes' general criticism of my "Washington and the West", my reply, after twenty-four years of additional study, is this present chapter, in which every point made in that book is reaffirmed and every deduction is emphasized even more pointedly. I do not overlook or underestimate Washington's landed interest in the West; more, probably, than any writer, have I exploited that element of

in more directions than could be counted. He had steadied a people's hope in the blackest days of war; now in peace he became no less a leader in pointing the way to expansion as the best assurance of future unity and development. "Be a Nation" was the burden of his message.

The coöperative movement which, I have said, supplemented this one of personal initiative, was very largely inspired by Washington's faith; for it was promoted by his captains in the late war and with his heartiest recommendation. The officers who became associated under General Rufus Putnam (in 1783) at Newburgh were unable to secure from Congress the grant of a western State on the terms they proposed; Congress could not act in the matter until it had previously determined both a land system and a policy of government. As these men now returned to their homes they in no wise forgot that dream of a western inheritance which they had been promised. One group of these men (including the Chairman, General Rufus Putnam) lived in the vicinity of

perfectly honest self-interest on Washington's part. But this does not blind me to the fact that the Master of Mount Vernon saw probable western development in a clearer light than most of his contemporaries, nor to the significance of the fact that he called every State's attention to the duty of opening its waterways toward the West in order that, by improved commercial connections, we might have "a more perfect union." Mr. Hughes is helping us to keep George Washington; he may change his opinion as to relative values as days go by; he may wish he had paid more attention to the great constructive influences exerted by Washington and less to whimsical idiosyncrasies which are relatively unimportant and which arouse pique and phlegm. And yet here a service may be rendered, especially if facts are used for the purpose of showing that Washington *grew up;* if he did that, he was human, he was real and influences lives; if not, he was a "God", removed from the field of common human experiences, unaffected by the facts of life with which we must all contend, and of vital importance only as a paragon, a marble image. This I have elaborated elsewhere under the title "The Washington We Forget."

Boston and were bound together by the ties of Masonry. In their lodge the plan of a coöperative association of emigrants was talked over and kept alive.[1] Meanwhile events were occurring that favored their plan.

In 1784 Congress appointed a committee to plan a scheme of government for the West. Hand in hand with this work another committee formulated a Land Law which described exactly how a beginning should be made to survey the West into townships and how land offices should be established to carry on the sale. Thus a scheme for the disposal of the land beyond the Alleghenies for the benefit of the national government was adopted.

This news aroused in the Revolutionary officers under General Putnam new efforts to secure a tract of land in partnership. They changed their method of procedure. Instead of asking the government to exchange their bounty-land claims and hard-earned, but almost worthless, certificates (soldier's pay checks) for land, they planned to bulk all these credits in order to form the capital stock of a land company and, with it, purchase of the government the desired land. This change of method was wise and well-timed.

It was wise because it placed these Revolutionary soldiers and the government in the way of dealing with each other on a business basis. These soldiers now appeared, not as beggars demanding that a promise be fulfilled, but as a business corporation proposing a contract — and with assets behind them of potential value.

It was well-timed because, at the moment, Congress was engaged in a very important debate over establishing firm government in the West. The original plans for such a government had been amended into a notable

[1] A. B. Hulbert (ed.), *The Records of the Ohio Company*, I, xlii–xliv.

ordinance. This now-famous Ordinance of 1787 proposed a plan of government and included a bill of rights which set a precedent as important as any American history records. But Congress, in its debates, was talking about a frontier in which no Americans lived — a wilderness. Who should put government into operation there? Who should hold up the hands of the proposed governor — enforce the ready-made laws — enjoy and guard the bill of rights? Who, indeed, but these very soldiers of the Revolution, men of unquestioned bravery and loyalty, who had already prophesied that they could "make that Wilderness the pride and glory of the nation?" They, on the one hand, needed firm government in the West if they carried out their plan of migration and settlement; no less, on the other hand, did the government need loyal men and true in the West in order to carry out its plan of extending American rule into the new frontier.

Such, in bare outline, is the story of the formation of the Ohio Company of Associates and the adoption by Congress of the Ordinance of 1787 and the formal erection of the territory northwest of the river Ohio. A million and a half acres of land were sold to these Associates — and with them, across the mountains, went the new governor of the territory, to be inaugurated at the Ohio Company's little wilderness-fortress, at Marietta, Ohio, in July, 1788. Great good was accomplished by Washington in his notable appeal to the nation to look westward with pride, confidence and boldness. It was a case of individual initiative of greatest importance. But from some standpoints the advance from New England of this coöperative movement of well-known Revolutionary officers, the Putnams, Greenes, St. Clairs, Whipples, Tuppers, Winthrops, Varnums and Parsons, carrying in their hands the famous Ordinance of 1787 was of greater importance.[1]

Despite the bungling, misadventures and peculation involved in some phases of this Ohio episode (anent Joel Barlow's selling lands in Europe for a non-existent Scioto Company which had never paid anything, even on an option) the resultant effect was to make all men say "Washington was right." Every step those New Englanders took westward formed a solid "link in the chain of Federal union." They turned a people's face westward. A study of the Atlantic seaboard press of these, and succeeding, years shows a surprising growth of companies and associations formed for the purpose of migration and settlement. The rush which followed into the Ohio Valley — at which so many looked askance in the days when Washington was writing to Governor Harrison — is clearly indicated by the mere fact that Ohio was admitted into the Union (1803) only fifteen years after Marietta, Ohio, was made the capital of the Northwest Territory.

Meanwhile a chain of events of epoch-making importance was bringing the States to recognize the hopelessness of creating a firm Union under the limited Articles of Con-

[1] Singular it is that the most famous writer, in some respects, on American political life, James Bryce, all but ignored the Ordinance of 1787 in his great study. In the main text he observes that the Convention of 1787 paid little attention to methods of extending government across the Allegheny Mountains. To this remark is subjoined a footnote of eighteen words in which the Ordinance of 1787 is dismissed with the mere adjective "great." On other pages the impotence of the Continental Congress is outlined at length. The reader is left to guess how such a Congress could have passed a "great" Ordinance. Webster paid this tribute to it: "I doubt if any law of any lawgiver ancient or modern has produced effects of such lasting value"; and of it Andrew C. McLaughlin wrote: "It was one of the wisest documents ever issued by a deliberative assembly."

federation. As a background sponsor in this splendid process Washington was, also, a leader of prescience and amiability. To help smooth out the age-long quarrel over tariffs between Maryland and Virginia his part was vital. In organizing a joint company for the improvement of the Potomac River, Washington had given a new impulse (with a fresh goal in sight) to interstate coöperation. To assuage the tariff question, he called a meeting of friends at Mount Vernon. Immediately was it seen that the compromise on the tariff question necessitated other compromises and that, to secure such, a meeting of delegates from other colonies was needful. This led to the notable Annapolis Convention to consider the state of the nation. In turn this assembly soon realized the enormity of the great problem, the need of complete representation of all the colonies and the need of the advice and deep loyalty of the nation's wisest men. By such a course the Constitutional Convention of 1787 came into existence — to forge forever the chain of Federal Union of our United States.

It is not our province here to do more than to make the great event of the adoption of the Constitution of the United States appear (as sometimes it does not) as a culmination of a long process. Hardly a single force or influence exerted of a centrifugal character in the long story of the making of the Americans but was now voiced by some pessimist at some time in those torrid summer convention days at Philadelphia. And surely no centripetal influence, working for unity and harmony, but was brought to bear on the discussions that were waged. In the hard school of adversity under the weakly empowered (but not weakly spirited) Congress, real lessons had been learned. In forming and operating State constitutions, experience had been acquired. The western movement had inspired the sense of new nationality. Before the bulk of such argument, adroitly advanced by the Jays, Hamiltons and Madisons, reinforced by the Washingtons and Franklins (whose influence perhaps was more effective because they did not make speeches), the friends of centralized power and firm government won over those who stood for a radical independence which would never have brought real unity.

Considering the great world-influence of the American Constitution it is exceedingly singular that it presented but one genuine novelty in ideas of government, a Supreme Court with nullifying powers. Yet, on the other hand, nothing proves more clearly than this what a victory had been won for liberty. Practically every plan proposed in it had somewhere been tried — somewhere succeeded — somewhere failed — somewhere been discarded as inefficient or dangerous. A chief executive, for instance, had never seemed desirable for Congress or Confederation, but the office had proven a success in some State governments. Systems of checks and balances over executive, legislative and judicial departments had been tried, successfully and unsuccessfully. Both one and two Houses of Legislature had been on trial in the States. Large States who complained at the power men now proposed to give small States, knew what they were talking about; some of them had refused proper representation locally in State legislatures to large outlying counties. Hardly a single discussion in that notable assembly but had, in one form or another, attracted the attention of men and been debated in earlier days. We think of our Constitution as having been *made;* but James Bryce has gone so far as to say that it "is almost as truly the matured result of long and gradual historical development as the English Constitution itself."

It was typical of the new spirit of compromise for the sake of unity that the heated debate over allowing equal representation in a Senate and proportional representation in a House of Representatives came to a satisfactory end. It was typical, too, that, as in forming the Declaration of Independence, questions (on States' rights, for instance) over which no agreement could ever have been reached were allowed, like sleeping dogs, to lie. This has been called a blunder. To sympathize with that view one must agree that a longer period would have to lapse ere a constitution could be adopted; and also to admit that the risk that no compromise on it could ever have been reached was a good risk, at this time, to run. I cannot agree to these things.

The result was the adoption and final ratification of the Constitution and the forging of the links of Federal Union which have served our nation to these times. It was an outgrowth of a long-developing spirit of unity. The ultimate success of our American experiment in self-government in the generations to come must be answered by our children's children to the tenth and twentieth generations. But it is the thesis of this book that only by encouraging the self-same spirit of unity, by means of an alert but patriotic coöperation, can the experiment be the success which the memory of its wise founders deserves.

Since the adoption of the American Constitution, that greatest document, according to Professor Channing, that man has yet written, amid all the astounding developments of nearly a century and a half, much has been done to reassure the world that our Fathers builded well when they signed its final page — "in the dark, in witness of the Dawn."

PART TWO
"BE AMERICAN"

VIII

THE EMERGENCE OF HIDDEN FORCES

SANGUINE indeed one would be, if not wantonly arrogant, to try even to catalogue all the factors which have made the United States a unity in these six generations since our Constitution was adopted. Many and many of these have been treated at large by experts. But it is not impossible, following the line of that last command from Mount Vernon, to analyze some of the ways in which we have, consciously and unconsciously, been true to the command: "Be American." Perhaps the chief art of patriotism (in contrast to cracker-box theories) is to see through the meanness and pettiness of everyday life — our "night" — and be inspired by the potent fundamentals. Too often, forsooth, are we like the Eastern lady who once rented a summer home in the exquisite Broadmoor environ of Colorado Springs. Behind her rose peak upon peak of snow-lit beauty; before her lay the grandeur of a hundred thousand acres of plain, flecked with constantly changing islands of shadows, gorgeous in their bewildering transformations. When asked how she liked her location she replied, "I don't like it a bit; you can't see out one way and there's nothing to see out the other."

The cares of the world and the deceitfulness of riches or poverty tend to give us all eyes that see not and ears that do not hear. And one of the most interesting things to see in all the world to-day, as the Great War proved, is the fundamental unity of our country. Among the catch phrases most used by our calamity-howlers is the fact that we are "going the way of all the earth"; and frequently are we asked to pause and consider the tottering and crumbling nations of the past, the decay of Greece and the fall of Rome, in order to see exactly what we are coming to. Any who thus wrongly read history cannot "go to the devil" too quickly for the best interests of posterity. Nothing is more alive to-day than the actual assets which Greece bequeathed to the world before she "decayed", or than those Rome gave before it "fell." So far as they can be said to have "fallen", it was due, as Rostovtzeff clearly points out, to their inability to transfer the benefits of civilization from classes to the masses. And that author closes his great work with the query: "Is not every civilization bound to decay as soon as it begins to penetrate the masses?" Much depends on your evaluation of words; for what Rostovtzeff terms "decay" is described by Ferrero as "emergence" when he says: "The law of life was the same then as it has been in all ages . . . the great men . . . were the plaything of what in history we can name Destiny, though it is nothing more than the unforseen coincidence of events, the emergence into action of hidden forces which, in a complex and disordered society such as that of Rome or of our own day, no contemporary can be expected to discern."

The numerous similes we have offered from the various sciences to show the likeness of the laws of *all* life testify, every one of them, to the emergence theory in the insensate, physical world; yet if the maple *knew* that its business was to grow strong where it is, not somewhere else, develop all its powers in its own environment — not some other environment — and be preëminently centripetal in its every fiber, could it be any more lavish in carrying out its other mission, namely, to personify the centrifugal as it sends its seeds out to all the world? Although those seeds may illustrate every centrifugal passion in leaving "home" — practice every art of separatism, every dogma of particularism — the most delicate instruments of science we know cannot find in their tiniest organism or cell one throb of life which does not chant the paean "Be a Maple."

Our remaining chapters will deal with phases of this development of the emergence principle which was so instinct with the call to "Be American." If our topics do not always correlate themselves one to another it is because the hope has been to present types of the processes at work. Men who cried out at the danger of planting frontiers little dreamed that those frontiers were to perform a more "terrible" function still — create new ones! We shall also follow the seed of a family tree repeating the lesson of the maple; see the unconscious laying of a basis for a great industrial nation by those who broke open dusty trails and those who laid steel rails; and note the emergence, from an utterly unsuspected source, of an ethical theory which to-day makes possible the integrity of that enormously busy nation. Introductory to those divisions of our subject, I would point out two specific instances of emergence; they are unrelated, in a way, and have no chronological connection; but both illustrate how delightfully unconscious a people may be of the greater things which happened as, on the one hand, they fought for the physical conquest over Nature, and, on the other, how, amid sectional jealousy and rivalry and even internecine warfare, and from the very depths of despair, a common bond of intense respect — almost affection — could be forged.

How close might be the relationship of character-making to mastering a physical inheritance is vividly apparent when you ask foreigners for a definition of our outstanding American trait. Eagerly we are reminded of the skeleton in our closet. We are big. We love bigness, ostentation, braggadocio, showiness; quality with us is of less consequence than quantity. All this and much more our critics and rivals gleefully reiterate. Little do they dream, and nonchalantly do we forget, the root of this matter — how inherently such predilections were bound up with us in Mother Earth's womb; and how the business of planting frontiers on this continent made such ominous characteristics emerge.

A man doing a real work necessarily becomes a part of that work; the tools used crease his hands; the grime, perhaps, discolors his features and clothes; worry seams his face — whether he is building a half-faced camp in the Ozarks or a railway merger in Wall Street. Rarely has the physical cost of our job of continental conquest been properly estimated, nor has its effect upon us as a people — for better or worse — been satisfactorily appraised. Little attention has been paid, on the one hand, to the lack of our forefathers' mental training for the mastery of a continent three thousand miles wide, or, on the other, to their lack of conditioning for the work; in fact, behind all this lay a seeming handicap in the shape of inherited traits which made for slow, careful building, rather than the blithe, care-free penchant for hurrying hither and yon which dominated their rivals from Old France.

Is it not extraordinary that beside the names of Brulé, Champlain, La Salle, Cadillac, Frontenac, Joliet, Marquette, Radisson, Grosielliers, Brébeuf, Lalamont and a score of other French explorers in America you can write no contemporaneous Nordic name? The valiant Captain John Smith pierced the "continent" — as far as the White Oak Swamp in Virginia where, one day, a brave Stonewall Jackson should be killed! The bold Lederer threaded mountain fastnesses until he believed that he had found water flowing into the Pacific Ocean. He had reached a tributary of the Ohio River! The hardy Batts explored the "continent's interior" — and we know now that he gained only the summit of the Potomac bluffs at Harper's Ferry! "Our country has now been inhabited more than 130 years by the English," wrote Colonel William Byrd of Virginia in 1728, "and still we hardly know anything of the Appalachian Mountains, that are nowhere above two hundred fifty miles from the sea." One wonders why the good Colonel did not explore them. It was not for lack of venturesome blood in the family stock; for Mary Byrd gave George Rogers Clark to Illinois and William Clark to the Columbia; and the brother of our own Governor Byrd is the hero of Arctic and Antarctic aero-exploration!

But tiny England itself, the homeland of those "stuffy", "stay-at-home" American pioneers, as the French dubbed them, was itself little mastered at the time. Queen Elizabeth was congratulated over being thrown out of her chariot only once while making an inland "progress"; and noblemen's sons were sent to school over narrow trails a-horseback, with outriders testing the water holes and marshes with long poles to find where a crossing was safe! What training had such men for overcoming the

Alleghenies, the Mississippi, the Rockies and towering Sierras? But note; there was unity even in this "sluggishness" at which Frenchmen (a-slapping their strong thighs) laughed. The English borders everywhere spread in singular unison. New England was not much outrun by Maryland or Virginia. Solid building was the rule for a century and a half. And when the thrusts across the Allegheny wall came, only some ten years separated the advance of Virginians into Kentucky and that of Yankees into the Ohio Valley!

Oddly enough, no sooner had the nation come to itself, and Independence had been secured, than did the self-made penchant for continental mastery become a passion — not, however, without arousing alarm in many quarters. "All the passions which are most fatal to republican institutions," said the pessimists, quoting an Old World theorist, "increase with an increasing territory; the love of country, which ought to check these destructive agencies, is not stronger in a large than in a small republic." Echoes of this resounded, faintly, when the northwest frontier was secured from Great Britain along with Independence. In homely phraseology, the young Republic already was said to be "biting off more than it could chew." The purchase of Louisiana brought a shrill outcry — with many "Down Easterners" threatening to carry New England out of the Union and form a republic of their own! Another lunge and Florida was ours; then Texas, California and Oregon. Those were not lacking, indeed, in the "days of gold" to prove with figures that the possession of California in 1849 was far from being an unmitigated blessing. H. R. Helper (the optimistic name of a pessimistic man) took pains to show that in labor and capital the East lost upward of half a billion dollars through migration to the Pacific Coast; and that when the value of all gold found was deducted, the East was loser by about two hundred million dollars. Numerous details of this story — "glorious" to many, "absurdly preposterous" to others — it will be our business to outline on later pages. Our concern at the moment is to note the character-influencing forces produced by those lunges forward.

The gist of the thing is here. Each successive physical task, forced by the exigencies of the case upon our people, was greater than the last. The illustrations of this follow in fast sequence. Little mountains, rivers, animals, grasses, trees, deserts, plains, mines, lakes always gave way to greater, as the western progress went on. Reverse the case and you get the point. If our fathers who planned roads, canals and railways had mastered the Sierras first (transplanting that range, in imagination, to Pennsylvania and Virginia), with what ease would the Rockies, the Alleghenies and the Berkshires have been handled later! If the Columbia, Colorado and Mississippi had been bridged first, how simple would have been the bridging of the James, Connecticut and Hudson! If the vast western deserts had been first overcome, how insignificant would have been the "York Barrens" or the Pine Barrens of Virginia or eastern New York or New Jersey! If the great plains had first been mastered, how simple would have been the mastery of the glades of the Alleghenies and the beaver meadows of New England!

But it was always the other way. The easier tasks came first. Spanning the Berkshires or Alleghenies with railways brought the experience needed for the Rockies and towering Sierras. Bridging the Connecticut and Susquehanna taught men how to bridge the Ohio and Mississippi. Developing the smaller Eastern meadows, "oak openings" and glades, paved the way for mastering the greater vistas of the Central States, and this task made the invasion of the great plains seem less hazardous. Fashioning the boundary lines of smaller States in the East was succeeded by running the lines for giant States beyond the Mississippi.

At every step westward men met the imperative challenge of greater distances and harder tasks. It aroused their initiative, their courage, their hardihood. The one-horse plow or rake or reaper gave way to great engines for plowing, raking and reaping. Men, we have said, became a part of their work. Americans became a part of their giant task of continental mastery; they were compelled to dream constantly bigger dreams; they were forced to overcome constantly greater handicaps — open constantly greater farms, build constantly greater roads, canals and railways. The process became a part of them. They thought in terms of bigness; it became their obsession. Blue grass never blossomed more spontaneously from limestone soil, cactus never came to life more naturally from sterile desert, than did this skeleton in our closet — crass worship of bigness — become a national characteristic. Ignorance as to its imperative naturalness makes it seem a gross, uncultured, reprehensible thing; but a realization of its place in the orderly sequence of our national phenomena makes it seem splendid because it is a direct and natural fruit of performing our first great duty — frontiering.

To paraphrase an Eastern legend, the "scroll of a nation's fate is bound about its neck at birth." Fate gave us and our children this continent to occupy. Nothing makes for harmony — in a family, factory or nation —

like bending heartily to a great task; although every one's task may not be of the same nature, all are working for the same end. Nothing unified the Children of Israel like the rebuilding of Jerusalem. Nothing unified Belgium so much as reconstructing its devastated areas. Nothing more completely unified America than the common enthusiasm, earnestness and initiative for the great task of continental mastery which conditioned our having so unique a republic of continental dimensions. "Millions of men are marching at once towards the same horizon," wrote a clear-thinking man in 1833, of American expansion; "their language, their religion, their manners differ; their object is the same." In their heart of hearts our people gloried in the victory of "Clinton's Ditch" over the swamps of old New York, in the rich blossoming of a Kentucky blue-grass region, in the planting of a firm Chicago on the shifting dunes of a lake shore; in My Antonia's growing that first crop of wheat on her Nebraska "mountain", in the completion of a transcontinental railway, in the recovery of an Imperial Valley from its Gila monster sterility.

"Never, indeed, it would seem," Owen Wister exclaimed, "have such various centuries been jostled together as they are to-day upon this continent. We have taken the ages out of their processional arrangement and set them marching disorderly abreast in our wide territory, a harlequin platoon." Love of bigness was our doom and our pride. But out of it emerged an astonishingly virile love of country, pride in its growth, confidence in its integrity.

Yes, and more vitally than even friend or critic often realizes. For in the emergence of such Americanism were there not ever present the obstacles of old, the jangling of interests, the rivalries of sections? Was this not always true, both on a small scale as well as on a big? How fondly proud were men of their own clans, upon whom irascible neighbors looked with suspicion if not with disdain! While dressing in the morning my father used to "sing":

> "All to the borders, Vermonters come down,
> In your jackets of buckskin and breeches of brown."

Passing the question (although at times it occurred to me) of what raiment a college president could boast that it should lead him to break out in song o' mornings, I wrongly supposed that it was red coats or red skins which made the Vermont pioneers rally. But I learned in time that it was to black the eyes or crack the heads of Hampshire "thieves" on one side, or of New York "cutthroats" on the other. The affection of the Green Mountain men for these neighbors of theirs reminds me of the brotherly love that was wasted between some Kansans and Missourians a few decades later. Vermonters took great pride in their own stock. Speaker Champ Clark felt equal pride in the men of his Missouri frontier when he said:

"All Missourians were native of Virginia, North Carolina, Kentucky and Tennessee. They were the flowers of their respective stocks — the salt of the earth — courageous, hardy, intelligent, honest, industrious, honorable, patriotic and God-fearing . . . the finest specimens of manhood and womanhood betwixt the two oceans."

But Senator Ingalls of Kansas saw the frontier Missourians in another light. He said that that part of Missouri was a place "where climate, products, labor and tradition have conspired to develop a race of hard-visaged and forbidding ruffians, exhibiting a grotesque medley of all the vices of civilization. To these fallen angels villainy is an amusement, crime a recreation, murder a pastime. To the ignorance of the Indian they add the ferocity of the wolf and the venom of the adder. . . . Their continued existence is a standing reproach to the New Testament, to the doctrines of every apostle, to the creed of every church."

The art of hating has certainly not kept pace with the other arts. Were Miss Martineau to return to America she would not hear to-day, as she did a century ago, Philadelphia ladies aver that Baltimore ladies would never learn how to put on a bonnet; nor meet a Boston citizen who was ready to take oath that Cincinnatians did not eat "sitting down like Christians."

The Missouri-Kansan border story serves as a reminder that no European can hear American unity mentioned without citing the Civil War as one of the most bitter episodes of internecine conflict known to history. This we must, of course, look into, later, but it is in point now to mention that an Americanism emerged from that struggle — hard though it would be for a foreigner to understand its full significance. A group of Ohio boys had been wont to float flatboat cargoes down the Ohio and Mississippi to the old South before the war. After 1865 they expected to give up this lucrative commerce, but essayed to make one experiment by carrying with them as a passenger a neutral "Copperhead" agent to do the dickering with their erstwhile foes. Never was a greater tactical blunder made. "Where are you from, stranger?" "Which side did you fight on?" "Why did n't you fight for the Yanks?" "Then why 'n hell did n't you come and fight for us?" Such was the Copperhead's greeting — and, with cries of "quitter" and "black leg", reinforced with stones and brickbats, he was harried back to the refuge of the flatboat. A "Yank", who had met the rebel yell at Shiloh, Stone River and Vicksburgh, now hesitatingly attempted to sell peach brandy and wheat where once he had peddled only bullets. "Hello, pard, what was your regiment?" was his greeting. "Stone River? No! Sho! Put 'er there! We made you smell hell fire and you made us drink brimstone an that 's God's truth!" They were instantly comrades — welded together in the memory of a mighty courage each knew the other had possessed! The war proved to the North that, behind a sword-eating, swashbuckling bravado, the South could produce leaders hard, if not impossible, to match, and a self-sacrifice worthy of the purest cause for which men ever fought. It proved to the South that, to her surprise, the North thought less of money-making and profits than it did of "union and liberty, one and inseparable, now and forever." What a remarkable emergence was this — of loyalty to race, to tradition, to a common country! Where else could it have happened?

That question provokes another: "How has Europe fared meanwhile — its Vermonts, Missouris and New Yorks?" How much have its Chinese Walls of jealousy been battered down? Its bottomless wells of hatred filled up? Its vicious policies of trickery and duplicity reformed? "They neither understand each other better," said Maurice Muret, speaking even of the present European States, "nor feel more kindly toward one another. . . . Europe has never known such disorder as since the democratic spirit has tried to divide it according to the principle of nationalities." Only yesterday did the Boston *Transcript* say, relative to a long-mooted international engineering problem involving the most advanced of

European countries: "Americans who enjoy the fruits of untrammelled economic development can only look on regretfully at the failure of the old world to sink the prejudices and fears which balk an object so transparently for the advancement of many interests." In essence Europe has changed, if at all, only slightly; some would say, not at all. Ferrero, pointing out that hatreds such as persist in Europe are unknown in America, explains those of the Old World as resulting from nations being closely crowded together, and from the age-old caste systems which have limited individual freedom and engendered ill will. Nothing in Napoleon's career is more interesting than his blind fumbling with the cardboard nations which, for some strange reason, would not go together to make a United States of Europe! "Out of each of these peoples," he said, "I wanted to make a united national whole. . . . That would have supplied the best chance of establishing a general unity of laws; a unity of principles and thoughts and feelings, of outlooks and interests. . . . Then it would have been possible to think of founding the United States of Europe after the model of the United States of America. . . . Sooner or later this union will be brought about by force of events." But at that time the chief "force of events" was the inordinate ambition of the builder — Napoleon himself. The one specific instance of Europe's actually adopting something distinctively American was in the case of Switzerland which modeled so closely upon our Constitution and then left out the one distinctively American thing in it — a Supreme Court with nullifying powers — being accustomed, as Gallieur puts it, "for centuries to invest the State with omnipotent authority."

I like the utter frankness in one of Owen Wister's outbursts in his very first book: "But, oh, my friends, what a country we live in, and what an age, that the same Stars and Stripes should simultaneously wave over this [Gila] Valley and over Delmonico's." There are lessons for mankind in the processes which have brought these changes since the brief "yesterday" when the Great Virginian said: "Be American." The movement has ever followed the rule of "cell" reaching out to vivify "cell" — the physiologist's law of the dominant gradient. Or, a scientist has expressed the idea that before there is a heart in the human embryo a palpitation takes place where the heart is going to be. Something suggested by those processes became a fact when the "Babel Towers" on eastern frontiers went down, because of sterile soil, over-population or the lure of new countries, and scattered the atoms of different races and languages which soon began fresh building. Palpitation occurred in the wildernesses of Kansas — Oregon — California, where a heart was going to be. That story is as bewildering as human nature, as fantastic, as bizarre.

IX

FRONTIERS BREED FRONTIERS

"The West" was always a common phrase in American parlance from the very beginning of colonial life on the Atlantic seaboard. No sooner did the members of Hooker's church at Newtown stride off across the Worcester hills to the Connecticut Valley than "a West" was established — to be looked upon askance by many a person in a smug, conservative, older settlement on or near the Atlantic Coast; and, conversely, a new, raw, uncouth frontier community came into existence in a "Land of Do Without", which looked with a kind of proud commiseration backward upon an "effete East" seventy miles away!

The story of the American Republic, territorially speaking, has been the story of the planting of one "West" after another, from the Atlantic to the Pacific; and, in a measure, the political history of our Republic has been the story of reactions of "Wests" on "Easts", or vice versa, with reference to almost every problem of national life. Therefore what was "West" and what was "East" was almost always, and is yet, a matter of personal viewpoint. To many a typical "Down Easterner" anything beyond the Hudson is the "West" to-day; to the sons of the Middle Border nothing is really "West" until the Great Plains are reached; while a friend of mine, hailing from Bellingham, Washington, remarked to me within the year: "When I cross the Rockies and get off the train at Denver I can tell where I am by my nose — it just *smells* East." And all the antipathy of East to West or West to East to-day can be found reproduced in what was said by the "Boston people" concerning the "Connecticut people", or vice versa, two hundred ninety-two years ago; no clergyman ever came nearer swearing than did the Reverend Mr. Hooker when he tried to describe, in language which reeked of Biblical phrases, what he thought of the outrageous fibs told in Boston about the Connecticut Valley.

From our point of view nothing is more interesting in our history, and nothing surely is more human, than the sectional antipathies produced by the creation of one West after another across our longitudes; they are so real, so honest; the contrasts so hit the newcomer, from whatever section he hailed, in the face. Not long ago I met a sojourner from "mine own people" of Yankeeland who had whiled away a space of time in Montana with no more satisfaction with the view, or the memory of it, than had the lady I mentioned who rented the Broadmoor home under Pike's Peak. "There are more square miles and less land," he mourned, "more cattle and less beef, more to look at and less to see in Montana than any State in all the world." I was once playing cards in a Pullman, while making the transcontinental journey, with friends of many years' standing. As I reached to raise the window curtain which had been lowered to keep out sunlight the wife of a well-known university professor seized my coat sleeve firmly. "Don't you dare raise that curtain," she said impatiently; "if I have to see any more of those dreary plains I'll trump every ace you play." The rebuke had an interesting effect on me. I had just recently taken my children to Sunday School in Boston, in a church known around the world, after quite an absence from my homeland. I accepted a hearty invitation to be a guest in an advanced class of grown-ups. It consisted of at least sixty elderly people. To illustrate the day's lesson, which appertained to keeping the heart clean with all diligence, the silver-haired leader took from beneath the speaker's stand a ten-cent tin washbasin and with it a cardboard heart, "all done 'round with woolen yarn." "You must wash the heart," he harangued the class, dousing the cardboard into the empty tin, "wash the heart, wash the heart." I felt a peculiar sympathy now for the good unacclimated lady who was afraid she would lose her mind on the plains — out of tune with environment; if that man had "washed" that heart just once more. . . .

What is strange usually seems uncouth, if not forbidding. No spectacle in America was so uniformly commented upon by travelers in pioneer days as tawdry and desolate, as were the fields covered with the stumps of felled trees. It takes an out-of-the-ordinary person to look upon what others deem an "eyesore" and *see into it* magic pictures which forever haunt the brain. Such was the incomparable Dickens — looking at one of those slaughter fields (as so many had visioned and described them) in Northern Ohio:

> These stumps of trees are a curious feature in American travelling [he wrote]. The varying illusions they present to the unaccustomed eye as it grows dark, are quite astonishing in their number and reality. Now, there is a Grecian urn erected in the center of a lonely field; now there is a woman weeping at a tomb; now a very commonplace old gentleman in a white waistcoat, with a thumb thrust into each arm-hole of his

coat; now a student poring over a book; now a crouching negro; now a horse, a dog, a cannon, an armed man; a hunchback throwing off his cloak and stepping forth into the light. They were often as entertaining to me as so many glasses in a magic lantern, and never took their shapes at my bidding, but seemed to force themselves upon me, whether I would or no; and strange to say, I sometimes recognized in them counterparts of figures once familiar to me in pictures attached to childish books, forgotten long ago.

In most repects our many Wests have been much alike in origin, in development and spirit up to the time when frontier conditions disappeared. To the staid, cosmopolitan centers this "Back of Beyond" has usually been a mystery, a sordid, squalid mystery. But, in the same way that one can never righteously indict a people or a country, so one may be wrong indeed in passing judgment on any of these provinces of ours; they are too varied in character. Some one, for instance, showed his ignorance when he coined the quip: "The thermometers of Arizona have but four reading-points: blood-heat, boiling, Phoenix and Hell." The starlit splendor of White's "Arizona Nights", with snow-capped peaks often in sight the year 'round, was as unknown to this "dude" joker as the traps on the ninth hole at St. Andrews to an Esquimo; or as unknown as was the general good health of Thomas Hooker's cattle on the Connecticut to the Eastern "liars" who said that all but one died the first winter.

The outside world was probably never surer of anything than of the unalloyed wickedness and treachery of the "bad men" of the American West in the days when it was at the mercy of every "Dead-Eye Dick" and Billy the Kid. Little is it realized that such classes of men preyed very largely on themselves. Wrote Judge Kuykendall, who presided, for instance, at the first trial of Jack McCall for the murder of "Wild Bill" Hickok, and who resided in Cheyenne, Wyoming, when it was at its "worst": "My long and varied experience with such men had convinced me that there was little or no danger from them, and that so long as a peaceably disposed man attended to his own business and was not hunting for trouble, he enjoyed their respect and confidence." Some one has well said: "The price of improvement is that the unimproved will always look degraded."

No matter, then, in what regard it was held, the pivotal fact remains that some West always beckoned to adventuresome Americans. As a rule these frontiers exerted their magnetic influence only on men and women who were physically fit and spiritually brave. James Lane Allen said that the Kentucky pioneers who crossed the towering Cumberlands were not unlike the ants who scaled the fortress wall: only the strong could do it and only the brave dared to. And Roosevelt, in one of his vivid flashes that usually hit the nail squarely, said that the American pioneers "had to be good and strong — especially strong."

In the days before the Constitution was adopted the frontiers were, comparatively, near by; in after years they lay at increasingly greater distances — at the end of the Oregon, California and Santa Fé trails. Their whereabouts never seemed to matter. The call of the Columbia or Sacramento was no less clear, insinuating and captivating than had been the call of the Susquehanna, Genesee or Shenandoah in constitution-making days. This may seem, on the surface, to have been a disintegrating, centrifugal influence on American development — a sort of confusion of tongues which scattered people widely, broke up homes and hindered methodical building. Such it might have been but for the law which makes the wind's scattering of maple seeds an exceedingly constructive process! The parallel is not too strong. It was invaluable to our national life that these outlets were constantly available; and when they cease to exist an ominous factor of large proportions will face us as a nation. The famous president of Princeton, James McCosh, riding with my father across the Vermont hills, thrilled his listener as he pointed to a lone chimney (a true sign, in some eyes, of provincial decay) standing stark and gruesome in the twilight over the remains of what had been an old Green Mountain homestead and said, in his biting Scotch brogue not to be imitated: "That, Sor, is no monument of decline or dissolution; the proudest shafts Vermont possesses are the glorious chimneys of homes from which sons and daughters went out to educate, Christianize and conquer the world; Rutland marble nor porphyry could add to their glory." This migratory process made for unity in the end, even though men looked upon it in dismay and sought to regulate it — with the same inability to see the thing in the large as was displayed by the youngster who wanted to pare down his puppy's huge paws "to make them fit."

All of our frontiers have had a type of unity that was on the one hand physical, and on the other moral, intellectual and spiritual. In the first place the physical unity of each was that of position, of geography. It was a "poor man's land", if you know what I mean; a "Land of Do-Without"; but if you do not know what I mean the sense of the thing will not be apparent. On every frontier the people had so few possessions that one of them, at least, said, "To move, all I hafen to do is to put out the fire an' call the dog." We hang their simple pioneer tools in our museums to-day — but oh, that we might really own and relish our "possessions" as they did theirs! They made the most of nothing and are a lesson to all who make so little of everything and say the world is "going to the devil."

There was a prevailing type of moral code on all the old frontiers; a code which frequently smacked of a practical Christianity. I do not mean that the expert would feel comfortable in trying to recognize frontier religions by that name — holy rolling, for instance, or the incantations of hectic camp meetings, where fences had to be erected to prevent young folks from holding petting parties in the outer gloom. I do not know how the religious expert would view the religion of Kephart's wrangling lumbermen who, amid curses that all but scorched the bark on their logs, would argue heatedly all day as to whether or not Saul was damned; or how he would rank the pious faith of the mountaineer who, when surprised by his circuit rider in a leafy ambush beside the trail, calmed his unexpected visitor with the words, "Pass along, Parson, pass along; I 'se waitin' for Jim Johnson, and with the help o' God A'mighty I 'm goin' to blow his damned head off." The men of the old frontiers were men with rugged convictions; this may not be accounted religion — but the thief on the cross was promised Paradise "to-day" for nothing else than a conviction.

Blood feuds existed, it is true; killings were not uncommon; debauched characters were as plenteous in proportion to the population, no doubt, as in the civilized hives on the Atlantic shores which had once been the frontier — though I have no proof that any borderland man ever ate his wife up, as once happened a very few miles from the seashore before the frontier had migrated. The Allegheny and trans-Allegheny frontiers were unified by real moral codes. For example, if any one inferred that the inevitable lack of privacy, necessitated by pioneer conditions, permitted wanton intrusions; if one took advantage of a seeming callousness to formal decencies of more cultivated society and crossed the unmarked, but no less absolute, dead line of respectability, he most likely came back across that line feet foremost. There is a very real tang to Kephart's description of his first night in a one-room mountain cabin:

> I will never forget [he wrote] my embarrassment about getting to bed the first night I ever slept in a one-room cabin where there was a good-sized family. I did not know what was expected of me. When everybody looked sleepy I went outdoors and strolled around in the moonlight until the women had time to retire. On returning to the house I found them still bolt upright around the hearth. Then the hostess pointed to the bed I was to occupy and said it was ready whenever I was. . . . I lay there awake for a long time. Finally I had to roll over. A ruddy glow from the embers showed the family in all postures of deep, healthy sleep. It also showed me something glittering on the nipple of the long, muzzle-loading rifle that hung over the father's bed. It was a bright, new percussion cap, where a greased rag had been when I went out for my moonlight stroll. There was no need of a curtain in that house. They could do without.

I suppose that, if the religions of the mountains and Mississippi Basin would assay as "terrible" in the City of Brotherly Love, those of the far West would be classed as mawkish sentiment. But on no one of these frontiers could the pious pretender be half as sure of his neck as he could be east of the Delaware. There is local color in the cattleman's query when he asks his friend if the latter realizes

That a heap of stock is lowing now
Around the Master's pen,
And feeding at His fodder stock
Will have the brands picked then?
And brands that when the hair was long
Looked like the letter C,
Will prove to be the Devil's,
And the brand the letter D.

I wonder if some cowboys were not more religious than some would suppose, as they "sang":

"I 'm scared that I 'll be a stray yearlin',
A maverick unbranded on high —
And get cut in the bunch with the 'rusties'
When the Boss of the Riders goes by."

Who gave to the Western frontier its romantic flavor of hospitality, friendliness, *happiness?* The trapper? The miner? The prospector? The lumberman? No — the cowboy. And nothing — not the engaging cowboy ways and dress, not their intriguing, half-Spanish lingo, not even their perfectly delightful songs — gave to the life of the typical Western ranch that charm, which is the despair of novelist and scenario-writer, so much as the *morale* developed in the cattle country. To the picturesqueness of the *voyageur*, this modern unselfish hero added a note of chivalry not common to all frontiers. "The cultivation of the unselfish part of our natures," said W. E. H. Lecky, "is not only one of the first great lessons of morals but also of wisdom."

The intellectual unity of the frontiers has been a byword in our national story; practically every foreigner who visited our hinterlands in early days marveled at the class of books our Pyncheons, Lincolns and Jim Bridgers carried into the wilderness. "Please send me the *Youth's Companion*," wrote the first white woman to cross the Rocky Mountains. No one so well as De Tocqueville has painted the contrast between the squalor of appearances on our frontiers and the robustness of intellectuality there displayed:

> Nothing can offer a more miserable aspect than these isolated dwellings. The traveller who approaches one of them toward nightfall sees the flicker of the hearthflame through the chinks in the walls; and at night, if the wind rises, he hears the roof of boughs shake to and fro in the midst of the great forest-trees. Who would not suppose that this poor hut is the asylum of rudeness and ignorance? Yet no sort of comparison can be drawn between the pioneer and the dwelling which shelters him. Everything about him is primitive and wild, but he is himself the result of the labor and experience of eighteen centuries. He wears the dress and speaks the language of cities; he is acquainted with the past, curious about the future, and ready for argument upon the present; he is, in short, a highly civilized being, who consents for a time to inhabit the backwoods, and who penetrates into the wilds of the New World with the Bible, an axe, and some newspapers. It is difficult to imagine the incredible rapidity with which thought circulates in the midst of these deserts. I do not think that so much intellectual activity exists in the most enlightened and populous districts of France.

Harriet Martineau in the wilds of the Michigan of 1835 wrote: "At Ypsilanti I picked up an Ann Arbor newspaper. It was badly printed; but its contents were pretty good; and it could happen nowhere out of America, that so raw a settlement as that at Ann Arbor, where there is difficulty in procuring decent accommodations, should have a newspaper." One California '49er, going to hobnob with a neighbor of a Sunday, took "a pair of stockings to darn, one of my old shoes to mend, and the *Democratic Review* to read."

The gist of the thing is that the poverty of our frontiers was not abject poverty. "Frontier life has in it ordinarily less of poverty than any other condition of society," wrote Thomas Condon, "a fact doubtless due to the continuous effort necessary there to keep at all abreast of the incessant struggle against the savagery of its surroundings . . . indeed along this [Mississippi River] border no one could be classed as dependent poor." Longing there was, of course, because, save for eccentric exceptions, the pioneers in our formative days were people who looked up. The difficulties of their position were many; long, rough roads to markets; isolation from good schools and churches. Such outcries as were voiced in Shays' Rebellion and the Whiskey Rebellion were based on economic hardships which time, and only time, could alleviate. When a horse on a mountain trail could carry, in one load, eight times as valuable a cargo of corn juice as he could of corn, there seemed something wrong to Pennsylvanians in prohibiting the traffic. They felt that government was no friend — even of horses. The frontiers of Washington's time had vociferously endorsed the Revolution and poured into the Continental armies reinforcements far beyond their proportionate quotas. But, in the main, they were skeptical of the strong centralized government organized at Philadelphia in 1787, and one of their spokesmen, Patrick Henry, formerly Governor of Virginia, voiced his frontier's opinion when he again cried out (in effect): "Give me Liberty or Give me Death" in opposition to the Constitution. Most frontiers had suffered from centralized power and had temporary antipathies against it. They, in common with the nation at large, had to learn that "nothing but might," in Sumner's words, "has ever made right."

For, with "poverty", frontiersmen always had an intense spirit of independence — often the kind which leans backward. If it was a bane, it was also a blessing. It created at times a spirit of seeming disloyalty, of separatism; but it often bred nationality. This is uniquely illustrated by the fact that the frontiers were potent nurseries of territorial growth. In them the instinct of boldness and a headstrong willfulness swerved the nation into paths to which conservatism and convention did not spontaneously beckon. In this, so to speak, frontiersmen were influenced by the knowledge "given to babes" and denied to the elders. In this respect one might paraphrase Bagehot and say of our nation: "Alone among modern nations the United States exhibited the deference to usage which combines nations and the partial permission of selected change which improves nations."

It is worth while to look a little carefully into this phenomenon of our frontiers as nurseries of expansion; it had its very marked influence on our national growth; it had, also, its bearing on internationalism. Enough has been said of the planting of the outlying New England settlements — on those islands of good soil — to show this frontiering process at work in earliest colonial days; the conditions under which planting of settlements took place along the Atlantic Plain and nearer West, as in the limestone region of Pennsylvania, have also been described. Among the scores of specific cases of pioneering in the further West, let us look at the governing principles which dominated two of outstanding individuality.

The good soils which Penn found, rather to his amazement, in the interior of his province soon received into their ample bosom thousands of pioneers. The resulting miracle has been described: splendid wheat fields; stone roads; Conestoga horses and wagons — a new era in the development of seaboard transportation. But the price of land inevitably went up; more people crowded in; congestion resulted, even though the Scotch-Irish (fearful of limestone lands which, in their homeland, were known as "dry lands") pushed on past the Germans, in many instances, and banked themselves up against the Alleghenies on the slate and shale lands farther west. Economic pressure was bound to burst the Pennsylvania shell as soon as the white of the egg (free or cheap lands) should be eaten up. When the bursting took place, it is plain that the overflow would follow the soil-line of least resistance — southwest across the Potomac, up the limestone pathways marked by the beautiful Shenandoah and its sister streams.

It is never safe to say of any American, "He was the first pioneer." The old records show that many a hunter and trapper had been "feeling out" that splendid Valley of Virginia in those first decades of the eighteenth century — as well as land on all those glittering finger tips of the Tennessee and Cumberland beyond, the Clinch, Holston, Watauga, French Broad and Powell. If there had been, however, no outstanding leader to cry "Come on" the movement would have taken place just the same. Unwittingly, those strong peoples, who had founded so substantial a kingdom in the Pennsylvania limestone land, had planted a breeding-place of expansion; and they had created, also unwittingly, the necessary tools of expansion. These, in the main, were the factors in transportation mentioned; but of major consequence, too, was the developed aptness in working in iron which Pennsylvania, Maryland and Virginia now began to produce. Lancaster, Pennsylvania, early became the gunsmith emporium of the frontier; and in this and other neighboring towns the making of all the tools necessary for farming — and pioneering — was carried on extensively.

Finally a real leader appeared. This was the foreign nobleman who could boast the proud name of Baron Heydt. He had come to America in his own ships. But so quickly was he Americanized on this very typical American frontier of Pennsylvania that he readily doffed all trappings and became plain "Joist Hite." He broke open a pathway through the York Barrens to the Potomac and the Valley of Virginia, which became one of America's important routes of national advance — a road made famous by the Lewises, Findleys, Boones and Lincolns to — Where? Who can name its real termination? Over its curling stretches thousands poured down into Virginia's valley; other thousands pressed on the same track to Kentucky; a perfectly defined extension of the same path led to Louisville and on into the Missouri Valley, whence diverged the great routes of the Far West, the Oregon and Santa Fé trails. A Valley of Virginia breeding-place of migration was now planted from Pennsylvania; a Kentucky breeding-place of advance in turn was founded by men of the Valley; and the Missouri frontier breeding-places, such as Franklin, Liberty and Westport, were settled, in the main, by the surging vanguards from Virginia, Kentucky and Tennessee. The story of those lunges forward, from Lancaster to Winchester to Staunton to Crab Orchard to Louisville, and ending on the Missouri, the Platte, the Arkansas, the

Colorado and Columbia — what a part of republic-making they were! We shall catch a picture of this again when we see the members of the Lincoln family moving by generations from one of these breeding-grounds of expansion to another — and would (but for the wise advice of Mrs. Lincoln) have gone the whole length, had Abraham Lincoln accepted the proffered governorship of Oregon!

But let us turn to another type of initiative on such breeding-grounds, one termed by the late Professor Dunning the most "delicious" instance known to him of that irrepressible instinct of American frontiersmen. We have seen General Rufus Putnam lead to Ohio that interesting company of Revolutionary soldiers who founded, at Marietta, the capital of the territory northwest of the Ohio River, and there put into operation the great ordinances of 1785 and 1787. Many of these New Englanders were from the seafaring towns of Rhode Island and Massachusetts; block and tackle, mast and jib, hawser and anchor-lore were a part of their very blood. At their feet they saw the "Beautiful Ohio" stretching away to the Mississippi and that, in turn, to their own beloved ocean — two thousand miles away.

Washington had foreseen in 1784, as we have noted, the phenomenon of ocean-rigged vessels descending the Ohio River. I suppose many of the "Going-to-the-devil" morbids of those hard days of Shays' Rebellion and St. Clair's Defeat laughed loud and long at this prophecy of the Virginia planter. But within three years of Wayne's victory at Fallen Timber those irrepressible Yankees had a brig of one hundred and ten tons on the stocks at Marietta, Ohio. From the forests they had dragged the black walnut for the hull; from their fields they plucked the hemp for cordage; and soon iron works at Pittsburgh were, to quote a pious contemporaneous newspaper advertisement, "sufficiently upheld by the hand of the Almighty" to be able to furnish the necessary metal. In every major port on the Ohio shipbuilding yards were soon echoing with these strange tools of migration and commerce. Far up on the Monongahela men of Delaware were constructing the *Monongahela Farmer*. This ship and the *St. Clair* set sail for the Atlantic Ocean in the first year of the nineteeth century. Without a doubt pessimists smiled broadly at the idea of their ever getting there! "How can they make the innumerable bends in the rivers?" laughed the iconoclasts. Yankee ingenuity met this test as nonchalantly as all the others — and the heavy tubs were let down backwards, with anchors dragging from the prows; by alternately tightening and slacking anchor lines, the ships were safely eased around the bends. Within seven years a hundred ocean-rigged vessels, some with a tonnage of five hundred rating, had been built between Pittsburgh and the mouth of the Ohio. How far afloat these "landlubber" ocean vessels went will never be known. The first to arrive at Liverpool was the *Duane* of Pittsburgh, on July 8, 1803. Two years later, "in the Year of Human Salvation 1805", the nonplussed harbor master of Trieste, Italy, at the head of the Adriatic, made out papers (now in the Marietta College Library) which permitted the *Louisiana of Marietta* to set sail from Trieste for London with a cargo of oil, wood, boxwood, apples, juniper berries and "other things!" [1]

And not the least "delicious" phase of this unique episode in pioneering was the consciousness of those

[1] A. B. Hulbert, "Western Shipbuilding", *American Historical Review*, XXI, No. 4.

unconquerable Yankees that they were doing clever things!

> He hath oped the way to Commerce,

sang a poet, on the gala occasion of the sailing of the *St. Clair* from Marietta, and in honor of the captain of the ship. This was none other than Admiral Abraham Whipple, who had helped to fire the *Gaspée* in Narragansett Harbor and precipitate the Revolutionary War.

> Sirens attend with Flute and Lyre
> and bring your Conks my Trittons
> in chorus Blow to the Aged Sire
> in welcome to my Dominions

continued this poet of the day, Colonel Jonathan Devol, picturing Neptune welcoming to his Gulf of Mexico a hero of Narragansett Bay from the Ohio River!

Again, our frontiers played a vital part in international questions. That independent spirit developed on them was of large importance in extending our national boundaries until the United States became a Republic of continental dimensions. We would doubtless have come to our present dimensions in any case; but the United States grew in size when it did, because the frontiers demanded it — and would have fought for such extension if they had been denied — especially in the case of the Louisiana Purchase and the annexation of Texas.

The East was little interested when Thomas Jefferson began seriously to study the question of American advance beyond the Mississippi; it was not altogether fear of Napoleon which led the politician of Monticello to plan *secretly* an investigation of that region; he knew the Northeast would never sympathize with the scheme. But land ownership was only a phase, and a lesser phase, of the Louisiana Purchase business; the crux of the matter was the control of the Mississippi River outlet to the sea. And there, Thomas Jefferson had no choice. For do not suppose that the sudden burst of shipbuilding we have described in the Ohio Valley frontier originated merely from a desire to play in the water. As Pennsylvania would never have had Conestoga horses and wagons and stone roads but for the immense crops of wheat to be hauled to market, just so there would have been no ocean-rigged ships on the Ohio save for the rise of immense cargoes to be transported.

The surplus which the Ohio Valley was ready to export by 1800 was surprisingly large. In three spring months of that year cargoes to the value of $700,000 in present-day values passed the revenue office at Fort Massac on the lower Ohio; the list included twenty-three thousand barrels of flour, eleven hundred barrels of whiskey, thirteen hundred pounds of pork and seventy-five thousand pounds of cordage. With assets of such value steadily mounting to huge proportions (for a "Land of Do-Without"); with a hundred ocean-going ships on the stocks involving the investment of what would be to-day at least a million and a half dollars; with Natchez and Memphis merchants purchasing goods (shipped by wagon across the Alleghenies and floated down the Ohio-Mississippi channel to them) to the amount of a million dollars in values of to-day which they could pay for only with cotton sent *down* the Mississippi, can you not see what it meant to this frontier world to let the Spaniard sit in the seat of custom at New Orleans and charge what duties he pleased — or prohibit, if such was his pleasure, *all commerce whatsoever?* In all the generations during which France and Spain had owned the Mississippi Basin the export trade from it amounted to very little. But those lusty Americans had created all this wealth there (and the promise of billions more) in the short space of forty years. Should Spaniards block its passageway to the world's markets?

The self-respect of such a frontier, filled with bold pioneers, could never have brooked that hazard and indignity of such interference. The frontier had been thinking fast on this subject — faster, I am sure, than the East commonly realized. You know the stereotyped story — of Jefferson's commissioners going to Paris on their mission to unlock the Mississippi by the purchase of the Isle of New Orleans and of their alleged sudden trepidation on being confronted with Napoleon's proposal to sell *all* of Louisiana? They may have been startled at the proposal; if so, it was because of fear of exceeding their instructions and not because the idea was new, for it certainly would not have surprised even the far-away citizens of infant Pittsburgh! A paper in that city had carried a news item twelve months before, without headline and without editorial comment, stating that Napoleon would sell Louisiana to the United States for fifteen million dollars — the exact price later agreed upon.[1] Jefferson was made to understand that the Ohio Valley demanded the freedom of the Mississippi and that his securing it would be the price of its remaining loyal.

This frontier influence in international affairs appears again in the sequel to the Louisiana Purchase. It was the same frontier, with extensions due to growth, which forced the War of 1812 upon an unwilling East. The insults offered to the "free ships, free goods" theory by England and France aroused the touchy patriotism of

[1] Pittsburgh *Gazette*, April 9, 1802.

the pioneer West and South. The "War Hawks" of those sections forced the War of 1812 which the seaboard regions opposed. Only in recent years have we realized to the full the significance to America of fighting that last struggle with the Mother Country and making that stalemate Treaty of Ghent at its close. It gave birth both to the sense and fact of the true independence of our land from Europe; it freed our southern shores of the Great Lakes from further fear of hostile occupation and hastened armies of pioneers thither; it paved the way for the new conquest of the Atlantic by the doughty American clipper ships of later days.

Nor is the story of that old trail opened by Joist Hite, the Boones, Lincolns and Findleys complete, unless we see in the large a mighty southwestern section, west of the Alleghenies and south of the Cumberlands, come into virile existence, fill with eager people and become, itself, the breeding ground for another expansive movement. The War of 1812 was hardly over ere another "Joist Hite", hailing from the far-off Missouri region, fared southwest across the Mexican border and received a large grant of land in what is now our Texas. Stephen Austin turned at once to the sections from which he came to secure pioneers for his adventure; and by the hundreds from that Old Southwest, came Americans to Texas to open a new frontier under a beneficent Magna Charta granted to their leader, Austin, by Mexico.

The swiftness of the movement and the unexampled prosperity of these settlers soon led Mexico to doubt the wisdom of her liberality and to annul important promises made to those pioneers of "life, liberty and pursuit of happiness." The Texan Rebellion followed. It was successful; Mexico then had no more chance of reconquering

Texas than Norsemen have to-day of reconquering Labrador. The United States (along with other powers) recognized the international right of Texas to be reckoned one of the nations of the world. Our annexation of those Texas Americans was as natural and normal a process as history records, for the region was economically eclipsed automatically unless, by annexing California, Texas could establish a great rival republic along and around the flanks of its own Mother Country. The Mexican War followed. Once more a northeast seaboard objected and once more frontiers said "Fight." President Polk, who declared a state of war to exist, was denounced by the Northeast as "scoundrel", "thief" and "pilferer" — as a tyrant land-grabber intent on robbing a peaceful neighbor, and everything thus said by those Northeastern papers was copied into the Mexican press. Mexicans therefore very naturally believed in the righteousness of their cause — believed with certainty that Mexican armies, if they marched northward, would be hailed by the people of St. Louis and Chicago as armies of liberation, come to free a land of tyrant and a despot! At the close of the war Texas, New Mexico, Arizona and California were added to our Republic — the gift to the United States of frontier spirit and initiative. Simultaneously the Mississippi frontier had conquered Oregon — with the broadax. No sooner was this clearly recognized than the kindly Lord Aberdeen ordered the Canadian-American line to be drawn in conformity to our government's desire, along the forty-ninth parallel.

We became, thus, a republic of continental dimensions; and, very truly so, because frontiers bred frontiers. How many there were of such frontiers depends on the range of one's vision. Take the oldest frontier known to man —

the sea; what new frontiers, in a real sense, did not American initiative and boldness discover there! Frontiersman, indeed, was the hero Paul Revere, as he patiently practiced rolling copper plates which finally did give American ships a mastery of the South Seas which no other nation then possessed, because barnacle and borer could not pierce the bottoms of ships so protected. Frontiersman, too, was Captain Andrew Robinson of Gloucester who first successfully applied fore-and-aft schooner rigging to ships — a Yankee trick which gave American privateers the phantom-like flexibility which won many a victory on the sea. And how this "frontier" bred another when, in the 'fifties, men of the same blood and stock quite outwitted the world with their clipper ships! Flaunting every conservative principle of marine architecture, these Houdinis of Atlantic America built their long, rakish, Norselike "monstrosities." And when conservatism gasped because these impish builders raised on their craft the whole complement of eighteen sails known to the great galleons of the past, those irrepressible "frontiersmen" added a spencer and then a stunsail; they then made place for moon and water sails, ran up a ringtail and broke out a studdingsail from the gaff of the spanker. The best "authorities" said these abnormally besailed clippers would only turn somersaults in a stiff wind; but English merchants gave them six pounds per ton for carrying tea from Canton to London when British masters, who had not broken all the written and unwritten laws of the sea, could only secure from three pounds to four pounds! In 1851 the *Flying Cloud* made her world's sailing record of three hundred seventy-four miles in twenty-four hours. The American privateer "frontier" bred the clipper "frontier."

But that meant the passing along from decade to decade something more than saws and adzes, gimlets and screw-drivers. In troughs of thought and experience family-seed carried forward the sum totals of past errors and failures, mistakes and misjudgments, past successes, conquests, triumphs. In fact frontiers mean little except as they are visioned from the physiologist's viewpoint of cell feeling out cell, bringing it to fruition. This family phase of the problem, and one singular example of its manifestation, might well ask for attention as it survived the melting pot, survived "submergence" and flowered astonishingly in a far distant country.

X

THE PATERAN OF YOUR LINCOLNS

I ADMIRE what I see in the story of the processes of American unity as they have been worked out in some of our families which the leaven of restlessness so astonishingly dispersed across the face of the continent. Sons may have resembled fathers but little in face and figure, likes and dislikes; they may have ignored or repudiated the advice of parents and callously stridden forth from old homesteads to cast the family seed by rivers whose very names were unpronounceable. Yet they carried that selfsame seed. Principles unrecognized by them — or perhaps ardently flaunted in "flaming youth" — unconsciously dominated their lives; old precepts, homely dogmas, intellectual leanings, deep-seated antipathies, followed them in their blood. In curious ways, over and over again, this family flowering on distant plains, strange mountains or unknown valleys, was instinct with a unity with the past, and bound distant parts of our land together across rough roads in spiritual sympathy not less real because not recognized for its full worth in building a homogeneous nation — making the Ship strong.

Let us take what I believe to be a singular illustration of this; one all the more interesting because it concerns one of our greatest. It is not to be supposed that my analysis of this family line is accurate in the sense that all the facts can be historically attested; some imagination must be permitted in order to characterize men about whom almost nothing is well known, for the purpose of bringing out what I am sure were truthful and very important processes — even at the risk of arousing the biologist's ire.

With this foreword let us look to the curious pateran of your Lincolns for evidences of that subtle thread of unity, which surely did bind its scattered members as they passed along that famous line of American migration from Pennsylvania; became allied with other stock; but produced, in the end, a man not to be understood, I feel certain, unless you trace the family thread backward along that pathway.

Your first Lincoln is Samuel Lincoln, the English emigrant, who built his home in Hingham, Massachusetts. I see in him the typical Yankee, long of limb and jaw, hard-fisted, sharp in bargaining, a steady worker, and humble withal as he dickers devoutly with the Lord in prayer. He was a "forty-acre man", as the saying went; that is, he was a full-fledged citizen, with his right to a seat in church, to a vote on election day and to all the privileges and prerogatives of a juryman who could send men to death for any one of eleven minor misdemeanors and one major crime. The long winters invited this Yankee Lincoln to absorb such books as came within his reach; and especially did he become master of that literature of literature, the King James Bible. Its splendid English colored and made vital his speech; its beautiful allegories and alliterations wove themselves into his thought and dreaming. So stands Samuel Lincoln, founder of a family line, a distinct figure. He had raw faults; he was narrowed by bigotry; he was intolerant of all the "lesser breeds without the law"; he was penurious to wife, son, daughter, church and God. But he was a real man — a *vir*, plumed knight, not a *homo*, an animal that wears pants. His austerity was softened by a tender conscience, and his callous indifference to some of the niceties of life was relieved by his passion for the unexcelled beauties of speech which he drew from his Book of Books.

Your second Lincoln was the grandson of Samuel, and known as Mordecai Lincoln, of Pennsylvania. But note this man's full title, "Mordecai Lincoln, Gentleman." With a pause for a generation in New Jersey, this Lincoln tribe was following the normal line of American migration — southwest. They were the type of folk who build houses "by the side of the road where the race of men pass by."

But Mordecai was a gentleman. He lived in a land flowing with milk and honey. He met life on terms unknown to his father or grandfather. His fields were broad, like his limestone roads; they burned like burnished brass with acres of yellow wheat. His blue and red Conestoga wagons groaned with heavy freight as his big Conestoga horses sweated in the harness on the broad, white Lancaster Turnpike to the Philadelphia market. These fields, roads, horses and wagons bred complacency. Mordecai had little quarrel with the world — or with his fellow bank directors who voted with him "aye" on the topic of dividends. This complacency bred toleration. Mordecai Lincoln, Gentleman, was surrounded by Shakers, Quakers, Scotch-Irish, Huguenots, Mennonites, Hittites, Amorites and Perizzites. It was all one to him. These were not lesser breeds without the law but brothers who carried balances in Mordecai's bank. Mordecai knew

Henry Smaltz and Oscar von Austenbroiser and Herman Von Schmertilz and all the little Smaltzs and Austenbroisers and Schmertilzes. When Katharine Schmaltz was sick "by her bedside" Mordecai sent her some Ben Davis apples. They cheered her. They made her remember Mordecai's laugh. For Mordecai loved a joke and his horses turned their heads when he laughed. It was not a "te-he" laugh. His laughs began away down deep; they surged up first in ripples; then they broke into a swelling tide threatening vast destruction. They ended with him out on the porch wiping his eyes.

Mordecai was not a Samuel Lincoln. Yet, he was a staunch church pillar and as upright in character as he was in stature. He read the Bible, but he did not mouth it. His conscience did not prey on others for its daily food. Along with the sheets and bread box Mordecai let it bask in the sunshine for exercise. Over his rotund face no cloud settled — save when he found his "queer" son John looking down the rough road across the York Barrens.

This queer son John is your third Lincoln. The consensus of opinion in the home was that he "heard things" and "saw things." No steaming pudding was so good that John would not turn from it to watch, long and dreamily, a dusty emigrant's team plodding on Joist Hite's road through the York Barrens. He came in the house at night from rendezvous with other boys on the roadway, breathing strange words. He spoke of Opequon Creek and the Northern Neck, of Lord Fairfax and Winchester, of Watkins Ferry, the Shenandoah and Rockingham. When Mordecai talked about "all the comforts of home," this John asked if, out of all this plenty, he could have a horse and wagon and some cows. To him that road through York Barrens to the Valley of Virginia was a pathway to "Treasure Island." On it mocking birds sang at night in magnolia trees — which helped to make the pateran.

The lure of those olden trails through and beyond the York Barrens of pioneer American history — who nowadays can depict their romance and compelling mystery? Mary Johnston was surely sensing it when she made her tobacco roller curl up to sleep "in the lee of his thousand pounds of bright leaf," while Lewis Rand

> . . . and the hunter sat late by the fire. "We crossed that swamp," said Gaudylocks, "with the canes rattling above our heads, and a panther screaming in a cypress tree, and we came to a village of the Chickasaws —"
>
> "In the night-time?" asked the boy.
>
> "In the night-time, and a mockingbird singing like mad from a china tree, and the woods all level before us like a floor, — no brush at all, just fine grass, with flowers in it like pinks in a garden. So we smoked the pipe of peace and I hung a wampum belt with fine words, and we went on, the next day, walking over strawberries so thick that our moccasins were stained red!" . . . The boy rose to throw more wood on the fire, then sat again at the trader's feet, and with his chin in his hand stared into the glowing hollows.
>
> "The West," said Gaudylocks, between slow puffs of smoke. "Kentucky and the Ohio and the Mississippi, and then Louisiana . . . and Mexico like a ripe apple — just a touch of the bough, and there 's the gold in hand! If I were a dreamer, I would dream of the West."
>
> "Folks have always dreamed of the West," said the boy.

This fever of the westwarding pioneers, the passing Boones and Findlays, was not to be quenched by any home comforts. Soon the lank, brown mountaineers of

Rockingham County, Virginia, found John Lincoln with them behind the Blue Ridge. Like his fellows, John was poor. In him began the Shirt-sleeve Era of Lincolns. But he married a daughter of the South. Life was seen from new angles never caught by his Samuel and Mordecai forebears north of Mason and Dixon's Line. I fancy that, as John Lincoln's "half-faced camp" became a farm and that metamorphosed into a plantation, as children came to bless this union of North and South, the stark, old words of Leviticus or Deuteronomy used by Samuel were well known in that home, even if the *r*'s were dropped; and the echoes of Mordecai's robust laughter were heard, I imagine, ringing merrily here on the Shenandoah. Once more, a Lincoln cabin was built beside a road where the race of men passed by. Did I say road? This valley pathway blazed by Boone was, rather, a gangway to Kentucky. Every day, we may suppose, Mrs. John Lincoln of Rockingham looked out anxiously to that pathway to see if the surging crowd had sucked in her stalwart son, Abraham. For this boy was hardly grown ere — irony of ironies — he spoke of stranger, far-off things than ever the queer John had talked in Pennsylvania — of Cumberland Gap, Colonel Henderson, Limestone, Crab Orchard, Pilot Knob and the "Falls of the Ohio."

This fourth Lincoln of yours, Abraham Lincoln, faced the Cumberlands, I suppose, with only a pack on his back. I rate him as quite the typical poor white mountaineer. Moving, to him, meant only to put out the fire and call the dog. He had, no doubt, large capacities, but I imagine his capacity to enjoy silence was, of them all, the one best developed. You see him now, in 1780, in the crevasse on the mountain summit, Cumberland Gap. In his linsey-woolsey and jerkin he seems taller and more gaunt than

Yankee Samuel. Yet, in him, Samuel Lincoln goes down into the Mississippi valley. No rotundity of his frame bespeaks Mordecai Lincoln — but I fancy that that urbane Pennsylvania gentleman's sense of humor lights the wan face of this determined Kentucky pioneer. Most certainly of all, this Abraham Lincoln carries into the fresh new West a real blending of the blood of the North and the South; Pennsylvania and Virginia hold equal parts in the throbbing soul of the man. But he was a man of the "Country of Do-Without." He knew pinching hunger. Monotonous diet gave his cheeks the wan frontiersman's look. He became one with that gaunt, mountain race in whose eyes obesity was almost a high crime. "I named that boy from the best man that ever walked God's footstool," said one of its typical representatives, "and then the fool had to go and get fat on me. A fat woman is bad enough but a fat man ought, pintedly, to be led out and shot."

Cove and mist-enshrouded peak lit in this Abraham all the flickering fires of superstition common to his class — in a land where, to quote W. E. H. Lecky, "the dream world blends so closely with the world of realities . . . that men become almost incapable of distinguishing between the real and the fictitious." Here the raven grunts, barks, cajoles, pulls her cork, whets her scythe and files her saw — all with her tongue — imitating, no doubt, the language which she thinks the mountaineer speaks. In turn, that white invader of her forest-empire (who can doubt it?) got tones and expressions, if not actual words, from her. Who but ravens could teach mortals a language which was based so absolutely on bird's-eye-view standards that a traveler, on inquiring how to reach a certain destination, should be told to "Go two looks and a go-by" — meaning that he should breast the horizon twice, pass the first turn-off, and take the second?

Here the razorback hog, who can run like a deer and climb like a goat, taught the mountaineer (who will doubt it?) the proper mood for mastery in a wilderness. What courage, what sagacity that four-footed emigrant embodied — so strong to bear grudges, to brood over indignities, to follow his pateran of rich mast onward to new lands! Here, then, "submerged", amid ravens who taught him language and razorbacks who taught him diplomacy, where Nature said "Provide with thine own arm against frosts and famine and skulking foes or thou shalt surely die", another Lincoln built a house beside the road on which the race of men went by.

The point is that this Kentucky pioneer's son, Thomas Lincoln — your fifth Lincoln in this category — was bred in a home of the poorest of the poor, and that on a distant and distraught frontier. I fancy Mordecai Lincoln's fat Conestoga horses alone, back three generations in fertile Pennsylvania, represented a value far beyond the total assets which Thomas Lincoln could boast in his most opulent days. In other words — let us mark well the fact — this family seed had fallen, in the providence of the Almighty, on thin soil amid thistles and briars. It had known Pisgah Heights and it had seen its Sloughs of Despond. The intellectuality of a Yankee Lincoln and the solid prosperity of a Pennsylvania Lincoln had become refined in the fires, first, of a catholicity of sympathy by being blended with the blood of the South; and, second, by the fires of poverty, destitution, hunger and want.

The pioneer instinct led this last Lincoln, Thomas, to take the rough road as his father and grandfather had done. But it was not a stray track leading nowhere. It was the main-traveled highway of national expansion from Kentucky northward into the free soil of Indiana and Illinois. Once again a Lincoln built a home by the side of a pathway of common men. I do not need to tell you that with this Kentucky Lincoln there went northward a boy — the last of your six Lincolns — our Abraham Lincoln.

Teachers have a harder time "selling" Abraham Lincoln to college classes — at least to the best thinkers in those classes — than any other of our great Americans. Of him, those young men and women ask the hardest questions to answer that come in a whole college year. I have no disposition to discount environment or material inheritances, but I cannot explain Lincoln from environment.

His marvelous influence on American history never became plain to me until I caught the sight of the six of him. I never seemed able to explain those classic pieces of American literature to which he gave utterance until I knew his great-great-great-great-grandfather, Samuel, the Yankee who knew his Deuteronomy and Leviticus so well. I never thought I understood Lincoln's fondness for humor (which so exasperated Seward and Stanton) until I knew his great-great-grandfather, Mordecai, the jolly, complacent Pennsylvanian. I never thought I understood Lincoln's impassioned sympathy for the South until I knew of the queer John, his great-grandfather, who blended North and South in Lincoln blood in Rockingham County in the Valley of Virginia. I never thought I understood those strange half-unbalanced moods of Lincoln's young manhood — which made friends fearful for his sanity — until I knew that mountaineer Abraham, his grandfather, a man bred in the coves of the southern Alleghenies, acquainted with "hants" and moved by the superstitions of those underfed denizens of that "Land of

Do-Without." I never thought I understood Lincoln's singular ability to mingle with all sorts and conditions of men until I knew that every Lincoln behind him had built a house beside the road where the race of men passed by; until I saw that a map of the migrations of these Lincolns was the best map you could draw of the main procession of pioneering Americans in their respective generations. From the standpoint of the longitudes, what family line unconsciously reëchoed the refrain "Be American" more concretely than the Lincolns'?

You will find flaws in this explanation. You will say, "Lincoln's immediate ancestors never showed enough of the intellectual traits of the Yankee Samuel to warrant your saying that Lincoln's astonishing use of English was an inheritance." I repeat, they were "carriers" of a germ from which they were immune. Americans were often surprised, and foreigners utterly astounded, as we have noted, at the erudition and taste of the uncouth "carriers" of the germs of literary ideals found on our frontiers. "Think of a rough fellow in a bearskin robe and blue shirt," said Bret Harte of a Missouri Valley pioneer, "repeating to me 'Concepcion de Arguëllo'!" You will say, again, "The money-making, business administrative ability of Mordecai Lincoln, Gentleman, was not inherited by the poor men who were Lincoln's immediate ancestors." To that I will answer that they, too, including Lincoln, were "carriers" of that germ, and that it awoke to life in Lincoln's millionaire son, Robert, who for so many years was president of the Pullman Palace Car Company.

Something better went westward across our longitudes with the Putnams, the Greenes, the McCormacks, the Clarks, the Ameses, the Palmers and the Stanfords than guns, cannon, plows, reapers, monkey-wrenches and frying pans. The call of "the Beyond" was insistent, alluring — whether it was New Jersey, Pennsylvania, the Valley of the Virginia, Kentucky, Indiana, Texas or Oregon; and, in essence, it always said: "Be American." The delicate gossamer cables of love of home, deep-down affection for family traditions, old unremembered loves for forgotten haunts, unconscious predilections for old ways of reacting to given stimuli, held firm. Men who were many leagues distant from home reacted at times to codes which were far from being practiced by them personally at the moment. I like such unconscious harking back as is shown by "Silver Jack" who, although perhaps as besotted a "carrier" as the Plains knew, was ready to fight across the Western barroom floor with an airy upstart who ridiculed the religion in which his mother "lived and died":

And they fit for forty minutes
  And the crowd would whoop and cheer
When Jack spit up a tooth or two
  Or when Bobby lost an ear.

* * * *

But at last Jack got him under
  And he slugged him onct or twict,
And straightway Bob admitted
  The divinity of Christ.
But Jack kept reasoning with him
  Till the poor cuss give a yell,
And 'lowed he 'd been mistaken
  In his views concerning hell.

Countless errant sons like Jack became living sum totals of generations long passed away; as such they preserved one of the strongest bonds of unity which could weld a nation in common purposes and lead men, far-scattered, to work unconsciously for common ideals.

XI

STRANDS OF DUSTY TRAILS

THE splendor in the unfolding story of American unity, to me, lies in the fact that, although so many of our pioneers, in every age, loved their old Eastern homelands with true affection, they yet had the enterprise and strength of conviction necessary to uproot themselves like the Lincolns and trudge off to almost unknown sections and provinces; and that there, under other suns, they reïncarnated a like love for "home", a like affection and virile pride in a new local environment — without ever seriously impairing their sense and passion for American nationality. We may be too "close up" to catch the significance of it now; "it belongs to the idea of progress," said Bagehot, "that beginnings can never seem attractive to those who live far on." But the day will come, I fancy, when our people will relish intensely the memory that one generation of Americans could sing about their "Silvery Rio Grande" with the same robust pride that was felt by their fathers who had praised the "Moonlight on the Wabash" or that felt by their grandfathers when they glorified in song "The Hills of My Old New Hampshire Home"; and all because of the fact that so many of these could, at all times, sing "America" with so little trace of lessened affection for the nation they were building between the Atlantic and Pacific oceans.

It is this fact which lends the real air of romance to the old trails of America, those strands of twine which bound section to section, province to province, leading westward and ever westward. One wonders whether we could have had a republic of continental dimensions planted so swiftly, so timely, but for the lure of romance which cast its halo over the process. We have referred to the fact that only a few hours, comparatively, intervened between the signing of the treaty which gave us California and the discovery of California's gold fields. The imagination is strained to think what might have happened if those good Atlantic American Whigs had been successful in defeating President Polk's program in that campaign of 1844. If Mexico had been proven able to double the world's supply of gold, what alliances might not have been made and wars precipitated?

Then, too, there was an elemental satisfaction felt, consciously or unconsciously, in the fact that our Republic had attained so quickly her normal territorial objectives. Ambitions to reach chauvinistic dimensions have, as previously noted, been a bane of many peoples in world-history. But Americans sought only a reasonable limit. The Pacific, the Yuma deserts and long Canadian winters formed normal boundary lines beyond which only the erratic asked that we should step. This made for a solidarity that was as timely as it was salubrious. With no further territory to occupy, a very valuable backlash from our Pacific Coast helped in no small degree to fill and develop the thinly populated Rocky Mountain regions. Again, the fact that all objectives had been reached before the Civil War rent the land, allowed no hostile neighbor good ground then for making a sinister American territorial ambition an excuse for aiding one of our sections to break away from the Union.

As elsewhere stated, it has been the writer's chief form of recreation and exercise to find, traverse and sometimes to name many of these old-time human-seed arteries of exploration, conquest and migration, from the dim track which his forebears followed from Connecticut to Northern Vermont to the Oregon Trail, swinging down the Blue Mountains into the Columbia River basin, or to the California Trail, surmounting the Yuma Desert and gaining access to the now Imperial Valley, to join there the pathway of the *padres* of old, *El Camino Real.* And it has seemed to me, sometimes, that neither from book, library nor archive have I gained so certain a comprehension of what it cost to build this Republic as when I thought I could hear the low talk of Ethan Allen's men gathered at Catamount Inn across the Green from my birthplace, or on the trail from there to old "Fort Ti"; the raucous cries of Braddock's thirty sailors lowering wagons by block and tackle into Allegheny ravines; the creaking of the great wains that brought through Cumberland Gap the household goods which helped Virginians to plant a Kentucky; the squeaky rasp of an Arkansas fiddle by Wagon Bed Spring on the Dry Cimarron or the groaning of oxcart wheels, and the agonizing bellowing of cattle, hurrying frantically from the Sink of the Humboldt to Carson River. Curiously enough, I have an unconscionable lack of interest in the exact alignment of these famous pathways, unless it could be established from an actual early-day survey. Sometimes the monuments erected with the best of patriotic intentions to commemorate such routes have reminded me of Ikey's pin. You remember Cohen met his friend and looked with some astonishment at the unusual brilliancy of Ikey's necktie. "And vare did you git it?" was his excited query. "Vell, you see," said Ikey, nonchalantly, "my uncle left five huntred dollars in his vill for the erection of a stone to his memory; that iss the stone." In most cases, of course, these trail-markers are planted correctly and well perpetuate the story of the track beside them; but too often local jealousy or the desire to commercialize history has been influential in their erection.

The point about these trails which interests me may be expressed by saying that, in myriad ways, their relationships to the vast series of topographies which they cover bring out — if one studies the actual journals and diaries kept by pilgrims on them — the trials and dangers and sufferings of those who went to conquest over them; and that, if the actual experiences of those pioneers could be shown to-day on the silver screen, not one tenth of one per cent of our people would really care to see them. Drama has been turned into melodrama in both scenario and historical fiction; six-shooters are forever banging away *six* times — in the stories of those who do not know that the hammer in every old-time six-shooter rested, for safety's sake, on an empty sixth chamber. Emigrating parties to Oregon in the days of the rush thither are made to fight circling bands of Redskins on all occasions; but you cannot find in the many records left us of that migration of the forties a single description of day-by-day attacks, and very few accounts of any attacks at all; whereas scores of journals mention none whatever, and several explain that white men on the trail were much more dangerous than red. What happened on the trail in later railway-building days and fort-building days has been brought forward, chronologically, to the days of the great migrations to Oregon and California and made to seem commonplace. This could do no harm except for the fact that the real hardships endured are made to give way to the exotic sensations which are out of focus historically.

To an interesting degree these first pathways of the continent, in a bird's-eye view, resemble closely the more important main lines of railways of to-day; but in their time they relatively exerted greater binding influences than do our trunk railroads of the present, because the well-traveled ones were few in number; whereas hundreds of minor railways serve every section of our land to-day. No railway of the present bears the same strategical relationship to the Alleghenies that Nemacolin's Path once bore, nor one which singly serves so great a section as once did the Oregon Trail. From Atlantic tidewater the Old Bay Path and Mohawk Trail stretched from New England through old New York along the lakes to Lake Michigan; its shorter counterpart, in the South, was Nemacolin's Path which threaded the Alleghenies from the upper Potomac to the Pittsburgh region on the Ohio. From the Potomac, near the mouth of the Shenandoah River, a branch of this track led up the Valley of Virginia to Cumberland Gap and Kentucky. The Great Trail from the upper Ohio (Pittsburgh) wound across Ohio to meet the Lake Shore Trail in the Sandusky region; while southward from this shore of Lake Erie a famous Warrior's Path led to Kentucky and beyond. You can sketch these routes closely when you name the chief towns and cities on the Boston and Albany, New York Central and Michigan Southern, Baltimore and Ohio and Pennsylvania, Chesapeake and Ohio, and Ohio Central railway lines.

Beyond the Mississippi, the Missouri, Platte and Arkansas rivers were the keys of transportation to the Rockies; at the head of the Platte (near Casper, Wyoming) the

Sweetwater Valley offered a passageway through famous South Pass, beyond which the Green and Bear presented fertile oases for those who were pressing on by way of the Snake River and the Blue Mountains to Oregon, or by way of Raft River and the Humboldt to the Carson River passageway across the Sierras to California. At the head of the Arkansas the Purgatoire (called "Picketwire" by cattlemen) led to Raton Pass and, beyond, the trail ran down through the wide levels and uplands of New Mexico, taking the traveler or wagon train to curious old Santa Fé. Gaining thus the Rio Grande River, a California path diverged from that valley below Socorro and led by later Cooke's Spring (near Deming, New Mexico) through the modern Apache Pass to Tucson and the Gila River; crossing the Colorado and the sand hills, the parched (now luxurious) Imperial Valley opened the way either to San Diego or the pueblo of Los Angeles. By the Oregon Short Line and the various connections of the Southern Pacific you may view these historic pathways for much of their route west of the Rockies, just as, from the Union Pacific and Santa Fé trains, you may trace their course in the main from the Mississippi to that mountain barrier.

Frémont has gained the name of "the Pathfinder" of the West; Boone or Christopher Gist or even Washington might be called the pathfinders of the East, although the Catholic missionaries of Canada antedated them a century. These terms are rightly used — more so than the average person knows. They all found many, many trails; and so did the Indians of a thousand years before find the selfsame paths. When a plateau was being built, through which a Colorado River might (milleniums later) begin to carve out the first hollow which should in after ages become a Grand Cañon, Nature was disposing of her hills and rivers and Continental Divide in such a way that through Wills Gap and Kittanning Gorge in the Alleghenies, and through Cajon Pass, Walker's Pass and Truckee Pass in the Sierras, the buffalo would find a line of least resistance or least elevation, eons later; and Indians and covered wagons, Golden State and Overland limiteds would profit by the same conveniences amid tortuous surroundings in a still more distant age. This view shows how idle it is to think of any man of our race, or the red man's, as being a "pathfinder" in the sense of creating any routes of early travel. In every case, the heavy game animals pounded out these strategic lines of travel from the Alleghenies (where Washington found their broad roads in 1784) to Oregon and California.

We have noted the slight training which our English ancestors possessed for the task of continental mastery in this land. For the most part that conquest was made over the network of these narrow trails; doubtless no other evidence of their pluck and boldness and virile power is so impressive as this. Strands of twine they were; but they connected and bound together New England and New York; Pennsylvania and the Valley of Virginia; the upper South and Kentucky and Missouri; the eastern seaboard and the Ohio Basin and Great Lakes; the lower South and Texas; and the Mississippi Valley and Oregon and California.

James Lane Allen caught that deep fundamental throb of the thing as he paused one night in the darkening shadows of Cumberland Gap, that high uplifted hinge, so to speak, on that vital pathway from the seaboard to the Ohio Basin:

As we stood in the passageway [he wrote], amid the deepening shadows of the twilight and the solemn repose of the mighty landscape, the Gap seemed to be crowded with two invisible and countless pageants of human life, the one passing in, the other passing out; and the air grew thick with unheard utterances — primeval sounds undistinguishable and strange, of creatures nameless and never seen by man; the wild rush and whoop of retreating and pursuing tribes; the slow steps of watchful pioneers; the wail of dying children and the songs of homeless women; the muffled tread of routed and broken armies — all the sounds of surprise and delight, victory and defeat, hunger and pain, and weariness and despair, that the human heart can utter.

These lines trenchantly bring out the fact that while the old trails were links, the real binding lay never in them but, rather, in the unmeasured courage of the men and women who overcame all obstacles and made their far-off destinations whether or no, carrying with them, it must be remembered, hearts bowed down in many cases with the sorrow. Overdosed, as we are, with what is technically called "sob stuff", it is difficult not to become callous to honest sentiment. Homesickness tends to render the sufferer's body susceptible to diseases which otherwise would be harmless. It would, indeed, be a moving picture if we could know what it cost to say the good-byes spoken audibly by departing pioneers to friends, and unspoken (for what lips could frame the words?) to beloved fields, rivers and hills! The erroneous notion that yelling Indians encircled the Western emigrant's wagons every night drives from our minds correct ideas of the real pain endured by these westwarding Americans. Let a faded letter before me give its inkling of what was passing through an emigrant's heart while on the Oregon Trail; it pictures one rarely remembered phase of "their night":

The boys is all writeing back I believe — tell our sweet children howdy and that pap thinks of there sweet pratling constant and all the gold in 10 californias with out my family would be no comfort to me I have dreams — my mind when I am a sleep is like an uncaged Bird it is as ungeovernable as the wild roe that runs over these mighty planes I can see Sally woods wateing on her Grand Mother with her mild countinance I can see China a wireing over the floor I can hear the pratling of Sweet little nank I can see your own Dear Self I can see you in affliction and trouble. I can see that sweet smile whitch without all this worlds vane store would be no more to me than the chaff be fore the mighty Storm. Tell Sister Nerve that we have her Edwards a cooking and he does well tell her it would make her laff to see him putting in bread with his tongue between his teeth Tell her he is just like he is at home all wais mudling at some thing cant ceep him still — I want all of our friends to ceep cheer full.

Thus, for many, the struggle to go forward amid difficulties that were frequently appalling was rendered the harder because of thoughts which, like the stray horses and cattle, always took the backward track. "A study of the psychology of homesickness," states an eminent authority, "would no doubt throw light upon the still unknown aspects of the intricate moods of home love." For a laboratory for such investigation no psychologist need go further than the one hundred eighty diaries of American overland migration in the Ayer Collection of the Newberry Library!

The summer storms on the plains often greatly frightened those unaccustomed to such sights on great level spaces; but, except for a temporary wetting and delay through loss of horses and cattle, these inflicted no lasting harm. When caught in a winter blizzard on the Santa Fé Trail, for instance, as outfits sometimes were, the story was different. Colonel J. W. Abert was once so overwhelmed a few miles west of Council Grove, Kansas; of those days he wrote:

> I now saw that it would be an eventful night for us. Our fires were blown out by the tremendous violence of the wind, and we were forced to get into our beds and there abide the fury of the storm. Such was the force of the wind that it drove the snow through the canvass wall of my tent. Next morning as the sun began to appear I forced my way out and looked around on a scene of utter desolation; most of my men had lain down on the ground to sleep, but now not one of them could be seen. I called aloud; they heard me not. One man who had slept in a wagon came rushing toward me half distracted. "O, Lieutenant, take me to a house," he cried, "I shall freeze to death! I 'm freezing! I 'm freezing." I put the poor fellow in my own bed. We now searched about and found the men by the aid of the cracks on the surface of the snow, caused by the movements of the restless sleepers; covered by the heavy mantle of snow they had kept extremely warm and now the chill air felt to them intolerable. . . .
>
> This morning [eighteen days later] is the first time for thirty-six hours that any one has ventured out of bed. After some time we missed Preston and the sick man. It was now evident that they had been buried beneath the snow drift. . . . The snow was six feet deep and we had only a little piece of board to dig with and the cold was so great that no one could work very long before his hands became perfectly rigid. After a good deal of hard digging we found a pair of boots, which were recognized by the men as Preston's property. This urged us to renewed exertions; at length we cleared the snow from a portion of his buffalo robe, and lifting it up, we got sight of the poor fellow's face; he cried out in a weak voice, begging us for God's sake not to leave him to die. We assured him that we would not forsake him, and again covered his face until we could remove more of the snow; having dug as far as his waist, five men caught

hold of him to drag him out, but the snow had been moist and was packed very hard, and he was held tight by the tent which had been broken down by the pressure of the snow; however, we dug a little more until we could get at the ridge pole of the tent, which we cut in two with our axes. We now drew Preston out of the drift, which had like to proved his grave. His bedfellow, who had been much weakened by sickness, was already dead. . . . Preston told us that when he first awoke, he felt very comfortable; at length he perceived that his companion was dying. The full conception of his awful situation now burst upon him; he struggled violently but not a limb could he move, and he had sunk into the depth of despair, when we fortunately rescued him from his icy tomb.

The well-known film, "The Covered Wagon", brought to millions of interested spectators much of the atmosphere of the old transcontinental migrations. Present-day efforts to reproduce with faithfulness historical detail is in some instances highly commendable, a fact impressed upon the present writer by the receipt one morning of the following night letter: "Can you wire collect Yale University Press 522 Fifth Avenue how Saint Pierre in command at Fort Le Boeuf in 1753 covered his missing eye and which eye was gone." And yet events which can be made picturesque, whether or not historically accurate, force their way upon some picture-makers. This is illustrated, in "The Covered Wagon", by the great expense laid out on a spectacular crossing of a wide river by an outfit trending toward Oregon. The Kansas River below Manhattan, Kansas, was the only stream on that twenty-two hundred-mile track that was not usually fordable; and here outfits ferried over; at other dangerous crossings the alert Mormons had established ferries long before the 'forty-niners were faring westward. But the point is that by emphasizing the crossing of sizable streams spectacularly, the average person wholly misses the fact that it was not the infrequent streams of real size which were the nightmares of the migration — but the crossing, perhaps a dozen times a day, of dangerous cut-bank creeks, coulees and ravines along the trail. To be continually getting heavy wagons or carts down into these almost perpendicularly banked ravines; to keep from becoming mired in their bottoms, and to get up out of them again, became the constant dread of men and the terror of women and children. Little Coal Creek, south of Lawrence, Kansas, delayed one outfit longer than did the crossing of either the Kansas, Platte, Green or Snake rivers on the long road to Oregon!

No moving-picture audience would ever care to see enacted accurately the terrible sufferings of many of the 'forty-niners who fought their way through the burning sands of the Sink of the Humboldt country in Nevada to Carson River. In many cases it was an instance of dropping everything beside the road and making a rush for the far-off mountains. Whole outfits here became terror-stricken, men fighting frantically for the possession of such animals as were still fit to carry them away to safety — leaving behind wagons, equipment, food, clothing, and, pitiful to state, any and all who could not race away with them to the distant mountain streams.

One spectator of the scenes in this desert in 1850, after the wild rush of the year previous, A. W. Harlan, wrote:

I find there is about 30 [abandoned] waggons to the mile for 40 miles of the road — 1200. the dead animals will average about 100 to the mile for 40 miles — 4000. water is being sold at $1.00 a gallon. . . . I think here [on Carson River] in one place of say 20 acres of ground that there is the remains of 800 waggons, some persons think 3000. there is perhaps 2000 along the bank of the River in 6 miles. I have seen say 50 waggons that had been fired and went out. others pile them up and then pile on their ox yokes and harness and consum all together. such bonfires are common . . . people arrive all hours of the night. Those that reach here with more than half the team they start in with are considered fortunate.

The silver screen might portray something of the havoc wrought to the migration in this hotbed of death in the very sight of the snow-capped Sierras; but it would mercifully leave to the imagination the experience of wending one's way eight or nine miles a day along a road lined with thousands of dead cattle, which lay rotting in the sun. It is known that the frightful stench which arose from these carcasses proved too much for many who had endured heroically all the vicissitudes of the long two-thousand-mile backward track. Of the many graves dug beside the Carson, not a few were filled with the remains of those who went, almost instantly, stark mad in the heated putridity of this true Valley of Death.

We too easily forget that these wayfarers who were binding a nation together across leagues of desert and mountain were, very frequently, rendered unfit, physically and mentally, to do a normal day's work. It is difficult to believe that men could endure the day's work of cooking, packing, traveling and camping, for instance, when so utterly reduced in the matter of food as was sometimes the case. For example, how many calories were there in worn-out, grimy, sweat-soaked leather saddle girths, that a member of the McMahon party could contemplate eating them with equanimity, if not satisfaction, as follows:

The next day found us without food; and now came into use the long, narrow strip of raw-hide which first bound together the old, rotting logs of which the raft was made, then later to secure the mule of nights. It was now almost as hard as bone, and nearly round, having been dragged through the hot sand while it was yet green and wet, closed up like a hollow tube with sand inside. Two or three yards of it at a time was cut into pieces about five inches long, the hair singed off, the sand scratched out, and these pieces were dropped into our camp kettle and cooked until the whole formed one mass of gluten which was, to us, quite palatable. When the lasso had all been thus prepared and eaten, the broad girth which had served so well in holding the pack-saddle on the mule's back, was cleaned, cooked and eaten. These substitutes for jerk sustained us very well.

While the outdoor life was astonishingly invigorating and the climate favorable to many constitutions, the character of the only food which could be carried or secured was heavy diet and monotonous; and the risks run by drinking every known kind of water along the way were innumerable. Scurvy, which led to the disastrous cholera epidemic of 1849–1851, and bowel complaint, were common; and those whose constitutions were weakened succumbed easily to serious attacks of these and kindred diseases. Any one at all experienced in administering medicine or in nursing was in much demand in the heydays of the migration — and the stories they could tell would hardly make popular material for the silver screen! Edwin Bryant, later first mayor of San Francisco, was so held to be a good "medicine man" on his trip across the plains, much to his embarrassment. Once he was hurriedly summoned to a neighboring outfit to administer to a boy suffering from an injured leg:

I found him stretched out upon a bench made of planks, ready for the operation, which they expected I would perform.

. . . I soon learned . . . that the accident had occurred nine days previous . . . last night he called to his mother, and told her that he could *feel worms crawling in his leg!* and . . . it was then discovered that gangrene had taken place and the limb of the child was swarming with maggots . . . I was satisfied that he could not live twenty-four hours, much less survive an operation. . . . A Canadian Frenchman was present and stated that he had formerly been an assistant to a surgeon . . . and would amputate the child's limb if I declined doing it. . . . The instruments to be used were a common butcher-knife, a carpenter's hand-saw and a shoemaker's awl to take up the arteries. . . . The knife and saw were then applied and the limb amputated. A few drops of blood only oozed from the stump; the child was dead — his miseries were over. The scene of weeping and distress which succeeded this tragedy cannot be described. . . . Between eight and nine I was invited to attend a wedding. . . . After we left the bridal tent, in looking across the plain, I could see from the light of torches the funeral procession that was conveying the corpse of the little boy. While surveying this mournful scene a man arrived from another encampment about a mile and a half distant, and informed me that a wife of one of the emigrants had just been safely delivered of a son, and that there was, in consequence of this event, great rejoicing. . . . A death and funeral, a wedding and a birth, had occurred in this wilderness, within a diameter of two miles, and within two hours' time. . . . Such are the dispensations of Providence — such the checkered map of human suffering and human enjoyment!

But no matter what may have been the state of health of members of any outfit, the inexorable Law of the Trail insistently and inevitably demanded "*Go On, Go On.*" The amount of time between spring, when the rich rain-soaked Kansas soil became firm enough to bear wagons, and the first snowfall on the Blue Mountains (the Oregon route) or the Sierras (the California route) was just sufficient in which to make the transcontinental journey; the illness of any member could not be important enough to jeopardize an entire outfit. To be caught in those snows might be the death of all and the average emigrant train could make but ten to fifteen miles a day.

Get On was the cry, therefore, no matter how deep were the gorges torn by the floundering wagons in the Black Pool of the Little Blue. *Get Along* was the order, though wagon hounds snapped as the wagons with their smoking brakes plunged down the three-hundred-foot drop into Ash Hollow. *Catch Up Your Mules* was the stentorian command at break of dawn in burning Goshen Hole — no matter if funerals, weddings or child birth had been the accidents of the night before. *Ride Out* was the command at dawn, even if you had spent an exhausting day scraping pitch from spruce trees with which to "grease" the hot axles of the wagons. It was to cross the flooded "Kaw" (Kansas) and move out — and On. It was to bind the shrunken wagon-wheel felloes with strips of oxhide — and Go On. It was to burn and scrape the swollen stumps of oxen's hoofs, coat them with tar, and Go On. It was to travel a desert track all day, with moaning cattle, only to find, at the end, the long-looked-for spring sucked dry — and Go On into the night toward the next. It was to find at the end of a terrible day the spectacle of dozens of putrid cattle around an alkali lake or poison spring, and fight till you could drop to keep your cattle from rushing in to their death. It was to meet with single individuals, or a full company of them, hurrying eastward and breathing anathema upon the lands which were your goal and haven and Promised Land — and hold the *morale* of your outfit and struggle ahead. It was to Go On, although you knew in your heart some one in your company was becoming mentally unbalanced by the struggles, the fears, the stark lonesomeness, the stifling columns of dust, the doubt of what the future held in store. One catches here the true inwardness of John H. Finley's words which pictured the pioneers as "far-conquering people." Their determination canceled mere space out of the national equation and made the Ship strong.

Those trails were, it is true, only thin strands of twine, but over them brave hearts, impelled by an ardor almost unexplainable, bound the eastern "Mother Country" to a Colorado, an Oregon and a California. And what true Acts of Faith — signed in a night of doubt, signed in the desert sand of the Humboldt, with wagon-tire rust, with the lava dust of the Snake, by graves of babes and strong men — in witness of the Dawn; dawn of a Republic of continental dimensions, bounded only by the Pacific Sea; dawn of a day when no Spanish menace from the South or British menace from the North or Oriental menace from the West should alarm those whose dream of empire was flanked only by oceans!

But the processes of history, served in one generation by strands of twine leading to wilderness frontiers, demanded fresh, new building along other lines if our nation was to become what its dreamers hoped. Thus it is for us to turn to the story of stronger binding — of the laying of stone roads, the building of canals and railways, to the new frontiers of commerce and business.

PART THREE

"BE TRUE TO YOURSELVES"

XII

BANDS OF TEMPERED STEEL

WHILE the Western trails were guiding afar those who should make it certain that the United States would be a Republic of continental dimensions, Americans could not have been "true to themselves" unless, in the busy centers of population in the East, a foundation was being laid for a great industrial nation by promoting extensive plans for swift and sure methods of transportation. Thus, during the half-century when the Oregon, Santa Fé and California trails were serving to develop the splendid provinces to which they led, a great game was being played in the East over the development and control of new lines of transportation on the routes of those Indian trails we have mentioned, which connected the Atlantic seaboard with the empire washed by the Ohio River and Great Lakes.

The ringing advice of Washington to the young nation to "Be true to yourselves" demanded that the basis of a united, industrial country — improved transportation — should receive attention. This meant that the new States should look to their river-valley avenues to the west as the main chance of binding the rich interior to the Atlantic seaboard. That Virginian himself set the pace, upon his return from his tour of 1784, and became the president of the Potomac Navigation Company which now began the improvement of the Potomac River. Not far from Washington, D. C., you may find the moldering, ivy-clad ruins of the first locks built in America for the purpose of canalizing an American river. Washington's company spent something like two millions, as values are to-day, in the impossible task of controlling a large river's current. In other States, as on the Susquehanna and Lehigh in Pennsylvania and on the Mohawk in New York, similar experiments were made but with the same discouraging results. "Rivers are unmanageable things," the Sage of Philadelphia had declared, after reviewing efforts of the same kind in England; and, for a full century, American engineers found that Franklin was right; never until the new Erie Canal was constructed has a river been made to behave like a well-mannered canal.

But the gist of Washington's philosophy of American unity remained always true; the tools by which every West was to be made to feel at home within the folds of the Union might not be those Washington had in mind; but the process of making the Union inviolate by creating coöperation between separated sections, by bringing about a healthy exchange of raw materials for manufactured products, was of preëminent importance — although the methods of doing this would change with every era of development from roads to canals and from canals to railways and aëroplanes.

If rivers could not serve this great purpose, recourse must be had to the trails and pioneer roads — widened out and changed into macadamized boulevards. After that first fitful rivalry to improve rivers, all the seaboard States began seriously to study the method of Pennsylvania and Maryland in building stone roads. One of the prettiest games ever played for commercial conquest now began. The figure of a chess game fits the case, at times with some aptness; and these rival commonwealths (in order to secure the rich benefits Washington prophesied would come to the States which reached out westward for them) now moved out their "pieces", so to speak, on the mighty Allegheny chessboard — and hard roads were pitted in a game against hard roads, canals against canals and railways against railways. Every move in the contest only welded a growing nation together by the strongest bonds of a material character known to the modern world.

No sooner was it recognized that the stone roads of Pennsylvania and her neighbor Maryland (likewise favored with the wide Hagerstown belt of limestone soil) made the surest all-the-year-round pathways for freighter and stage than Baltimore countered Philadelphia's famous Lancaster Turnpike with a rival metal roadway that reached out to Reisterstown, Hagerstown and Frederick toward Cumberland in the eastern foothills of the Alleghenies. In turn, New York hastened forward with her "knights" and "bishops" (to continue our chess figure) in order to match the advance of these southern rivals; in less than a decade New York had put on foot an eight-million-dollar campaign for stone roads.

The incentive to conquer the Alleghenies with stone highways was now notably accelerated by the government. When Ohio applied for admission to the Union in 1802 she requested that her isolation from the Original Thirteen should be made less forbidding by the construction of a highway from Atlantic waters to her borders. In response, the government promised that a proportion of the money accruing to it from the sale of government lands in Ohio should be appropriated to that purpose. As a result, in 1806, President Jefferson ordered a survey of routes for such a roadway and, in 1811, the construction of a great road began from the chosen eastern terminus, Cumberland, Maryland. By 1818 this National — or Cumberland — Road was opened to Wheeling, West Virginia, and a new era of trans-Allegheny commerce began. In a most interesting way, therefore, Washington's challenge to the nation of thirty-four years before had now been met; and the welding of the seaboard to the Ohio Basin proved all that that real Father of his Country (a title as much deserved for his advocacy of commercial unity as for his stalwart struggle for Independence) had foretold.

This National Road became increasingly important as its respective sections were completed in the seven years, 1811–1818. Over its broad stone surface "a nation is moving westward", exclaimed an excited spectator. Simultaneously with the completion of the road to the Ohio, the Ohio-Mississippi steamboats proved that they were strong enough to come upstream; in 1816 the steamboat *Washington* had conquered the currents of the Mississippi and Ohio without taking advantage of backwater. Thus the completion of a great highway from the East to the Ohio, and assured steamboat navigation in the Mississippi Basin, opened at once a prospect of real significance. Western produce could now go eastward by either land or sea; Southern produce could be sold in Northern markets on either side of the Alleghenies; and, perhaps most interesting of all, Eastern manufactured goods, Pittsburgh ironware and Southern and Western produce could be laid down by steamers at that strategic great bend of the Missouri (the present Kansas City region) from whence diverged the trails to Oregon and California and Santa Fé. It therefore really seemed that the building of the National Road through western Maryland and Pennsylvania to the Ohio (with convenient eastern offshoots and extensions to Philadelphia, Baltimore and Washington) had settled important questions as to the main line of American commercial expansion and the methods by which it should be conducted.

It can readily be seen that this prospect of a monopoly of this great trade by these southern rivals did not one whit please the Yankees of New York. Should Pennsylvania and Maryland, which were blocked off from the West by the ragged Alleghenies, enjoy advantages denied to New York? Could their pathway which traversed mountains almost three thousand feet high hope to compete with one which might be built through the Mohawk Valley and Finger Lake country, where there were no mountain heights to scale? Should Philadelphia and Baltimore hold the Golden West in fee, and New York City, with the best harbor on the Atlantic, not get its full share? Such questions as these had not long been on men's lips ere the New Yorkers were ready to counter knight for knight and bishop for bishop in this game for one of the world's richest prizes, Western American commerce.

In far-off Revolutionary War days a keen-minded Knickerbocker had dreamed a dream out loud before a camp fire. He drew an accurate picture of the Mohawk Valley, the waterways between it and the Genesee, and that latter river's course to Lake Ontario. "Do you not see," Gouverneur Morris had then said, "that New York has almost a natural waterway to the Great Lakes? Allow me to lead your imagination to the very brink of daring. Some day the waters of the lakes shall break down the slight barriers which stand in the way, and, by man's assistance, flow uninterrupted to the Atlantic."

All of the early efforts of New Yorkers to canalize the Mohawk River had led to but little more success than had those of her southern rivals to improve the Potomac or Susquehanna. For a time stone-road building was essayed, as we have seen. But the building of the National Road across the Alleghenies shocked New Yorkers into renewed activity to open their natural water route. In the very same year (1806) that Jefferson had authorized the survey of the National Road, Jesse Hawley, than a pilgrim within Pittsburgh's gates, penned a forceful broadside in favor of digging a canal across New York — his native State. In detail he now showed how the very streams which could not be successfully canalized were still mighty assets because they provided a never-failing head of water for a canal.

The idea was received with enthusiasm by all New Yorkers who looked up and forward — and with ribald jests by all local adherents of the "going-to-the-devil" school of philosophy. No canal of such length existed in all the world! Floodtides which ruined the locks on canalized rivers would surely run riot in any such canal and wash its banks away! In dry summers the channel would lack sufficient water, and in winter a canal would be frozen over for months! When the ice went out it would carry all before it. Thus the pessimists argued.

But New York could not sit supinely by and let Pennsylvania and Maryland monopolize the trade of the West, or let Philadelphia and Baltimore outstrip New York City. It was pointed out how greatly all States beyond the Hudson would be benefited by any water highway that New York might open to the Great Lakes — how every State bordering those Lakes would profit by a natural highway to the Atlantic over which their cargoes of grain could float much more cheaply than they could be carried by wagon across the mountains, no matter how good the road. It was argued that not only could subscriptions be secured from at least ten interested Western States, but that, because of the interstate importance of such a waterway, aid might be had from the national government. The effort to float loans and get government assistance was undertaken. But the fact that the canal lay wholly within one State militated against these efforts. Also, the practicability of a canal so long, fed by so many various systems of waterways, was doubted from an engineering standpoint. "If New York needs a canal let her build it," said both the government and New York's neighbors.

How was proof of New York's real need to be established? By one of the innumerable "upsets" of the philosophy of history — the War of 1812–1814. That war proved the vulnerability of New York's lake frontier. It was found that it cost more than a cannon was worth to haul it across the State. Was so princely a State always to be subject to this nightmare of invasion? The belief that England had agreed to a *status quo* Treaty of Ghent because of European complications was well based. The further belief that, once the Napoleonic ghost was laid, she would begin a new American war was not well based — but it was proclaimed no less ominously and insidiously for that reason. The bill inaugurating the far-famed Erie Canal — New York's answer to the National Road — was authorized by the vote of the Council of Revision solely through fear of a third war with England. In the space of seven brief years these New Yorkers performed the "impossible"; "Clinton's Ditch" moved steadily onward, despite the enormous physical difficulties and the psychic handicap of sneer, jest and contumely. How "true to themselves" were these Nordics as they worked in "their night" to lay the basis for a great Empire State!

It was now the turn of New York's rivals to bestir themselves, for those northern neighbors had now moved out upon the continental chessboard in an exceedingly bold way. As sections of the Erie Canal were completed, and tried out in actual practice, they proved the practicability of the system long before the whole canal was completed and could take its place (as it did) as a great interstate artery. As a feat of engineering this canal exerted an influence strong and far-reaching. Floods in places did injure the banks and locks as was prophesied by the critics, but these damages proved comparatively slight and schemes to counteract their effects met with success. The canal was ice-bound each year for months; but ice proved inconsequential as a serious menace. The Erie Canal was an unqualified success — and had to be enlarged within ten years to take care of the great commerce which flooded it. It was a real factor in the upbuilding of New York City, which now for the first time passed Philadelphia in population and importance; it paved the way for the growth of that whole galaxy of splendid cities in the interior of the State, — Buffalo, Rochester, Syracuse and Utica.

With ominous forebodings Pennsylvania, Maryland and Virginia now viewed New York's triumph. True, the canal could not supplant their stone roads as local avenues of commerce, but might it not divert the bulk of Western trade? This fear seemed to be realized to the full by the action now taken by the State of Ohio. The farmers of that State had found themselves greatly handicapped because their wheat frequently soured on the long river journey in ship's holds to New Orleans. In one instance only the innate ingenuity of a typical Yankee could avail to turn a year's labor into profit; in dismay at the condition of his soured cargo, which no longer was fit for bread-making, he palmed the whole load off on New Orleans cracker-makers! The success of the Erie Canal turned Ohio's eyes northward. It was seen at once that if canals were built through Ohio to Lake Erie it would make possible the shipping of wheat via the Erie Canal outlet to the East — always on the cooler route such as wheat demanded. This idea won the debate in the Ohio legislature; bills calling for the construction of a thousand miles of Ohio canals, giving a northward outlet for grain, were passed; and the hero of New York, Governor Clinton, was brought all the way to Ohio to lift the first spadeful of earth in this great undertaking.

New York's southern rivals now saw their stone roads, and everything else, going straight "to the devil." Alert, however, to match the Empire State's powerful position in the exciting game, Virginia and Maryland brought up their laggard chessmen, and planned a great rival interstate canal by way of the Potomac and Youghiogheny to Pittsburgh. Canals themselves, a little before this, had been discountenanced — even when a comparatively level country was to be traversed. Now, however, the gigantic task of throwing a canal across mountain summits was boldly undertaken! Southern knights and bishops should meet those of the North in this contest for supremacy; and, ere the Erie Canal was completed, the much-heralded Chesapeake and Ohio Canal was surveyed; by it Baltimore and Georgetown (Washington) would still hold the ancient trade-prestige won in the old colonial days on stone roads!

But, suddenly, the Maryland surveyors threw a bomb into camp. They found that tide-water Baltimore could not be linked up to the Chesapeake and Ohio Canal. No generous Hudson River (such as New York had) existed in Maryland whereby the necessary gradual change from a lock canal to ocean tide-water could be made. Engineering science was not then able to effect an abrupt change from the two different types of navigation. Baltimore, the Queen City of Chesapeake Bay, and long the proud mistress of Western commerce, was about to be checkmated! Consternation reigned in the minds of Lord Baltimore's offspring. What move in this interesting game could they make to ward off isolation and decay? The move decided upon was no less startling than New York's former decision to build a canal.

Baltimoreans castled — to save their "queen." If canals could not maintain the prestige of their city, then a railroad should! Loud laughter from New York followed — such laughter as its enemies had once showered upon the Erie Canal! Railroads were now in their infancy in England and steam engines were utter novelties. Even if these could run on a straight track (a very doubtful hypothesis), how could a straight track be laid across the Alleghenies, where even the bald eagle had to mind his *p*'s and *q*'s to fly straight? Curves would certainly ruin the whole plan if both passengers and freight had to be transferred at every curve. The delay that this could cause can be fancied, if, for instance, such transfers had to be made to-day at every curve on the Baltimore and Ohio Railway!

But the Baltimore men in "their night" heroically swallowed their fears and sent to England for experts and the designs of necessary railway equipment.[1] On July 4, 1828, two pageants were, therefore, enacted in this Southland, the lifting of the first spadefuls of earth for both the Chesapeake and Ohio Canal and the Baltimore and Ohio Railroad. Patriots hurrahed and pessimists grinned. Speechmakers foretold the glory of a new age — some in terms of a mountain-scaling canal, others in terms of rails and steam engines. And on into the wilderness rival crews of men forged, making America "true to herself" at every step.

The advance on this mighty chessboard (to continue our figure of speech) of Baltimore's "castles" and "queen" set men to thinking for the safety of their "pawns", "knights" and "bishops" — weaker tools, confessedly, than those their Chesapeake rivals now so brazenly brought forth. Pennsylvania, quick to realize the strength of New York's canal as a "go-getter" of Western business, but temporarily skeptical of railways as the solution of the problem, rapidly planned and energetically pushed the Pennsylvania Canal toward the Altoona mountain crest. With splendid daring a new system of transporting canal boats across the summit was now adopted. This consisted of a series of inclined planes on which cars of cradle-like form operated; these cars were attached by cables

[1] That this plucky exhibition of initiative was not an altogether sporadic thing, but was, rather, more or less typical of Baltimoreans, is suggested by the fact that on water, as well as on land, these Marylanders were ready to exploit innovations with singular confidence. For while the first rails and ties were being riveted together to form the first American railway, hammers, saws, mallets and chisels were fashioning in Baltimore harbor the frame of the world-famous *Ann McKim*, first of American clipper ships. This boat had lines which utterly defied all the hackneyed rules of the past; its dimensions had the "insane", "silly" and "preposterous" ratio (length to breadth) of 4.6 to 1. It was launched in 1832 and such clippers finally conquered the seas as railways conquered the land.

to stationary engines at the top of each incline; they were lowered into the end of the canal and the boats were floated upon them and securely fastened for the upward ride. This was the most difficult piece of engineering performed in our country up to that time and it elicited the interest of engineers the world over. The reader may remember that Washington in 1784 affirmed (page 99) that Westerners would do their full part toward the welding of the Atlantic seaboard to the Mississippi Valley beyond the Allegheny mountain wall. In its way it is an interesting fulfilment of that prophesy that the stationary engines which hauled up, on these inclined planes in Pennsylvania, the first loads of freight that ever crossed that rugged barrier by mechanical means were built in Pittsburgh.

But that same imperial integrity of sections, which made it easier for mountainless New York to build the most practical and profitable canal, still held. As railway engineering progressed, those wide-awake New York cities we have mentioned began to join themselves together by little, independent railways. In time New York City was linked to Albany; Albany to Utica; Utica to Syracuse; and Syracuse to Rochester and Buffalo. That these were planned as local lines originally perhaps actually accelerated their growth, and the creation, in fact, if not "on paper", of the nucleus of the later New York Central Railroad which came into existence as such in the 'forties.

Meanwhile the Chesapeake and Ohio Canal only reached to Cumberland, Maryland, and not that far without saddling Maryland with an enormous debt which was to be the sport of politicians for many years. Slowly the Baltimore and Ohio Railroad crawled westward by way of Mountain Lake Park, where Washington slept in the snows on his memorable western trip of 1784. Very quickly Pennsylvanians became converted to a belief in railroads and, though late in starting, the Pennsylvania Railroad made brilliant progress. As a result both the Pennsylvania and the Baltimore and Ohio railroads were completed to the Ohio River in 1853. By that late date a score of local railways had linked together most of the important cities of the East, South and West. An especial rivalry had grown up between proud, old St. Louis and an "upstart" town, which claimed to be a city, at the foot of Lake Michigan. And it was only a few years ere Chicago proved to have a location which would make it one of the world's great railway centers.

Looking back upon that exciting game in which rivals eagerly pitted road against road, canal against canal, and finally, railroad against railroad, let us not miss one interesting fact before we survey the struggle in the large. It is very plain that geographical conditions had been fundamental factors, as they always are, in transportation problems. At the same time we see that geography was, in reality, only an item. When the task was easy, work went fast; when it was hard, work moved slowly. Great swamps swerved the Erie Canal; high mountains swerved inclined planes and railroads. The importance of geography, then, appears in its most interesting and important aspect; and, more clearly than usual, does it seem that what was done was done by men — not by geography — on lines of least resistance.

In the large, the picture of those thirty-seven years, from the beginning of the Erie Canal to the arrival of railway trains at the Ohio River, is remarkable in the annals of man's conquest of our continent. No such increase of railway mileage in any land approached America's record for the years 1830–1860. And every blow which drove home a railway spike echoed the call, "Be True to Yourselves." Though rivals may have quarreled boisterously in that interesting game to conquer the Alleghenies and secure Western commerce, what, so much as rivalry, would have hastened the forging of links which made the nation one?

And in what era of our history have calamity howlers and pessimists had a richer flowering than in those days when new transportation methods were being tried? The art of destructive construction never so nearly approached a fine art as here. For everywhere and always the superceding of one system by another seemed to threaten "the very foundations of society", *i.e.*, the means of livelihood of the losers and the ruin of their investment. Enraged packhorsemen cut the traces, killed the horses and burned the wagons of the first wagoners who threatened their monopoly. Wagoners, in turn, in another generation, vented their rage on canals — broke their banks, scuttled the boats, killed the tow-horses. Hudson River boatmen were equally violent in their attacks on steamboats; Fulton's *Clermont* had her paddle wheels boarded up lest angry enemies should ruin them! And, in cases, canal-men were equally vindictive at new railroads. All innovations are revolutionary. "I come to bring the sword," said the Man of Peace. How full of meaning it is, in proof that civilization and common sense have made strides never suspected by your typical grumbler, that the Wright Brothers' first successful aëroplane of a generation ago was looked upon as a great asset instead of being hewn to bits by trolley, railway and automobile manufacturers; and that even the frightful loss of capital suffered by the investors in the decadent trolley lines in our country can be met so philosophically, the equipment junked and the results turned into newer and more promising fields of speculation!

But in the larger view, also, we must see and feel the patriotic thrill which warmed the hearts of these builders of old. Local jealousy there was, of course — serving as a spur; but behind that shone out a spirit to warm the heart of even a pessimist. Rarely did one of these enterprising promoters ignore the national viewpoint and outlook. It is illustrated, for instance, in Fulton's struggle to ship an engine of assured power from England for the *Clermont*. He saw the benefit steamboats would bring to *all* America, and of especial interest to him was the part they would play on our western rivers and lakes. "I consider steamboats of such infinite use in America," he wrote President Monroe, in his effort to have our government secure permission from England for the exportation of a Boulton-Watt engine, "that I should feel a culpable neglect toward my country if I relaxed for a moment in pursuing every necessary measure for carrying it into effect — I plead this not for myself alone but for our country."

When, in their old-fashioned high stocks and tall hats, those Fathers of New York joined in a pageant to celebrate the completion of the Erie Canal, a great flotilla carried a cask of Lake Erie water across New York Bay and out to the Atlantic. There, in a silence broken only by the lisp of the waves, the Governor of the State said:

This solemnity, at this place, on the first arrival of vessels from Lake Erie, is intended to indicate and commemorate the navigable communication, which has been accomplished between our Mediterranean Seas and the Atlantic Ocean, in about eight years, to the extent of more than four hundred and twenty-five miles, by the wisdom, public spirit, and energy of the people of the State of New York; and may the God of the Heavens and the Earth smile most propitiously on this work, and render it subservient to the best interests of the *human race*.

The words I have italicized show the breadth of Governor Clinton's vision as to the country-wide service which his much-derided "Ditch" would perform. That vision, in the face of the derision, rings with a true patriotic flavor.

When the first shovelful of earth was lifted in beginning the Chesapeake and Ohio Canal, the president of the company addressed the holiday crowd:

There are moments in the progress of time, which are counters of whole ages. There are events, the monuments of which, surviving every other memorial of human existence, eternize the nation to whose history they belong, after all other vestiges of its glory have disappeared from the globe. At such a moment have we now arrived.

Elegant bombast you say; yes, but behind the sophomoric phrases lay the love of country which sponsored them. On the same day, July 4, 1828, when the only living signer of the Declaration of Independence, Charles Carroll, raised the first spadeful of earth in the construction of the Baltimore and Ohio Railroad, Director Morris of the Board spoke these memorable words:

We are about opening a channel through which the commerce of the mighty country beyond the Allegheny must seek the ocean — we are about affording facilities of intercourse between the East and West, which will bind the one more closely to the other, beyond the power of an increased population or sectional differences to disunite.

Nothing more than improvement of transportation has awakened the fervid exultation of men; and inherently, despite tangible profits which might arise, the cause for gratification always lay in the sense of conquest and the fruit of conquest in renewed and more vital nationality. When the bands of steel which so truly bound our young West together, and to the East, had reached Chicago and St. Louis, men had already talked of railways which would link the Great Plains and Pacific Coast to the Union. The very thought of new methods of transportation to accomplish this conquest moved men sincerely. Even when the picturesque Pony Express began its brief existence in 1860, the feat called for repeated exultation. In these words did the editor of the St. Joseph *Free Democrat* relieve his pent-up enthusiasm:

Take down your map and trace the footprints of our quadrupedantic animal: From St. Joseph on the Missouri to San Francisco on the Golden Horn — two thousand miles — more than half the distance across our boundless continent; through Kansas, through Nebraska, by Fort Kearney, along the Platte, by Fort Laramie past the Buttes, over the Mountains, through the narrow passes and along the steep defiles, Utah, Fort Bridger, Salt Lake City, he witches Brigham with his swift pony-ship — through the valleys, along the grassy slopes, into the snow, into the sand, faster than Thor's Thialfi, away they go, rider and horse — did you see them? They are in California, leaping over its golden sands, treading its busy streets. The courser has unrolled to us the great American panorama, allowed us to glance at the home of one million people, and has put a girdle around the earth in forty minutes. Verily the riding is like the riding of Jehu, the son of Nimshi for he rideth furiously. Take out your Watch. We are eight days from New York, eighteen from London. The race is to the swift.

Though not expressed in the piquant language of sixty-eight years ago, the same exultation at the newest means of transportation as a factor for unity rings out in a recent editorial in the Los Angeles *Saturday Night:*

What more graphic illustration could we get of the oneness of the country than was offered Tuesday of this week when citizens of Los Angeles, 3000 miles from the national capital, sat in their homes and heard, more plainly than if the speaker were in an adjoining room, President Coolidge delivering his address on George Washington before a joint session of Congress.[1]

Now arose in the far West the exact condition for which Washington provided the true panacea almost a century before — the necessity of binding a nation together with serviceable methods of communication. With that patriot's ringing words (page 100) in mind, it is interesting to see how the same argument was used in the 'sixties of the nineteenth century that was employed by Washington in the 'eighties of the century before: "The west side of the continent," said F. H. Ludlow, "is overwhelmingly loyal, proud of the American union and its own position in it. But the Pacific States will in time grow, manufacture, import for themselves; and when that maturity arrives, the homogeneity of the two coasts will and should depend upon the degree of facility afforded to intercommunication. So long as it remains a formidable undertaking to pass between New York and San Francisco, so long will there develop an independence of interest and feeling

[1] In this Washington's Birthday Address of 1928, President Coolidge quoted the present writer on the importance of Washington's influence as a pioneer nationalist: "He calls him our first expansionist," said the President, "the originator of the idea of possessing the West through commercial relations. 'It was a pioneer idea instinct with genius and Washington's advocacy of it marks him as the first commercial American — the first man typical of the American that was to be.'"

which, however gradual and imperceptible, cannot fail to result in two distinct nations."[1]

Amid scoffs and jeers, "dreamers" and "lunatics" planned and began the two branches of a Pacific Railway, running west from Omaha and east from San Francisco toward that famous meeting-place at Promontory, Utah, where, in 1869, the laying of a polished laurel tie and the driving of a golden spike completed the binding of a continent with bands of steel. By a special wire, connected with the last rail laid, the news was flashed to Washington; the Liberty Bell heralded it beside the Delaware and cannon and fireworks in a hundred towns and cities passed along the pean. This feat piqued the imagination of all the civilized world. Critics, of course, were not lacking who pointed out that one thin line of parallel rails across a vast desert might be so often cut to pieces that the patriot dream of a united country was still but a fragrant fancy. Here again, however, operated the same sort of force which welded a nation together even while the pessimist talked. The connecting link was slight from the physical standpoint; it was a thin iron track amid vast wastes of mountain and desert. But it did *connect;* only by its breaking the connection could its power be realized. This is prettily illustrated in the case of the telegraph wire stretched across the same wilderness just previous to the building of the railway. "What a fragile thing," laughed the red man, looking at the thin wire; "I can break that with one thrust of my spear — with a rock, even." He broke it. Soon, as from nowhere, men appeared to mend the rent. Who told them a break had occurred? Could the wire *talk?* They broke it again. Again angry men appeared. The "hair in the air" *could*

[1] *The Heart of the Continent*, page 219.

talk! It was fearsome "medicine." They never broke it but men came at once. It was, truly, a Manitou! They came to fear and shun the devilish thing — some Indians were afraid, even, to ride under it! Just so, the impulse sent out by the brain cell seems feeble; but it is as strong as the cell. These iron tracks across the arid or mountainous wildernesses were just as mighty as the desire of the American people for unity; just as strong as their passion to "Be true to themselves." A few days ago the longest New World railway tunnel, the "Cascade Tunnel" on the Great Northern, was dedicated. President-elect Hoover on that occasion echoed the same "aroma of nationality" and century-old sense of conquest when he said of that feat of engineering, "It gives every American confidence in the vitality of our civilization."

XIII

A ROAD MADE ROUGH WITH BAYONETS

While Americans were being true to themselves by laying lines which, one day, would become the keys and channels of industry to bind a nation together, we must see the contradictory enigma of the normal rise of sectionalism which that very development helped to produce; this illustrates the fact that in civilization's every gain there seems to be some loss; and that a nation's life, like man's, seems to be a continual contest between centrifugal and centripetal forces. As the nation grew lustily, the business man and transporter formed a distinct class; the agriculturists and cattlemen also became distinct classes. The former contained two subdivisions, the farmer of the North and Northwest and the planter of the South and Southwest. As these groups grew and consolidated, provincialism became sectionalism — that is, we became a nation of sections (made up of combined provinces) which were distinguished by economic needs that were essentially different. The greatest French critic of American institutions, De Tocqueville, saw this clearly when he said, "These interests [the clash over the tariff of 1828] constitute, in the different provinces of so vast an empire, rival *nations* rather than parties." Nothing could have happened more normally than this seeming contradiction. A morning-glory comes into beauty no more naturally than our provinces grew spontaneously into distinctive life; a tulip develops no more naturally than our provinces metamorphosed into sections through the normal influences of economic pressure and, in the end, made the Road rough with bayonets.

Given a small acreage of fertile land in the North, together with large sections of sterile land, a profusion of fast-flowing rivers and an active, ingenious people — and you have the natural rise of mills, factories, cities. With this basis for a manufacturing civilization, all that is then needed for prosperity is markets. A huge population suddenly growing up in the Middle West provided those markets. Practically all the lines of transportation we have described were lines constructed from the Northeast to the Northwest. Even to-day the main lines of railways, telegraphs, bus lines and telephones lie north of the Potomac River. So dominant are the east and west lines, in railway parlance, that few if any roads in our country "run" in other directions. Can any American railway engineer whistle to "call in" a brakeman from either the north or the south? On north-and-south lines, "north", technically, is the east, "south" is the west. That miniature war on the continental chessboard we described, like practically all real wars, was most important because of its unpremeditated and unforeseen results. They welded ambitious provinces into one mighty commercial section. Even those which, seemingly, lost the battle found a jewel in the toad's head of defeat; found themselves a part of a very prosperous Nation-of-the-North. With great energy the Northeast was "true to itself" and prospected and exploited the Northwest; it linked that world to its own with magnetic chains that spelled prosperity for both — those bands of tempered steel. Provincialism remained, as the Cavalier and the Despot of Broomsedge Cove represented physical "provinces" within a great section of our country.

Now, it is no more instinctively human to close an eyelid or raise an arm in the face of an unexpected blow than it is for any people to ward off a stroke at their economic prosperity. We have already noted such incidents. The morality of President Jefferson's Purchase of Louisiana may have disturbed some Easterners. Their objection lay in the economic effect of attempting to absorb, protect, fortify and develop a vast barren wilderness no nation could ever want or use. "There is no telling," we can hear them say, "what a drain on our resources Louisiana will not entail; how many States may not be admitted from it to the Union; how may our prosperity not be swallowed up in raising legions to protcct this trans-Alpine Gaul; what Cæsar, fresh from victories, may not return, dragging Indians in chains behind his covered wagon and demand a crown." The morality of the cause of the War of 1812 may have interested some Easterners, but it was the anticipated shock to their business which provoked many to sympathize with those who would have had New England secede from a nation which could, willy-nilly, force them into a war with the strongest sea power on earth. "What if we do suffer indignities and insults," some of them said in effect (my authority is one of the keenest Yankee blue-bloods in Boston) "we can make money despite either England's or France's restrictions." In the hour of excitement and near-panic they had the delicious presence of mind exhibited by the Hebrew who was chasing a thief with a policeman and who, seeing the officer draw a revolver, exclaimed with his last expiring breath, "Shoot him in the pants—the coat vas mine."

New England did not want the existing, profitable peace with England shot through the heart, for the "coat" was hers!

It would be highly constructive if our modern psychoanalysists could solve this interesting historical problem of morality as it pertains to sectional welfare. So often what is "right" seems merely to be what makes for prosperity; and what is "wrong" is that which militates against prosperity. The men of Charleston cried out angrily over the "Tariff of Abominations" of 1828 and proposed to annul the national law because it threatened to undo their prosperity. It was, they said, "wrong", "wicked", "unchristian", "hellish." They threatened to secede from the Union, as New England men twice had threatened to do, and took many of their arguments from Northern speechmakers. The far West has cried out often at the injustice of their subjugation to money and commercial standards imposed upon them by the East. The Pacific Coast has expostulated heatedly over proposed new immigration laws. Material prosperity, in every case, was the basis of such outcries. And how easy has it been for sections to adopt an attitude of wide-eyed amazement at the "unpatriotic" deportment of other sections — to assume the "holier-than-thou" affectation — when innovations were proposed which in no way menaced their own material welfare!

The reader has no doubt wondered how one writing on the topic of American unity could philosophically hurdle the desperate Civil War which rent the country in twain in those black years 1861–1865 — a war which, it is said, could not have occurred, for instance, in a more perfectly united France. Nothing could have been further from my intention than to avoid that famous issue. For the platform on which our thesis rests is most perfectly depicted by it. But I must ask that you recognize that occasions of war and causes of war differ very greatly. Also that behind the sections lay the provinces; and that each province had a history millions of years old; that in them there was something of that imperial integrity which led them to produce their specific and essential products, blue grass or pennyroyal, the David Harums, the Shepherds of Kingdom Come, the Old Man Enrights; that in each one "right" and "wrong" were viewed as adjectives describing acts or policies which affected for good or ill *material prosperity*. Only thus can we reach the paradox — and the truth — that nothing but the emancipation of the South from slavery could bring genuine Amcrican unity.

The South was compelled to be "true to itself" and defend the individuality and integrity of its soils and products at the very outset of its history. When Virginia became a royal province the King of England laid down the theory that the colony owed it to the Mother Country to supply such resources as she lacked; this would cxempt English merchants from paying the tariffs necessary to secure such from exorbitant foreign rivals. Therefore, Virginia must raise wheat and silk and wine. For some sixty years the contest went on between English kings and Virginia biology. But biology won. Virginia raised tobacco, and, when scolded, raised yet more and better tobacco.

Along with tobacco, the South found her soils well fitted for other staple crops, such as cotton and rice. Climate played a domineering part in these matters, for white men could not endure the field-work required by these crops. As slaves were brought from Africa they were disposed of in all the colonies, but were in greater demand in those hot summerlands than in the cooler North. It was no fondness for colored men that rendered them more valuable to the South; it was no antipathy to the slave system that made slaves less valuable in the North. Everywhere it was purely an economic problem; if two trucks do your business, you do not buy three; if one slave sufficed in a New York or Philadelphia family, the head of the family did not buy two; if fifty were needed by George Washington's grandfather, he could hardly content himself with less. How perfectly the economic value of slaves, and not moral or ethical questions, dominated men is illustrated in the case of California in later days. People had, by that time, been discussing widely whether a State had the right to abolish slavery within its limits. Thousands of both Southerners and Northerners had rushed to California to find gold. There was scarcely room for a slave system in those mining districts; economically, it had no place. So the Argonauts let other people wrangle over the "right" and "wrong" of the thing and went ahead and abolished slavery in their State — Southerners voting with Northerners "Aye" without any fuss or feathers about it. The national debate, however, ground on as to whether a State could do this long after California had done it and forgotten all about it! As we have hinted before, the morals of a problem, process or policy are, sometimes, never questioned until somebody's fat is in the fire. In all the earlier days the matter of slavery was purely a matter of dollars and cents, and if Northerners did not buy many slaves, their captain-skippers ("true to themselves") were glad to find, transport and sell them where the best price was to be had.

With insistent regularity economic laws worked on — as though men were only tools in the hands of the great gods, Soil-and-Climate and Supply-and-Demand. These gods dictated two lines of economic development in the South: one that, as tobacco and cotton wore out the thin soils, plantations had to advance and new lands be opened up; the other, that an increasing horde of domestic slaves brought unexpected hardships. Cotton and tobacco varied in price, but the demands of one's Negroes did not vary. They had to be kept busy and well; an idle servile population is a serious menace. This compelled the South to stick to large, staple crops; only these would keep the slaves busy all months of the year. This did not enable planters to do what they would have liked — branch out, speculate in new lines, experiment with other crops, engage in business schemes, go in for diversified agriculture. It was always a struggle to provide new lands to take the place of old; clothing and food for their dependents; seed for next year's crop; tools for the work. And, too, there was the maintenance of the health of these ignorant, but usually devoted, servants, who, in many years of infancy, childhood and old age could give but slight return for the cost of their subsistence and general welfare.

I wish Fairfax Harrison could have lived a century ago and, instead of running the Southern Railway, could have acted as personal conductor to about twenty thousand Northerners a year and introduced them all to the "Mistress' Room" on the ground floor of the typical planter's home, about which he has written so intimately. He could, perhaps, have prevented the Civil War. If you stop to think what a conscientious mistress of a hundred black families needed in her wardrobes, closets, cabinets, drawers and cupboards to meet the exigencies of sickness, contagions, accidents, childbirths, funerals, weddings, drownings, burnings, "miseries", fits, falls, Christmas, Fourth of July, sacraments, betrothals, toothache, earache, heartache, bad dreams, hookworm and nosebleed, you will have a faint idea of the ordered jumble which existed in that room. It was at once a hospital, infirmary and apothecary shop; above all it was a Shrine, and thousands of Southern women spent whole lives of sacrifice that made them the Florence Nightingales of a forlorn race. We hear of the immemorial loving-kindness of Black Mammies; it had its background in the self-sacrifice of White Mammies, of which little is heard and whose praises the jazz fanatics never sing. When you hear Southern women described, in a tone of commiseration (it may be), as "unreconstructed even yet", let your mind wander back to that room in the "Big House" and consider the inheritance of soul-qualities which came from ten generations of women who gave unendingly of their care and patience for a race no one ever loved, or will love, as they did.[1]

But all this costs money. By Washington's and Jefferson's time the slave system did not pay. The price of cotton was too low and the underfoot expenses, let alone the overhead, were too great. Men have reiterated in

[1] Keenly, indeed, did De Tocqueville in 1833 sense some truths regarding race prejudice in ante-bellum days: "In those parts of the Union where negroes are no longer slaves, they have in no wise drawn nearer to the whites. On the contrary, the prejudice of race appears to be stronger in the States which have abolished slavery . . . In the South the negroes are less carefully kept apart; they sometimes share the labors and recreations of the whites . . . and although legislation treats them more harshly, the habits of the people are more tolerant and compassionate . . . It is not for the good of the negroes, but for that of the whites, that measures are taken to abolish slavery in the United States." "Democracy in America", I, 460–462.

lofty phrases the fact that the Ordinance of 1787 forever prohibited slavery north of the Ohio River. As a political precedent it was invaluable; as a proof of a pious hatred of an evil system it has less significance. Many Southerners would, gladly, have had the Ordinance include the South too. It hurts the cause of "history" to have idealism used to explain things which happened in the humdrum way most things happen, and because economic interests suggest them to be best.

But then, suddenly, a Yankee brought forth one of those alleged "upsets" to the philosophy of history — the kind which but proved again the "emergence" philosophy. The cotton gin, lessening the cost and work of raising and cleaning cotton, made greater crops and profits possible. The foreign markets for cotton also opened now more widely. It became a profitable crop. The more land, the more slaves, the more cotton, the more profits. But this does not mean that the South escaped from the sinister bondage we have mentioned, a system now forged more strongly with the increased profit of the business. In fact, paying slavery still more enslaved the South with a wrong economic principle, namely, that it is more profitable to buy men and keep them, and be unable to secure from them an honest *quid pro quo*, than it is to hire labor and be able to demand a return for proper wages. "In the end, the slave has cost more than the free servant, and his labor is less productive," said a planter who knew. "Why continue a system," asked the Louisville *Examiner* in 1848, "which impoverishes the many and deadens the enterprise of the State? We want it removed." It is impossible for finite minds to conceive of a creator endowed with sufficient power to install a new galaxy of planets in the heavens which will operate on a principle out of harmony with those already fixed. It would mean chaos confounded. If all the miracles necessary to release the South from the system so irredeemably fastened upon it had been performed, there yet remained another huge one to be wrought.

Since days which no man could remember, plantation crops had been pledged in advance for the cost of the new tools, buildings, slaves and seed needed for "next year." This system, once installed, worked two serious handicaps. Banks could lend money only on a known staple crop to be grown on acres of known and tested fertility. They could not lend money on experiments, new crops or novel adventures. Thus planters were denied innovation and forced into a fixed routine. Again, in a way sometimes serious, the stability of the Southern banks, and the money they freely printed, depended on the success of crops and the strength of the market price which they brought. This fickle, varying foundation did not make for the true stability which weathers "hard times" buoyantly.

Under these circumstances, Southerners ("true to themselves") went on enslaving Negroes profitably, and a bad system of labor went on enslaving the South. Except for a handful of monomaniacs, slavery was never called either "right" or "wrong" — it had never been called that in the North. Whenever that moral question was raised by an eccentric, men pointed out that Jesus had criticized almost every social and political error and fetish of His day, but never slavery.

But now, as the years ran their course, wholly unforeseen complications began to arise. But for this the South might still be enslaved by the slavery system. The South became consolidated into a new kind of a section and the complications accentuated differences (which fundamentally were those of soil and climate) of opinion in matters of all kinds. The reader does not need to be reminded that the provincial differences of attitude and prejudice and opinion had, for long, maintained some of those ancient "Chinese Walls" of colonial antipathy. The new complications gave men of the two sections colored glasses which made every topic that came up look one way to the Southerner and another way to the Northerner.

One of the most important of these has been described. The North grew rapidly into a manufacturing section. Its lines of transportation, its mines, mills, factories, its cities and spreading network of mail (and later telegraph) lines, bound it together under the control of the gods of Commerce and Prosperity. Meanwhile, although prosperous, the South remained distinctly agricultural. Europeans who descant vigorously on the alleged fact that France, for instance, could not have been torn asunder by a Civil War like ours, would be put to it to find in France such a dissimilar development of two great sections such as American history portrays.

This development immediately gave men of the North and South utterly different views of the tariff laws. The North wanted protection for its manufactures. This put a tax on foreign goods which were shipped to all America, and for the foreign goods which the South needed it had to pay high prices. For others, it was at the mercy of the North. Much of Southern cotton, rice and tobacco was sold in Europe. How soon would Europeans retaliate against the American tariff by charging a tariff of their own? What, then, would become of Southern cotton profits? It is plain through what different-colored glasses Northerners and Southerners looked at the tariff.

The North wanted internal improvements which should be aided by the government's treasury. Such lines of commerce spread Northern manufactured goods; roads, canals and railways put new regions on the manufacturer's map. You can see that men of the South and North would differ on the question of spending national funds for improvements which would benefit the North far more than the South.

The manufacturing North wanted a stable financial system — a standard of money values which would not vary. The "wild cat" paper money manufactured profusely in the South and West was next to worthless in the North; and, because of the closer commercial connection which existed between North and West than existed between North and South, less difficulty was experienced in converting the West to the Northern view than the South. It is plain that the currency question was, also, looked upon from diverse standpoints by the people of the two sections.

Now, when such vital questions as these, tariff, internal improvements and money standards, are in dispute between men of different sections, they engender debates of every sort and kindle fires of suspicion and hatred. In the end, it would seem, Northerners and Southerners could hardly agree on the sphericity of the earth or the binomial theory. It was, in fact, common in those days for men even in the same section or group to differ diametrically on subjects of importance. The wide gulf which separated Ralph Waldo Emerson and Abraham Lincoln on the question of the "martyrdom" of John Brown is an illustration of this. To the New Englander (at first thought) John Brown was "the new Saint, than whom none purer or more brave was ever led by love of men into conflict and death — the new Saint who has achieved his martyrdom and will make the gallows glorious as the Cross." But to the straight-thinking Lincoln, immediately it all appeared in another light. "Old John Brown," he said, "has been executed for treason against a State. We cannot object even though he agreed with us in thinking slavery wrong. That cannot excuse violence, bloodshed and treason. It could avail him nothing that he might *think* himself right." Nor Emerson, either.

It is plain that although the North preached high tariff, internal improvements and monetary reform the only harm which could actually accrue to the South would come by putting those ideas into practice; *i.e.*, creating them by law of Congress. If this was done, the South feared it would suffer just the same kind of economic eclipse that Germany is said to have anticipated in 1914. To prevent that eclipse the South desired to keep even the balance of power in the Senate (her hold over the House of Representatives, whose members are chosen in proportion to population, being hopelessly lost from the start because of her smaller number of inhabitants) and so be able to block legislation inimical to her. In order to do that, just as many States friendly to the South had to be admitted to the Union as those which adhered to the Northern viewpoints.

For practically twenty years the important forensic battles in Congress were waged, in reality, if not in name, over this problem of balance of power in the Senate. No good argument against the admission of States friendly to the North was found — except those raised by all who feared the South's eclipse. Now what argument was found which made it seem objectionable to admit States which favored the South?

That slavery was wrong! And the argument was sound, as a premise. But the conclusion — that the South was "guilty" — was utterly false. The idea that slavery was wrong was of English origin. It was adopted as an English policy as soon as it was known that it would not work any serious economic loss. It was seized upon by religious leaders in the North, and was diligently pressed just as soon as it was clearly established (in the 'thirties) that New England had gone over to a tariff basis and that agriculture would never again be its chief means of wealth. The South had been alarmed at the thought of political (therefore economic) eclipse; it was angered at being adjudged "guilty" of the wrong of slavery.

How truly the slave system — in our era, if not in Christ's — was wrong is now understood. "Uncle Tom's Cabin", which did the South a great injustice by making the unusual seem the commonplace, yet gave the world at large facts which could not remain even exceptional in the new age. Slavery broke up families; no such system could long endure. How truly the South was not "guilty" is proven on practically every page of this book. In origin and in conduct, forces all beyond man's power to change or control had always been absolutely dominating. The South was no more "guilty" of slavery than soldiers are "guilty" of trench fever. To be handicapped by Fate with a system involving great hardships was unfortunate; to be deemed guilty of moral wrong for the system was intolerable. To injury was added insult. And Northern abolitionists seemed to like to make the insult sting in the same proportion as their economic interests were free from danger if the theory won. They were filled with the religious fervor of Crusaders. Their main tenet was correct; but the proposal that a system two hundred years old should quickly be abolished was quixotic and heartless.

For slavery would have run its course to freedom, and the South have been relieved of its economic octopus, without recourse to radical measures. Lincoln was never more right than when he said that a "House divided cannot stand"; but what really divided the House was not slavery but economic systems; if genuine American unity was to be realized, those systems had to be brought into working harmony. And Lincoln was never more wrong (in theory) than when he (and his Republican Party) declared that neither proposed to touch slavery *where it existed.* For slavery could not long exist "where it existed"; "like an army of locusts," said an observer, "it is compelled to shift its place, by the desolation it has made." As lands became sterile, new lands had to be acquired; territorial expansion was absolutely requisite.[1] And beyond the Mississippi, north of Texas, slavery would not have survived. The staple crops of the plains would never have supported the system. "Slave labor is a very expensive method of cultivating cereal grain . . . inapplicable to countries in which corn and

[1] "It is scarcely possible to foresee," wrote Miss Martineau in 1835, "the destination of the southern states when the curse of slavery shall be removed. Up to that period continual deterioration is unavoidable . . . no mismanagement *short of employing slaves* will account for the deterioration of the agricultural wealth of these states. When the traveller observes the quality of some of the land now under cultivation, he wonders how other estates could have been rendered so unprofitable as they are. . . . A wise friend [of an Alabama planter] thought that it was a great injury, instead of benefit to his fortune, that his labourers were not free. To use this man's expression, 'it takes two white men to make a black man work'; and he was confident that it was not necessary, on any pretence whatever, to have a single slave in Alabama." — "Society in America" (1837), I, 210.

wheat are cultivated," said an ante-bellum agricultural authority. Slavery had to expand and expansion would have altered and finally extinguished it. But Crusaders have little patience. Thus it was that Fate forced upon the South the revolution which should free it and bring an American unity totally impossible under the old régime. This was achieved in hatred, in blood, in great sacrifice of lives, hopes, dreams, friendships. It left its serious scar. How the same result could have been achieved except by traversing that terrible road made rough with bayonets can never be known; the best guess will always be made by the biologist.

I have reviewed what I deem the fundamentals of the Civil War. I have left untouched the time-honored tenets of that age of argument, quarreling and open strife. They are well known; States Rights, Gag Rule, Squatter Sovereignty, Nullification, Compact Theory. These were tools employed by the leaders of the two sections to advance each his own cause. Many proofs exist that these theories or methods or processes were only of major consequence in so far as they did advance one cause or another. As pointed out, while men of both rival camps debated the right and the wrong of Squatter Sovereignty, men of both sections had united in California without qualms or dispute, to put the theory in actual operation. The South had always shown an adamantine firmness in advocating the States-Rights doctrine, but in the throes of Civil War Southern statesmen exercised powers diametrically opposed to that doctrine. Alexander Johnston has stated, for instance, that President Davis exerted powers "more sweeping and general" than any wielded by President Lincoln. On the other hand, the North scorned all nullification theories advanced by her rival section — although the Southern orators drew many of their arguments from the very lips of Yankee advocates of nullification of the days of 1803 and 1812–1814! The North fought for nationality against a confederacy by using confederate policies; authority was greatly divided; General Grant exclaimed in anger after the Battle of Shiloh that he was not the commander of his army but only an "observer" — and would have resigned his commission but for General Sherman's quieting counsel. The South fought for a confederacy against a national government by using nationalistic methods; power was enormously centralized, and the States Rights policy was flagrantly repudiated, as speeches in the Confederate States' Congress attest.

In other words, men seized upon every tool, argument, theory, compromise or tenet that would advance their cause, and discarded each as it became dull or ineffective or passé. This is illustrated by Lincoln's frank statement which made famous his Hodges Letter in which he acknowledged that he had obeyed a "higher law" and ignored his oath to preserve the Constitution in order to save the nation — and the Constitution with it. A man, he said, with his usual trenchant directness, would give a limb to save his life — but never his life to "save" a limb! The war came on, in one sense, unexpectedly. Just as the colonies in 1775 began a struggle to compel England to withdraw measures which threatened their economic eclipse (and to give them their proper place in the scheme of British Government) just so now the South seceded in the expectation that such a radical measure as that — threatening the destruction of the Union — would compel the North to accede to its demands for economic freedom. But that outcome did not follow.

With the Union actually broken, the whole face of the controversy was instantly altered. There was nothing to do but weld the sections together with the sword — contrary to Horace Greeley's statement that he never wanted to live in a Republic so "pinned together"; and gallantly and bravely did the North set itself to the task and carry it through. Only the winning of that war could have made possible the united nation we have to-day.

Thus in haste, and in seas of blood, the South (against its will, so to speak) was freed from a system that would have blighted its real advance for unnumbered years. The shock was terrific and could only have been endured by a brave, resilient race. Problems of inestimable difficulty were left on its hands after the war, and made a hundredfold harder of solution by a tyrannical sort of mandate-rule exerted in the land after the war was over. After Lincoln's death the wild idea, with which no Lincoln would ever have agreed, that the whites and blacks in the South should be put on a political parity, was advanced and, temporarily, enforced. A comic political opera resulted, as bizarre as any extravaganza ever produced.

Emancipated from economic bondage, the South has run its race with splendid credit and presents possibilities to-day of inestimable importance. It could never have coöperated with the rest of the nation in the great economic revolution of the last thirty years under the old plantation-system handicaps. To become free from that incubus was the price of genuine American unity. It has its race problem — for the shackles which fell from the South's hands left them free; but those which fell from the slave's hands left him practically helpless. No man is free save as he can recognize the responsibilities of freedom. The North could free the slave and wash its hands of him; it left for the South the far more serious task of making freed men recognize their responsibilities. Yet there has been coöperation here; for millions of Northern wealth have come to aid in this work of amelioration.

You hear much about remaining Southern antipathy; about Confederate flags supplanting, on occasion, Old Glory. But I have told a story elsewhere which strikes one of the real chords of sentiment — of the mutual admiration the men of each hostile section had for the courage and bravery of each other. On that basis a nation can be built. The new freedom of the South has lured thither men and capital which could never have come under the old régime. North and South are being welded as, in the old days, Northeast and Northwest were welded. Sentiment may sound, now and then, a discord in the national anthem of unity and progress; old memories of heroism may intrude on a theoretical "perfect picture" of national bliss; giant reliefs may be hewn from mountain cliffs to perpetuate the glory of the men of stamina and uprightness who fought for the Lost Cause. For one, I take my hat off to such homage of hero worshipers. So long as it is from the heart, so long as it cherishes love of courage and steadfastness, I account it a national asset, not an echo of sectional bitterness. No music in our armies in the late Great War so quickly stirred tired feet and lagging hearts of men of our North as did the rollicking tune of the once despised "Dixie";[1] and thousands of Southerners sang without a qualm "The Yanks Are Coming!" That, after all, is the mighty proof of the unity that exists at heart to-day.

[1] Paradoxically, the song "Dixie" was originally inspired by Negroes who, having been taken from the Dix plantation in New York Bay, sighed to come back from the South to their former New York home!

XIV

THE FRONTIERS OF BUSINESS EFFICIENCY

AMID the enormous development of the industrial age which has followed the days of Grant and Lee few, if any, of the old factors of centripetal or centrifugal influence failed to exert their customary power, while many forces, bewildering in number and complexity, emerged. These years prove again that some things never seem to alter, and one of these is the fact that no generation, no era, has ever yet been able to adjudge the compensating "hidden forces" which accrue with change, innovation and progress — while evils, handicaps and infelicities stand out like mountain peaks. These pages have been written in vain, however, if the reader has not gained the impression that faith was needed no less in 1829 than in 1629; and without it 1929 and 2029, their failures and successes, advances and retrogressions, will, alike, be bereft of the one asset which money cannot buy and the "main chance" of national perpetuity.

Vain, of course, would be the effort to attempt to point out the factors which to-day are fashioning the United States of the future; as of old, these dismay some, perplex many, psychically unbalance others; but I believe that, as of yore, millions remain confident, sane and hopeful — and express in commonplace ways, in ordinary level-headed attitudes, in humdrum, steady ability to do and dare, as genuine a faith as the Fathers ever knew. If this is true it is because we have been "true to ourselves" by breeding a Sixth Sense, the sense of confidence in the outcome of the unforeseen. For, as of old and always, our history will consist of that "unforeseen coincidence of events which . . . no contemporary can be expected to discern." And what patriotism is so constructive, what loyalty is so imperial in its quality, as that which begets confidence in the creation of the compensations necessary to make the Ship as strong as the road is rough? I call that Americanism. I account the man possessed with that Sixth Sense (involving Bagehot's "delicate principle of progress") the man who is not afraid to go and come, to invest and make blue prints and build. His life is based upon the emergence, not the decay, theory. He is confident in what will emerge. I agree that this is sentiment; but Viscount Bryce said, as we have noted, that sentiment is the "growing strength" of our government. What alchemist can separate sentiment and faith? The best proof to be had that an age is producing great salutary compensations is to find that such work is being done by the very forces which ranter, mourner and pessimist are agreed must doom that day, age or nation to destruction. Such was the new frontier of "Big Business" in our modern era; from this "horrid" toad's head what a valuable "jewel" sprang!

Great firms which have determined to produce new models or products are compelled to retool their plants at vast expense in time and money. The metaphor is vague, but there is a true sense in which we can say that our civilization had to be retooled after the Civil War as the nation swung out from an agricultural age into the new industrial era; new tools for the mighty steel truss and mightier Steel Trust; new tools for the Empire State Express; new tools for converting Knights of Labor into men of the American Federation; tools for free public schools and State universities; tools for absorbing a million immigrants a year and for governing a population scores of millions greater than before. On the physical side, how perfectly Sam Walter Foss caught the surge of this process as the "Hammers of the World-Smiths" began beating out a new frontier:

Across the trellised landways
  The lifted steamers slide;
Dry shod beneath the rivers
  The iron stallions glide;
Beneath the tunneled city
  The lightning chariots flock
And back and forth their freight of men
  Shoots like a shuttlecock.
The moon-led tides are driven back
  Their waves no more are free,
And islands rise from out the main
  And cities from the sea.

* * *

What is this iron music
  Whose strains are borne afar?
The hammers of the world-smiths
  Are beating out a star.

As America was thus being retooled, and the crude and arrogant monopolies of early days developed their ghoulish evils, the greed of men urged them to devote all of their canny energies to wrest success from Dame Fortune. But in so doing they ruthlessly discarded, one after another, the commercial shibboleths and shackles which, in former days, had been considered the *sine qua non* of progress and success. Business beyond doubt remained just as tricky, just as dishonest, just as underhanded, as before. But the newer lines of activity brought in their own ways of being crooked and, because they were different, it seemed as though world's records for evil were being broken; whereas, in point of fact, they were novel, not new; the Trusts found very few ways of being dishonest which are not (in essence) described in the Old Testament!

No nation experienced a more fundamental revolution than was now wrought in the United States by the very success of these new-day reorganizers of business. With a callous indifference to the past that would have piqued an Alva or a Napoleon, these men discarded traditions, methods, systems, policies, tools, adages, mottoes and men which were not efficient. As suddenly they also inspired a perfect flood of inventions which would accelerate business transactions both in volume and accuracy. Whole libraries of old-style record books were junked, and those of new design, and capable of securing an accuracy and availability never practiced before, were installed. All the new paraphernalia and tools for office and field use, systems of card-indexing, statements, accounts for filing and classifying, were also assets to the same end — efficiency. Unlooked-for, unappreciated and uncontrolled, the movement spread; new methods and tools demanded many more; and the use of these by one firm or company compelled their adoption, willy-nilly, by others — by rivals and competitors. Standards were set which thousands had to follow for dignity's sake, if not for decency's and safety's.

Now, every efficient tool and system insidiously bred new ideals. Amid much that was wrong and gross and gluttonous, a nation, through them, gained the secular pathway to a spiritual unity. It was one thing for a people to be bound together with physical bonds of commerce — transportation systems; but it was a greater thing for psychic bonds to be woven which one day would make all men agree that efficiency must at least spell and compel honesty. Not, of course, that the Dawn has come; but never were there so many witnesses — no, not one tenth as many — per thousand inhabitants who were thoroughly conscious that business dishonesty is suicidal as to-day. This emergence does not appear so interesting or significant unless it is seen as a culmination of a long struggle in which the United States has progressed faster than the Old World. To see "the pit" from which we were "digged", we must vision those days when our first Get-Rich-Quick-Wallingfords operated in Old New York and Boston, while European systems of trickery and deceit still dominated business; see the day when men never wrote important letters in longhand; the day when theft of codes and the interception of rival's letters and the tracking of the round-about-town visits of important financiers was left to highly paid sleuths; the day when no man's real assets could even be guessed and when high finance required code systems involving names of seventy men in high position, from the White House down. With a curious persistency, business and diplomatic ethics have always maintained similar moral levels; and when Washington declared that the United States would treat with other nations internationally on the basis of the highest code of private morality he signified that his country was reaching out of its "night" of low business morality toward that ethical preëminence which Arnold Bennett frankly proclaimed it had achieved at the end of the first decade of the Twentieth Century.

The basis of this emergence rested in American character. De Tocqueville sensed it a century ago when he wrote, "The passions which agitate the Americans are not their political but their commercial passions; or, rather, they introduce the habits of business into their political life. They love order, without which affairs do not prosper; and they set an artificial value upon regular conduct, which is the foundation of solid business." Given, then, such a background, how true Americans were to themselves as they developed the hosts of tools of efficiency in an industrial era. But the great French critic also suggested the wider range which the "passion" for order might take. Splendid is the conception that, in the natural process of business frontiering, without much attention being paid to it, without subsidy and without domineering from any one man or set of men, there has been established a University of National Efficiency in our land which the vast bulk of our people must attend whether or no! For such, in effect, has been the result of the development of standards of business efficiency; for no business man to-day may ignore the law that efficiency compels honesty without risk of disaster. "It is Industrialism," wrote W. E. H. Lecky, "that has brought into the world that strong sense of the moral value of thrift, steady industry . . . which is now so characteristic of the moral type of the most civilized nations."

But finer still is the conception that we are moving on fast in learning that "the value of regular conduct", to reëmploy the old phraseology, applies to all life, all the new frontiers. Having learned its value in business, we are taking rapid strides in applying it to the whole range of human activity. To what new levels will business systems not rise, as America becomes still truer to herself under the sway of these new standards? The movement, you say, is not all that may be desired; but you do not have to cure a million patients of hydrophobia to establish the efficacy of Pasteur's serum; once the cure for inefficiency, double-dealing, hypocrisy and deceit is known, the wise will seek it. You may not be a Lion or an Owl or a Moose, but you are a Gila monster if you think such pacts and pledges, such affirmations of high ethical principles, such promises of devotion to "come clean" and "live and let live", as the millions of service-club men make each week (even on empty stomachs) create no new ideals and influence for good no lives. You have got to give men a blue print of the Fixed-Price idea or the Money-Back-If-Our-Goods-Don't-Please idea before these can shape themselves as tangible propositions worth adopting — before men can see that they must put something into a customer-soil that will return manyfold. Do we properly reckon the great compensation-value of thus putting a premium on efficiency in our national life? Yet it has been a process. You could no more have introduced it by preaching to business men than, to use Senator Ingalls' vivid simile, you could have made a Jersey cow out of a Texas steer by preaching to him in the cattle pens at Wichita.

And processes never stop. Can you imagine a rule existing in a Board of Bank Directors which would allow an obstructionist to discuss a proposed measure or policy endlessly? If no "cloture rule" existed, in spirit, among such bodies of busy men, boards would not know how to punish too drastically such an offender against progress and decency. Such rules of efficiency must prevail at last in any political body. Take the handling of our charities as an illustration. What blundering, purposeless and ineffective methods existed to help the unfortunate in the old days; how it encouraged, rather than abated, the evil, and led to wholesale hypocrisy and incorrigibility. Business efficiency stepped in. Organized charity now reaches with no small degree of directness the downright needy and, as readily, discerns the loafer and the fake. Consolidation of charitable agencies has produced the maximum of relief at the minimum cost. Thus great ethical good is accomplished. Again, what has not business efficiency done to revolutionize our educational systems? What may it not do to revolutionize our churches? You still see in country villages, sometimes, three lonely wooden churches standing on three isolated knolls; behind the three churches are three underpaid ministers; three furnaces eating up coal to warm a chosen *few;* three insurance policies, Sunday-school organs, sets of hymn books and all other equipment — where only one is needed. The most shiftless storekeeper in the town would hardly condone such inefficiency! And for what purpose is this waste? To serve the most emphatic apostle of efficiency this world ever heard — Jesus Christ!

Business efficiency has made marked strides in politics since that fearless pioneer, Grover Cleveland, said, half a century ago, "There is, or should be, no reason why the affairs of our city [Buffalo] should not be managed with the same care and the same economy as private interests." Of him, a little later, James Russell Lowell said. "This man understands politics to mean business, not chicanery." Despite all the wrong-doing in high places to-day, what a story of improvement is seen as we glance along the years.

The birth and history of civil-service reform has been only the introduction of business-like methods of handling public office work efficiently. While we have been hoaxed by statistics on this matter (great numbers of small pay offices being put on the classified list while the real "plums" are not included), progress has steadily gone forward; the Law of Efficiency stands ready with its poignant lessons. Public office-holding does not enlist the interest and service of our able men. Rarely are counties properly represented by first-class men in legislatures, districts by best men in Congress, States by their best men in the Senate, and the grade of legislation cannot rise higher than its source. You say patriotism must operate here; the best of men must, through love of country, give up good businesses, practices and professions and devote themselves to public good.

Toward that frontier we must build, and what so perfectly as business efficiency marks the road? For the very thing better men shun in public life is *the one thing they hunger and thirst for in business life* — office — command of men — recognition by the world as worthy of the honor, the perquisites and the pay. You say, "The moment you make offices paying propositions, you invite the man to whom money means more than patriotism; you will recreate the old-time boss, and, under a new guise, the spoils system will return." But we have proof that, in business, *the exact reverse has proven true!* Never was business office-holding so little a matter of politics and family influence as to-day; never was the really capable man so sure of advancement as at present; never did the chair-lizard in business sit on so feeble a throne as now. Business efficiency has become inexorable in its demands.

There was a day when the tariff was a football in politics; and every fourth fall, if not annually, this "football" appeared in elections as regularly as the pigskin appeared on the gridiron. Methods of altering tariff schedules varied with the glasses worn by the revisionists. These were always bifocal; one always made necessary revision upward; the other, downward. The Democrats inveighed against Republicans because they profiteered by allying to them tariff-made industries; Republicans scoffed at Democratic inability to master the "science" of tariff making. On one occasion a Republican senator found in the Wilson Democratic Bill a clerical mistake by which hydraulic hose was classed as wearing apparel. "Look you," he cried in glee, "ere long these incompetents will be classing spinning jennies and hydraulic rams as livestock!" But business efficiency stepped in. Tariff Commissions were mooted and at last established. We are on the road now to take the whole problem out of politics and put it where it belongs — in the hands of specialists with unbiased minds.

This process is at work everywhere. You encounter it on every hand. "Before the soft-coal industry can be made to operate satisfactorily," said the Philadelphia *Evening Public Ledger* the other day, "it will have to be reorganized on a more or less just and scientific basis." The Federal Reserve and the national budget system are only markers along the road. One by one political "footballs" are being canceled out of the equation.

But a true process — or emergence, if you please — knows no boundary lines. On the wide frontier of internationalism the Law of Efficiency, first applied in model business relationships and then, logically, affecting ethical relationships, will prove ameliorating beyond the dreams of our generation. Then, and not until then, will the "brotherhood of the world" become a fact. What a story of plunder, economic oppression, of wars for land, mines, trade routes, fields, fisheries and forests (often under the name of religion) does world-history present! Forget, indeed, all the past and come down to the China of yesterday and to-day. Those "Spheres of Influence" established in that land by England, France, Russia, Germany, Japan and who-not were but faucets by which the cream of a rich empire was to be drained off at rare profit. If objection arose, an Opium War or Boxer Rebellion followed.

International business honorably conducted will greatly shorten that road. The coöperation thus achieved will purify international politics and diplomacy. Age-long prejudices will proceed to sink into the oblivion where now lie a large part of the sectional jealousies which once played havoc in our nation — and others. Few wars were ever prevented by limiting armaments; as one tentacle of the octopus, War, was hewn off, inventors and chemists supplied another wholly new. Of what advantage is it to junk a few battleships if noiseless aëroplanes are perfected which can drop newly discovered explosives that will rub out a million people in twenty seconds? "We must have moral disarmament," said Premier Briand at the Washington Conference, "before we can have physical disarmament." One Dawes Plan put into successful operation is worth more than any disarmament conference! Outlawing war is moral disarmament.

Signor Nitti said, "Beneath the veneer of the American business man there lies hidden a man of upright and ingenious mind, a man who is willing to toil on behalf of the ideals of humanity." To those of us who disfavor the decay theory this very optimistic statement is impressive; to us the proofs, such as are here illustrated, that our business frontier represents a "hidden force" that is emerging into commerce, into politics, into society and into international relations (but which our own day may be slow "to discern"), represent compensations of value. In those ranks of efficient business men you do not find the ranter, the calamity howler, the pessimist.

XV

THE INTEGRITY OF THE OLD FRONTIERS

THE analysis of one fear of the ominous development of our modern industrial age brings us back to our original viewpoint of this Republic as made up of a great and singularly interesting collection of splendid provinces. That fear is one awakened by the so-called alarming centralization of political power at Washington — of a bureaucracy that will obliterate everything suggested by the words "province", "frontier", "section" or "State."

We are developing a big governing machine and, no doubt, we are over-governed. The outcry at the big machine reminds one, however, that not long ago "Big Business" was viewed with an equal alarm; yet we have learned that it was not because business was big that it was an evil. And, when analyzed, it becomes plain that the argument against a big governing machine is not, in reality, based upon its bigness but, rather, on its exercise of alleged unconstitutional powers. Such exercise of power is equally dangerous whether employed by a great or small coterie of agents. One of the greatest lines of governmental expansion in our day is the enormous addition of bureaus under the control of the Secretary of Agriculture. It would take a bold anti-administration politician to maintain that such expansion has been anything but a national asset. The process of establishing efficiency in business is always a centralizing process. The work which General Dawes boldly led to establish a budget system and eradicate frightful waste was, in fact and in spirit, a centralizing process. At the very time of its installation General Dawes wrote the author that his chief satisfaction in the success of the effort was due to the fact that then "for the first time in our history, forty-three departments and independent establishments of the government are placed under coördinate business control." We cannot escape centralization if our governmental business is to be done efficiently; and whenever it is plain that the government is usurping the powers of the States, the remedy for that is at hand; it is a matter of fact; no party whip could long be successful in protecting its partisans from the guilt of unconstitutional misuse of power.

If we are over-governed, over-regulated and over-supervised the remedy for that is automatic. As an illustration, take the States which went so headlong into campaigns for initiating legislation by the people. The principle was correct; but it was soon found that a good thing could be made ridiculous. So many laws were initiated that voters were utterly bewildered; ballots began to resemble the size of horse blankets; the rank and file of citizens was in no position to give sufficient study to a hundred and more proposed laws to have any conception of their practicability or efficacy. Over-legislation, in time, always kills itself. Moreover, if you carefully examine the claim that we are over-governed it will be found that the States are equally guilty with the alleged "bureaucracy" at Washington; nothing proves this better than did the erstwhile craze for passing whimsical legislation proposed by initiative. And there "We, the People" shared the blame.

It is human to long for ideal conditions; but the world shows many illustrations of men urging "new things" as a theory which, if given the opportunity, they would not really install as practical agencies. The South in 1861 said that it was preposterous that States which desired to leave the Union should not be allowed to do so. Eleven States left the Union and formed a "Confederacy." But that Confederacy made no provision in its Constitution by which one of those same States could leave *that* Union. To talk of a State withdrawing from the Confederacy was branded as reprehensible to the last degree. Wrote a North Carolina representative to his constituents: "What was loyalty in one man three years ago, in advocating the dissolution of the old Union, *is treason in another now.*" In other words the compact "States Rights" theory for which the South had argued for eighty years was quite ignored by it when the theory was put to actual test.

So long as sentiment plays its salutary part in the American's make-up I do not look for the passing of our States as political divisions. I am not at all sure, however, that economically an "emergence" is not taking place here; I am not sure if, from this standpoint, the United States does not in reality consist, now, of twelve "States", bearing the names of the twelve Federal Reserve districts. It is human to become accustomed to word-meanings which the times alter without knowing it. Marcus Whitman sent home from Oregon an order to his missionary board which included "one hundred scalping knives." "Good gracious," cried the amazed brethren of Boston, or whatever may have been the Beacon Hill expression of that day for supreme consternation, "we cannot be a party to murder; we can't send missionaries *scalping* knives." And the Oregonians had to skin their cattle and wolves, and perform all other pioneer duties requiring sharp knives, with what instruments they could secure from the Hudson's Bay Company.

I believe that the outcry against centralization of power, while not without its meaning, is most useful for putting us on our guard to enforce the constitutionality of national legislation. I believe that by invoking the aid of "States Rights", men are pleading for a very real, very essential national asset in a vague way, by the use of word-meanings which have become obsolete. We suffer from the by-products of a marvelous age of commercialism which brings us wealth and power. In all advance there is, we have noted, some phase of seeming retrogression. In the perfecting of a great governmental machine centralization of power is inevitable. We must create, augment and capitalize the compensations. To some degree this can be done politically, but not adequately so, not sufficiently.

No truer words have been penned lately than these which echo Royce's theory: "Our diversification of interests and institutions geographically and socially is itself a guaranty of stability and of freedom"; and none more false have been written than these: "Man is the product of his environment, and his government, to be effective, must be also." The two propositions kill each other. Our utter diversification of interests makes it impossible for one environment to "produce" legislation wholly compatible with another. Herein lies the secret of success of our Constitution. It laid down principles; and its failures have been recorded only when amendments have been enacted which dictated specific details instead of reinforcing a set of principles. When the Constitution said the Negro should have the right to vote, or that intoxicating liquors should not be manufactured, it was not augmenting its prestige as a medium of principles — salutary, or not, as those specific requirements may have been. For, if we could assay things truly, we would see that the most insidious influence possible to national existence was being exerted when men studied out ways to prevent the Negro from voting or when, in any district, the conduct of citizens was such that officers announced that prohibition could not be enforced. Some small lessening of sentiment, of faith in law, ensues in such cases; this shows itself in crass form by a common, if not hilarious, disregard for all regulatory measures. The old ladies who roll by this California orange grove in electrics are practically the only passers-by who are not potential outlaws so far as speed limit is concerned. No finer expression of Americanism exists than the effort of legislators wisely to adapt national laws, so far as possible, to the great diversity of interests which mark our innumerable differentiated sections; and never in any land or age have men shown a tangible, practical patriotism better than have Americans who conceded something or sacrificed something by quietly acquiescing to legislation which was deemed, locally, discriminating and unfortunate.

But when it is stated that our diversity of interests is our guaranty of stability and freedom Royce's great truth is again bared to us. We cannot put our sections and provinces in a melting pot. We remain, still, a land of David Harums, Huckleberry Finns, My Antonias and Ramonas. Times change; improved communications revolutionize city, town and country; but the imperial integrity of our provinces, in new guises, with altered bases of economies, remains curiously constant. In no way can we Americans be "truer to ourselves" than by strengthening the diversity-assets of these kingdoms, dukedoms and principalities. That can never be done by political agencies, although diligence must be used to prevent the usurpation of local rights, privileges and prerogatives by a national government; that will protect local differentiations but it cannot create them; this has already been done by geography and climate, by the development of economic resources, by plant-seed and human-seed — in the alchemy of Time and Providence.

Why did this diversity — why will this diversity — make for national stability and freedom? Every page of this book ought to hint at the answer to that query, although no one more quickly than the author would agree that the question suggests unfathomable depths. When you tell me why a York should spring out of the poor mountain white country to become a national hero in the Great War; why two Wright brothers in an Ohio field should master flying; why Baltimore men should have underwritten the first American railway; why a West Virginia carpenter should build the first steamboat to ply on the water instead of in it; why California should produce a Burbank, Michigan a Ford, Minnesota a Lindbergh, New Hampshire a Webster; why an "Ohio idea" should develop here and an "Iowa idea" there and a recall scheme somewhere else; why a map of the progress of an anti-signboard law and that of the progress of an anti-spitting law should resemble each other, perhaps, in no particular whatever — then I will tell you why diversity of environments and interests make for national stability.

A land or people lacking variety and individuality fall into humdrum ways of thinking, acting, and even praying. The basic principles of life become fixed and form Bagehot's "cake of custom." Much attention may be paid to refining the basic formulas of life and finding new uses for them. Hundreds or thousands of men before Whitney had studied to improve methods of cleaning the seed from the cotton; but an outlander from New England made the first cotton gin. There is a static quality in thinking when land, soil, clouds, hills, seasons do not unite to present a psychic quality radical in its influence, revolutionary in its results. Something cataclysmic springs out from new environments upon old ideas, so to speak, giving them a twist, a focus, they never had before. It is called genius in invention and literature, heterodoxy, maybe, in religion, and incendiarism in politics. An illustration of note comes from the United States First Assistant Commissioner of Patents, who states that despite the vast resources in tools, equipment, capital and assistance given to research experts in the great laboratories and experiment stations of this country, the inventions which have been made under such auspices are, in the main, only elaborations and refinements of processes, while "nearly all the basic new ideas during the last twenty-five years" have come from free-lance men unconnected with such institutions or organizations and often as destitute, financially, as they are powerful. Such great, successful companies tend, like civilization itself, to better processes (as we have illustrated) but not to develop originality. "Men are too fond of their own life," said the sparkling Bagehot somewhere, "too credulous of the completeness of their own ideas, too angry at the pain of new thoughts, to be able to bear easily with a changing existence." Provincialism is the source of individual eccentricity — of "genius" when a Ford car is the result. "The causes which give birth," said the above-quoted writer, "to the startling varieties of individual character, and those which give birth to similar varieties of national character are, in fact, the same." These "startling varieties" are the antidote for the professional conservatism which, as Glenn Frank states, "has resisted all of the major innovations that have made modern science."

Honest efforts are made here and there to conserve and strengthen provincial integrity, originality and initiative; one such success in encouraging and amplifying the flow from the fountainhead is of more consequence than all the orations on "States Rights." It seems very human to argue for rights and rights, while homilies on the responsibilities which presuppose rights are less popular. How fully are we conscious of the responsibility of maintaining this diversity-influence in national life which makes for stability and freedom?

The effort of Californians to honor their "native son" precept represents a tangible method of strengthening sectionalism and giving prestige to provincialism. All local efforts to encourage native poets, novelists, artists and musicians to evolve work which shall smack of section and be "racy of the soil" are greatly to be praised and encouraged. It is of no small moment that wealthy men in later years of life do recognize this something which no one can explain accurately and spend large sums for the benefit of the rural communities in which they were born or reared. So far as money can do this, it is an asset; elegant buildings, exquisite landscape gardening, libraries, art galleries and new institutions, so located, raise what may be a "submerged" district in local and even national estimation. This helps to create the feeling that a "town" or "county" may be something infinitely more important than what the drab tale of the nauseating, typical "county history" depicts. Despite the commendable father-to-son-and-grandson affection which may send a boy from his own "country" to a far-off famous institution of learning, the example does tend to perpetuate the virility of the diversity-influence. Such boys too often become one of a fixed type; originality may be suppressed and individuality dwarfed. That does not make for national virility. "In modern times," states a critic, "when society is more tolerant, new national characters are neither so strong, so featurely." Yet our molds do not, fortunately, outwit Mother Nature. Glance at the honor rolls in the graduating classes of our great professional schools and you will find they contain the names of more men, proportionally, from the often belittled "fresh-water" colleges than from our "great" universities. This fact may be misinterpreted grossly; but it is true that little, local institutions conserve individuality and foster initiative to a significant degree. "School education unless it is regulated . . . will produce men and women who are all of one pattern, as if turned in a lathe," said Sumner; "an orthodoxy is produced in regard to all the great doctrines of life. It consists of the most worn and commonplace opinions." In a like vein Bagehot warns us that "academies are the asylums of the ideas and tastes of the *last* [or former, outworn] age . . . and out of their dignified windows pooh-pooh new things." [1] On the other hand, individuality is

[1] "If our schools of learning have been instruments of good to thousands, may we also express the conviction that to not a few they have been an injury? May we not often say,

sometimes constructively conserved by provincial influences without the help of any institution of learning whatever. In such cases we have the "self-made man", a term enormously abused; for the self-made man is an undiluted product of environment and heredity; in him provincialism is incarnate. But never suppose his success (if success he attained) was due either to his not being spoiled by a poor lot of professors, or to his failure to miss the inspiration of good ones. By avoiding the one and despite the other Mother Nature performed in him a good work.

Let us hope that we are on the eve of a great recognition of the essential value of promoting the integrity of the physical and mental diversities of our splendid country. In no way can Americans be more "true to themselves." If every one of us will remember charitably his "own country" vast improvement will follow; it may seem poor, drab, run-to-seed; do something, build something, to relieve that condition. Offer prizes for songs or poems that will embody its charms; a mass of trash will result — but suppose one "Carry Me Back to Old Virginny" results? Offer prizes for novels depicting the best of the historic lore of "your" country; armfuls of rubbish may be created — but suppose you inspire one "David Harum"

"Perhaps in this neglected spot is laid
Some heart once pregnant with celestial fire;
Hands, that the rod of empire might have sway'd,
Or wak'd to ecstasy the living lyre

but he committed himself in his youth to an institution which, true to its false theory, instead of seeking to develop his natural gifts in harmonious proportions, adventured upon a reconstruction of him after its own ideal, and thus destroyed him? . . . It was the conceit of educators who, instead of developing God's work, assumed the right to do it over again." — President Calvin B. Hulbert, "The Distinctive Idea in Education", page 23.

or "Prodigal Judge"! Invest something in a struggling local industry. Buy, reclaim and beautify a mountain in your "homeland"; you will never have so grand a monument. Endow a piece of splendid highway; establish scholarships in "your" struggling academy or college; establish a fund by means of which "your" town can carry on public improvement at the lowest safe interest cost; make the "old swimming hole" a healthful center of recreation — it may tie some boy's thoughts to a Star tighter than your wet shirt sleeves were ever tied; endow "your" day nursery or "your" boy or girl scouts; make an old-time green out of the space occupied by ramshackle buildings. Forget prose arguments about local States Rights and remember hereditary local responsibilities. Does a church or chapel bell send its notes across "your" old countryside? You say "Oh, they are all foreigners there now." Lucky it was for Jefferson's cabinet a century ago that a foreigner was inspired to take advantage of every round on the ladder of knowledge and refinement in frontier Pennsylvania — Albert Gallatin.

Fine, indeed, have been the splendid things done by the fortunate in our country in our back-to-the-country campaigns. The work, however, is hardly begun. Forces are at work in this realm of nation-building which will achieve results not thought of in our time. The creation of national and State parks and reservations contributes. The automobile and good roads are vitally contributing. In the end the slogan "See America First" will be rewritten and in its place "Love America First" will become more than a slogan, more than a theory for school children. It will possess a people. The far-off building of our provinces, our "Goshen Holes", our "Egypts", our "Blue Mesas", our "Laramie Plains"; the story of their seeding and economic development; the flavor of their peculiarities and differentiations as expressed in human types, political theories and religious variations; the literature which they have provoked or still hold in suspension, will be raised above sordid levels and will be considered so infinitely respectable that doctors' theses will be ground out to celebrate them — and a wealth of poetry and novels will perpetuate the essence of true nationality because founded on those very diversities which, alone, are virile with stability and freedom. The debt of "national character", using Bagehot's words again, to "parish character" must never be forgotten. "Every locality has its own inevitable and destined writers", said Floyd Dell; ". . . their writing forever smacks of *that* soil, has the tang of *its* speech — it must be a part of that spot of earth which it celebrates and adorns."

The centralizing influence of business efficiency will continue its work in government without campaigns to further it. The compensations which accrue are many, despite the infelicities and the dangers which must come in due order — until the very Dawn. But only by giving thought to it, only by energetic campaigns to accomplish it, can the greatest of compensations — the revivifying and strengthening of love of province and section — be secured. This is appreciated and practiced to that degree only in which we conserve the fountain sources of national stability and freedom and, in the largest sense, are "true to ourselves." Only by owning our birthplace (in either a literal or a figurative sense) can we have and keep a "fatherland."

XVI

THE RESPONSIBILITY OF FRONTIERING

THE master of Mount Vernon, when bidding the nation he loved to be "true to itself", recognized a process of spiritual welding which always was a matter of personal responsibility he, himself, had felt. His life is fraught with lessons of exercising such a responsibility for the public welfare. He had felt it as a loyal colonial Virginian. As such, being true to his colony, he had attempted in 1758 to make General Forbes see that the opportune route to the conquest of Fort Duquesne was by the Virginia pathway of the Potomac; and, when nettled by Washington's zeal to give his colony the economic advantage of the great military road west, that honest but brusque officer wrote home that Washington was "no gentleman." George Rogers Clark in later years felt the same personal responsibility to be loyal to his colony when (as tradition puts it) he ordered the inhabitants of captured Kaskaskia, whom he surprised at a dance, to "Dance on, but remember you are dancing under the flag of Virginia, not Great Britain." Robert Fulton gave expression to his sense of personal responsibility, as we have seen, when he wrote Monroe that he felt he would be guilty "of culpable neglect toward my country" if he left any stone unturned to aid America to secure steamboats for her mighty rivers. Lincoln felt the same thing, in essence, when he declared he felt bound to break his oath to defend the Constitution if by so doing he could save the Union.

To be "true" to ourselves does not mean that we are miraculously to reënter the colonial womb and be born again; nor to alter our ancestries by some trick of legerdemain or transpose by some feat of necromancy the vast series of environments which were factors in producing national individuality. No one knew better than that Virginian that there were weak Americans, disloyal Americans, cruel Americans, despondent Americans; has any President since Washington said openly that he wished he was "in his grave" instead of in the White House? By being true to ourselves Washington meant that we must take a personal responsibility in the art of recognizing those of our characteristics which are constructive and buoyantly healthful and, laying hold upon them with faith and optimism, make the Ship of State always stronger than the storms which roughen the road. As of old, the task is to make genuine Americans from a vast, complex army of "colonials"; we did that; we can continue to do it — all the calamity howlers to the contrary notwithstanding. There is a blue-stocking fear of the melting-pot theory; but the only melting pot of old, and of to-day, that had and has any great element of danger is the one which does not melt. Let us remember the truth which Quatrefages brought home to the French people, namely, "that a race mixture may bring out a form of character better suited than either parent form to the place and time." We must bind a nation together, as of yore, with lines of communication as superior to those of to-day as railways were in advance of canals; we did that; we can do it again. We must fight the good fight for the principles of the Constitution and blot out sedition even at the risk of the Constitution; we did that; we can do it again. We must carry the war into the "country" of any "enemy" that would reap from any material soils or human soils without plowing deep into those soils purse-profit and soul-profit — any enemy that by finesse or trickery would play the Barbary pirate on the high seas of society or finance. We did that once in our weakness, when the strongest nations on earth preferred to pay toll to a Barbary skull and crossbones rather than smite the evil; we can do it again.

Is not our most serious national evil a psychic evil? It is the *dread of thirst*, when your well is full, said Gibran's "Prophet", that is the thirst unquenchable. With all our abounding wealth in money and enterprise and of economic possibilities, is not our true danger there — the psychic catastrophe of the dread of thirst? For, once thus obsessed, we cannot be rendered immune from dangers through the act of battling against them; like the seeds elsewhere mentioned *we can be made conquerors only by conquest.* Shall this dread of thirst, whether that take the form of comfortable pessimism, blatant calamity-howling or pious bemoaning, disarm us?

From Thackeray's day down, men have pointed out that our wide frontier — free land — has been the safety valve which has prevented local explosions of pent-up and riotous majorities that would eventually scuttle the Ship. On the contrary, we have shown that the explosive forces, which demanded new frontiers and made them, were usually frontier forces — frontiers always bred frontiers. Is that spirit missing to-day? Far otherwise. In no way are we being more "true to ourselves" than by pioneering the frontiers of our age — intellectual, social and political. "Virginians" are still planting "Kentuckys" in the laboratories of an Edison and a Millikan; Ohio Valleys beyond mountain walls are being explored in the study of a Cadman. Oregons are being discovered in the herbarium of a Burbank and the workshop of a Ford; rich Californians lie at the end of the trails pursued by such pioneers as a Grenfell and a Steinmetz; Rockefeller foundations are planting clinics all over the world, and no Ashley, Carson, Bridger or Manly ever threaded the dangerous pathways of the Sink of the Humboldt or Death Valley with a courage exceeding that of hundreds who are boldly creeping through the pestilential paths of tuberculosis-land and cancer-land to-day! How these genuine pioneers are holding America "true to itself"; how little are their energies being wasted or the keen edge of their zeal being dulled by fears that the well will go dry!

In each of them I see another Daniel Boone leading that first company over high-swung Cumberland Gap. You remember, perhaps, that Boone's party had been attacked and some were killed; numbers were ready to flee from a land where hopes ended only in death. With invincible courage that pioneer now wrote on his knee, in the gunpowder ink, that message to Colonel Henderson: "My advice to you, sir, is to come or send as soon as possible. Your company is desired greatly, for the people are very uneasy, but are willing to stay and venture their lives with you, and now is the time to frustrate the intentions of the enemy, and keep the country whilst we are in it. If we give way to them now, it will ever be the case." How all these modern pioneers on our frontiers of investigation and learning are calling back to us like Boones in the present-day Cumberland Gaps of Science: "Come on;

come on; now is the time to 'frustrate' the enemy and keep this new land while we are in it; if we give way now such will ever be the case!" And what an unending fight it is! As one of these men has said, "We strive for the Truth day by day, night by night, and then at last, after bitter conflict, find the Truth and know it to be a lie; for, having gained one summit in the range of experience, we see beyond another summit undreamed of; and toward that we press with the same irrepressible ambition — and new truths unfold to view the newer." All frontiers of thought breed new frontiers; and in that America is being "true to itself."

Our United States Government has officially declared that the old historic frontier no longer exists — that a continually moving population has crowded that former factor of American life into the Pacific Ocean. Not a few pages of this book have been devoted to those robust characters, like Boone, who have defied the unknown, wrought out new tools of agriculture, law and society for the conquest of new soils, new minerals, new rivers — unmindful of sudden death from any quarter. But has the passion to explore new worlds departed with that frontier? Has the courage to defy death disappeared, oh, bemoaner of this age of "decadent" youth? Far, far otherwise; and how strikingly typical of all that had gone before it was that, when the old frontier had been officially dispensed with, the new frontier, the frontier of the air above us, was being explored by the Wright brothers! The comparison between the problems of the exploration of the "Sea of Darkness" by Columbus and his school and the exploration of this new "Sea of Light" by the modern school of birdmen is interesting indeed. In each instance utterly new sciences had to be developed and all the new instruments fashioned necessary for each science. In each case moaners, ranters and pessimists denounced, viewed with alarm, and went through all the paces of professional incantation to their Great God, Futility. Arts of navigation had to be discovered through raw experience and at the cost of innumerable lives; currents and cross-currents had to be identified by a comparison, often of disasters and shipwrecks. Portions of the ancient seas, where ships became hopelessly becalmed, had to be located and platted on nautical maps by those who had hitherto been utterly ignorant of their existence. Just so our aërial "Sargasso Seas" — treacherous air pockets in our "Sea of Light" — are being found to-day, with all the accompanying dread felt by ocean navigators of the long ago. The comparison runs true, also, with reference to the problems of larger ships, larger holds and greater sails in the olden days, and our problem of larger holds and engines to-day. But has the earnestness to solve such riddles altered? Is the willingness to risk life lessened? Were the seaports of the Old World in the ancient day filled with young men more eager to battle with the elements and solve the riddles of navigation of 1492 than are our airports of 1929? Boones and Bridgers and Austins are at our elbows every day, unnoticed until helmets are donned; and every day Hudsons and Magellans and Cabots sail away once more — never to be heard of again! How perfectly in the new frontier of the air are our pioneers of to-day true to tradition, to the old spirit of adventure, to "themselves."

I wonder if we sufficiently recognize the deep significance of the fact that, after all the savants and theorists have explained the reasons for the loss of the late Great War by the Central Powers, the latter, to-day, explain it by saying that it was lost because the people behind the armies came to feel defeated and, almost unconsciously, wavered in their support of huge armies which were ready and willing to fight? We are the people behind our American armies of labor, armies of teachers, armies of ministers, armies of farmers, armies of manufacturers, armies of salesmen. In those busy camps devoted to a peaceful conquest of the material and spiritual, American traditions are recognized and honored. But their success depends very largely on our faithfulness, our optimism, our tolerance, our ability to distinguish between destructive pessimism and a healthy, constructive dissatisfaction with present attainment. In no way are we more typically American than in expressing our dissatisfaction with present-day tools, theories, engines, policies, buildings, systems. Peter Cooper's "marvelous" locomotive, the "Tom Thumb", no sooner stood complete than in dozens of machine shops, laboratories, and designing and drafting rooms all that proved inadequate in the "Tom Thumb" was being challenged, repudiated, reconceived, replanned and rebuilt. As a result, the cab of one of the mighty Moguls of to-day is greater than Cooper's little masterpiece of ninety years ago; and the only thing we are sure of is that the Moguls of to-day will not be able to do the work of the Behemoths of to-morrow!

I enormously relish all the proofs which exist, and repeat themselves down through the years, of the passion of Americans for scrutinizing the inventions of men for the purpose of improving upon them. In that passion they have been specifically "true to themselves" as the records of our Patent Office convincingly prove. I like to read of the "spies" New York sent down to examine the locks built on the Potomac by Washington's Potomac Canal

Company — that better ones might be erected on the Mohawk. I like Henry Shreve's objectionable investigation of Fulton and Livingston's first steamboat on the Ohio River and his production of another which made the New Yorkers hale him into court — unsuccessfully! I like that Yankee who, when a cocksure English manufacturer offered one thousand dollars to any one who could pick his inviolable lock, "raised Hobbs" with it (that was his name) and came home with the money to perfect the unpickable Yale lock. I get good fun out of reading how crowds pushed and shoved at the Philadelphia Centennial of 1876 to get near the wonderful "Four Horse Drag" there exhibited — and sighed because the future might never be able to improve upon it. But at the Columbian Exposition at Chicago in 1893 there was a similar crush to view the glittering safety bicycle; in extolling its miraculous future a writer remarked that the automobile was not practical and that centuries would lapse ere the riddle of flying in the air could be solved. Yet at the Louisiana Purchase Exposition in 1904 the bicycle was as taboo as a drag was passé — and the crowds looked nonchalantly on many types of automobiles and even on the Wright brothers' miraculous aëroplane. If the success of a civilization is measured by passing on the blessings once monopolized by the rich what a live-long nation we will be! How few could own a drag in 1876 — or even the horses to pull it. And automobiles are common to millions now whose fathers had never owned a safety bicycle.

With the building of Peter Cooper's engine, the "Tom Thumb", other building was going forward; a "Psalm of Life", a "Thanatopsis" and some "essays" by one Emerson. In the very nature of the case — the processes of history — could it be that a people so ready to challenge

Cooper's designs and develop the newer and the better should not question the art and philosophy of a Bryant, an Emerson and a Longfellow? Could a Law of Life in the material world so possess the very soul of a people without influencing their thinking and dreaming about things immaterial? How necessary it is for us to know that the coming of so sinister a shadow as an "Age of Doubt" was as normal a thing as could have happened; to see, in fact, that its failure to come would be a proof that we were stagnating intellectually. Again and again it must be remembered that only by conflict can we become conquerors. What a piteous number of people have been thrown "off center" in confidence, in poise and tolerance, because our students of matters of the soul, of social psychology, of deportment and customs and mannerisms, display in their investigations identically the same spirit, the same originality, the same self-sacrificing passion for conquest on their frontiers that our engineers and designers and inventors have shown in their laboratories and workshops! Oh, that such could know that principles never change; that in all the revolution in engineering, from the "Tom Thumb" to the Twentieth Century Limited, the "creeds", so to speak, of whole armies of mechanicians were altered over and over again but principles never. The cam cut-off did not alter the principle of steam, nor the incandescent bulb that of electricity.

How shortsighted and untrue to ourselves it is, then, to become disturbed because this same passion finds expression in the realms of philosophical and religious speculation. Oh, that Christian people could have the same reliance upon their Regenerator that the physicist has in his generator, instead of exclaiming gloomily with

Andrew Gide, "I think we are watching the end of a world, of a culture, of a civilization, that everything will be subjected to criticism." I only wish I could think that all of our unrest of to-day was due only to a spirit of honest criticism, and not in part to gross hysteria due to the attempt of a nation to assimilate a sudden deluge of time-saving and labor-saving conveniences. Are we not missing something vitally necessary if we fail to appreciate the salutary influence of the time element? It is the great and potent "medicine" — as the red men used the word, indicative of supernatural power. For its alchemy there is no substitute. You can make a "flower" but only Time can produce a flower. There is no reasonable fear in the vast work science is doing save here: by creating the illusion that everything can be done quickly, and that get-character-quick Wallingfords and get-culture-quick Wallingfords can be produced as ready as get-rich-quick Wallingfords and be as genuine. In all gain, as we have noted, there is some loss. In the face of the enormous triumphs of science must we not fight against this breeding of impatience?

How plainly, then, does it appear that to make America true "to herself" a personal responsibility rests upon us — upon the sanity, the optimism and the honesty of our questioning. We are the weavers in this great pattern of civilization; upon the strength of the threads which you and I insert depends the excellence of the design and the reliability of the product. Evils surround, as of yore, but they have not kept pace with the forces for good; tricky propagandists, politicians and promoters thrive, but in proportion to the total population they are less than in the olden time; criminals carry on scandalously but the channels of publicity are widening every hour;

outrages against public conscience are common, but in all the ten centuries of known history never were there such advances in business morality. We must not let our gooseflesh be overworked by every ranting theorist; the future will bring greater engines, wars, universities, strikes, cities, dynamos, robberies, skyscrapers, hospitals, defalcations and churches than the world has ever known. Well and good: "Let courage rise with danger!" The best American is he who goes forward least afraid; who is confident that he can and will aid in the development of the compensating factors which shall more than keep pace with prevailing evils. "If a noble and civilized democracy is to subsist," said George Santayana, "the common citizen must be something of a saint and something of a hero." A big order! Yes, but we do not want it lessened.

From beyond the Pacific, from a land to which Christian nations have sent many kinds of representatives, this official message came to Americans fifty years ago, inscribed on a Chinese screen displayed at the Atlanta Exposition: "As from far beyond the clouds in Spring, the moon, with liquid refulgence shines, so the lustre of a proper observance of what is right is reflected upon our country and our literature, causing both to flourish." The legend poignantly depicts the relationship of individual conduct to national welfare. American history is radiant with that "lustre"; it shines to-day in the unchanging threads inserted in our fraction of the pattern of civilization by our Winthrops and Hookers and Franklins, by our Washingtons, Lincolns and Roosevelts. "Despotism may rule without Faith — but Liberty *never*." The mightiest engine this world will ever know, backed by all the forces of Nature ever to be harnessed, will never make Faith, not even of the one-grain-of-mustard-seed variety; but you and I can make it, renew it, culture it; and through it make America a nation, make it American, and make it true to itself.

From the grove in which I write one can see across to the San Dimas Canyon, named from the horse thief who was crucified with Christ — to whom were spoken those strange words about meeting again "to-day" on a still stranger frontier. Doubtless it is these factors which made Gladstone say that such frontiering — in the spirit land — was the most important business to which a man can attend, that give rise not only to the host of fakirs and charlatans who would peddle "lots" in that far country, but, as well, have given rise to a host of miserable contests and quarrels over creeds and canons through all the years. What a frontiersman was that Jesus Christ! Who, more than He, was fearless in His "night" because of the undoubted emergence of "hidden forces" which no living man "can hope to discern"? Who so perfect a Witness "of the Dawn"?

INDEX

Abert, Colonel J. W., account of a blizzard on the plains, 170–171
Adams, James Truslow, quoted, 36, 73
Air, pioneering the frontiers of the, 248–249
Alleghenies, as a line of defense, 86–87; the National Road over the, 183–185
Allen, James Lane, quoted, 131, 167–168
America, difficulties of the physical conquest of, 64; a new concept of, by the colonists, 70; the great unifying influence in the growth of, 121; the succession of "Wests" in, 127–132; making, true to herself, 253
American, the local patriotism of the, 18; evolution of the new, after the French War, 74–76; the best, 254
American history, the background of, 13–33; old methods of teaching, 58
American River, discovery of gold on the, 52–53
American unity, the struggle for, 64–68; splendor of the story of, 161 *et seq.*; the Civil War and, 204–205
Americanism, true, 221
Amherst, General Jeffrey, 69
Annapolis Convention, the, 107
Apache Pass, 166
Articles of Confederation, proposal and adoption of, 83, 85; realization of the weakness of the, 106–107
Atchison, Topeka and Santa Fé Railroad, and the introduction of hard wheat into America, 51
Atlantic, the, a common highway of communication between the colonies, 65
Austin, Stephen, the grant of land by Mexico to, 146
Ayer Collection of Old Diaries in the Newberry Library, 169
Bagehot, Walter, quoted, 14, 25, 39, 78, 161, 238, 239, 240
Baltimore, and the failure of the Chesapeake and Ohio Canal, 190; sponsors railroad building, 190–191; the first, clipper ship, 191 *note*
Baltimore and Ohio Railroad, construction of, 190–191; completion of the, 192–193; 196
Bancroft, George, 79
Bennett, Arnold, 224
Bergen, Professor Joseph Y., quoted, 15
Bible, the inspiration drawn from the, by the colonists, 64–65
"Big Business", 221
Blue Grass, 48–50
Boone, Daniel, 166; letter to Colonel Henderson quoted, 247; 248
Bosanquet, Bernard, 75
Boundary lines, early importance of, and disputes over, 59–60; 83–84, the normal, of the Republic, 162
Bounty lands, offered by Congress as an incentive to enlistment in the Revolutionary War, 84, 87; organization of soldiers to secure, 92, 103–106
Boycotting, in colonial days, 61
Braddock, General Edward, 69; defeat and death of, 73–74 and *note*
Briand, Aristide, quoted, 230
Brigham, Albert P., 34
Brown, John, 212, 213
Bryant, Edwin, on illness in the emigrant trains, 174–175
Bryce, James, quoted, 29; 30, 48; on the Ordinance of 1787, 106 *note;* on the development of the Constitution, 108; 221
Budget System, the National, 229, 233

Buffalo, the, as the early trail makers, 167
Bureaucracy, the fear of, in government, 232 *et seq.*
Burke, Edmund, 77
Burt, and the Marquette ore beds, 56
Business efficiency, the frontiers of, 220–231; a centralizing process, 233
Byrd, Colonel William, 117

Cable, George W., 25
Calamity and ruin, the ever-present prophets of, 6 *et seq.;* 194
California, discovery of gold in, 51–52; early cattle industry in, 52; the soil factor in the history of, 53–54; 55, 56; and the discovery of gold, 162; abolition of the slave system in, 206
Canal, first suggestion for a, across New York, 185–186; State of New York builds the Erie, 187–188; the, question in Ohio, 188–189; the Chesapeake and Ohio, 189–190, 192
Cascade Tunnel, dedication of the, 200
Cattle industry, the early, established by the *padres*, 52
Census, dispute over the taking of a colonial, 60
Channing, Professor Edward, on the American Constitution, 109
Charities, business efficiency in the handling of, 226–227
Chicago, early rivalry between St. Louis and, 193
Chicago Public Library, 5
Chesapeake and Ohio Canal, construction of the, 189–190; burden of debt created by the, 192; 196
Chesterton, Gilbert K., 24
Churches, need of business efficiency in the management of, 227
Civil Service Reform, business-like methods in, 227–228
Civil War, American unity and the, 123–124, 204–205; 162; fundamentals of the, 216
Clark, Speaker Champ, quoted, 122
Clark, George Rogers, 244
Clay, Henry, 8
Clermont, the, Fulton's first steamboat, 194, 195
Cleveland, Grover, quoted, 227
Climate, and slavery, 205–206
Climatology, influences of, 35
"Clinton's Ditch." *See* Erie Canal
Clipper ships, development of the, 148; the first Baltimore, 191 *note*
College songs, significance of section in, 32–33
Collins, 94
Commerce, the old conception of the movement of, 89
Condon, Thomas, quoted, 137
Conestoga wagons, the, 40
Confederacy, secession and the Southern, 234
Congress, difficulties of the Continental, 79–82; legislation for government of Western lands by, 103–105; the struggle for the balance of power in, 213
Connecticut, dispute with Pennsylvania over territory, 59
Constitution, one secret of the success of the, 235–236
Constitutional Convention, realization of the need for a, 107; the labors, compromises, and final success of the, 107–109
Constitutions, rapid adoption of the State, 81; uniformity of ideals in the, 81–82
Continental Congress, difficulties of the, 79–82; election of the, 83; powers delegated to the, 83; offers bounty lands as an incentive to enlistment, 84; wise legislation for Western lands by, 87–95
Coolidge, Calvin, Washington's Birthday address by, 198 *note*
Cotton, in the South, 205; and the slave system, 206–207; and the cotton gin, 209–210

Cotton gin, invention of the, 209
"Covered Wagon, The", the well-known film, 171
Cowan, John, and the Montana gold region, 56
Cowboy, the morale developed by the, 135
Crawford, William, agent for Washington, 71
Crévecœur, J. Hector St. John, quoted, 75
Cumberland Road. *See* NATIONAL ROAD
Cutter, Manasseh, quoted, 18

DAWES, CHARLES G., and the Budget System, 233
Dawes Plan, the, 230
"Dawn", in witness of the, 5–6
Deane, Silas, on the trans-Allegheny country, 91
Declaration of Independence, the, 79, 82–83, 109
Dell, Floyd, quoted, 243
Democracy, the best definition of, 29–30
"Democracy in America", de Tocqueville, 208 *note*
Devol, Colonel Jonathan, 143
Dickens, Charles, impressions caused by newly cleared land, 129
Disarmament, the futility of physical without moral, 230
"Distinctive Idea in Education, The", Hulbert, 240–241 *note*
"Dixie", popularity of, 219 and *note*
Duane, the, first Ohio River ship to reach Liverpool, 142
Dunning, Professor William A., 141

ECONOMIC INFLUENCES, as factors in nation-building, 35
Economic interests, a people's concern for their, 203
Educational systems, business efficiency in the management of, 227
El Camino Real, the *padre's* pathway in California, 52
Emerson, Ralph Waldo, quoted, 78, 212
Emigrant trains, bitter experiences of the, 168–177
Emigration, the urge of, in New England, 71
England, the songs of, the songs of the colonists, 64; alienation of the colonies from, after the French War, 74–76; arbitrary action of, 78; conditions in, in Elizabeth's time, 117–118; and the Treaty of Ghent, 187
English, methodical system of empire building of the, 64; unifying influence of the, language, 64
Environment, the passion for, 12
Erie Canal, construction and success of the, 187–188, 195
Europe, national hatreds in, today, 124–125
Expansion, influence of the soil factor on, 36; predicated by discoveries of rich soils, 44–47; inspiration for, derived from the French War, 71–72
Exploration, colonists not adept in, of the interior, 69; the advance agents of, 69–70

FEDERAL RESERVE SYSTEM, the, 229, 234
Ferrero, Guglielmo, 55; on the national hatreds in Europe today, 125
Finley, John H., 177
Food, scarcity of, in the desert, 173–174
Forbes, General John, 97, 244
Fort Duquesne, the site of the future Pittsburgh, 71
Foss, Sam Walter, quoted, 222
Fox, John, 25
France, rivalry between, and Spain advantageous to the colonies, 66; effect of the war with, 69–75
Frank, Glenn, quoted, 239
Frank, Waldo, 24

Franklin, Benjamin, 59, 182
Frémont, John C., as Pathfinder so called, 166
French explorers, the early, 117
French War. *See* FRANCE
Frink, Chum, 24
Frontier, the building processes of the, 4–12; a mystery to frontier, 28
Frontiers, comparison of the New England and Pennsylvania, 39–40; breed frontiers, 127–149; the "bad men" of the, 130–131; the type of unity of our, 132; moral code of the, 133–134; the spirit of hospitality and friendliness on the, 135; intellectual unity of the, 135–137; lack of material comforts on the, 137; the spirit of independence of the, 138; as nurseries of expansion, 138; international questions and the, 143–147; of business efficiency, 220–231; integrity of the old, 232–243; pioneering the, of today, 246–249
Frothingham, Richard, quoted, 79
Fulton, Robert, 194, 195, 244

GALLATIN, ALBERT, 242
Garden, Mary, 32
Geographical factors favoring growth, 65
Geography, the influence of, on history, 34 *et seq.;* early ignorance of the, of the Pacific coast, 51–52
"George Washington", Rupert Hughes, 102 *note*
German, the Pennsylvania, 39
Gide, Andrew, quoted, 253
Gist, Christopher, 166
Gladstone, William Ewart, 255
"Going-down" places, the, in early pioneering, 10–11
Gold, first effect of the discovery of, 51 *et seq.;* timely discovery of California's, fields, 162
Government, no enlargement of the concepts of, in England, 76; the three branches of, in the State constitutions, 81–82; developing proficiency in the art of, 82; planning the form of, for the new States, 90–91, 93–94; fear of the centralization of political power in the, 232 *et seq.*
Grant, Ulysses S., 217
Great Trail, the, across Ohio, 165

HARRISON, FAIRFAX, 207
Harte, Bret, quoted, 159
Hazard, Miss, 24
"Heart of the Continent, The", Ludlow, 198, 199 *note*
Heat, the intolerable, of the western desert, 172–174
Henderson Company of North Carolina, purchases "Kentucky" from the Cherokees, 71
Henry, Patrick, 137
Heydt, Baron, and the pathway into Virginia, 140; 146
History, backgrounds of American, 13–33; the new handmaidens of, 34; influence of geography on, 34 *et seq.;* "upsets" and the philosophy of, 54, 55
Hite, Joist. *See* HEYDT, BARON
Holland, in the New World, 66
Home, the passion for, 12
Homesickness, the burden of, 168–169
Howells, William Dean, 61
Hughes, Rupert, 102–103 *note*
Hulbert, Archer Butler, "Washington and the West", 101 *note*, 102 *note; The Records of the Ohio Company*, 104 *note;* "Western Shipbuilding", 142 *note*
Hulbert, Calvin B., "The Distinctive Idea in Education" quoted, 240–241 *note*
Huntington, Professor Ellsworth, 35 *note*

IDEALISM, Americans united in, 82
Illinois Central Railway, early circular of the, quoted, 45

Independence, events leading up to the struggle for, 76–78; the War of, 79; the spirit of, on the frontiers, 138
Indians, 66, 87, 89; the early pathfinders, 166; their fear of the telegraph line, 199–200
Industrial age, development of the, 220; fear of certain phases of the, 232
Ingalls, John J., quoted, 48–50, 122, 226
Initiative legislation, misuse of, 233
Inland water route, Washington's outline of an, 101 *note*
Internal improvements, Northern demand for, 212
International questions, the frontiers and, 143–147
Internationalism, ameliorating influence of business efficiency on, 229–230
Iron, the working of, in Pennsylvania and Maryland, 140

JEFFERSON, THOMAS, and the Louisiana Purchase, 143–145; 183, 203
"Johnny Appleseed", 56
Johnston, Alexander, 216
Johnston, Mary, quoted, 154

KEPHART, HORACE, quoted, 21–22; experience in a mountain cabin, 134
Kino, Father, 52
Kipling, Rudyard, quoted, 10
Kuykendall, Judge, his opinion of the "bad men" of the West, 130–131

LANCASTER COUNTY, PENNSYLVANIA, 39
Lake Shore Trail, the, 165
Land Law, formulation of a, by Congress, 104–105
Land System, adoption of a, for the new States by Congress, 90–95
Lands, the Western, ceded to the embryo nation by the States, 84–85; wise legislation by Congress for disposition of, 87–95
Lecky, W. E. H., quoted, 135, 225
Liberty, the universal demand for, 79
Limestone belts, the staple wheat lands, 39
Lincoln, Abraham, 141; sources of his outstanding characteristics, 150–160; 212, 213, 215, 217, 244
Lincoln family, pateran of the, 150–160
Little Coal Creek, an obstacle to the emigrant trains, 172
Local governments, vital importance of the strong, 80–82
Locality, the passion for, 12, 13
Louisiana, outcry over the purchase of, 118
Louisiana Purchase, the reasons for and consummation of the, 143–145; objections of the North and East to the, 203
Love of country, birth of the mesmeric, 75
Lowell, James Russell, quoted, 227
Ludlow, F. H., quoted, 198, 199 *note*
Lyman, Robert, a Forty-Niner quoted, 31–32

MACAULAY, THOMAS BABINGTON, 80
McCosh, James, quoted, 132
McKay, Captain Lauchlan, 56
McLaughlin, Andrew C., on the Ordinance of 1787, 106 *note*
Manufacturing sections, influences making for, 202
Marshall, James Wilson, and the discovery of gold in California, 56
Martineau, Harriet, 123; quoted, 136, 215 *note*
Maryland, and the question of the cession of Western lands in the national interest, 84–85; the stone roads of, 182–185
Mason and Dixon's line, 59
Massachusetts Bay Colony, domineering attitude of the, 63
Mather, Increase, 6
Mathews, Edward B., 34
Melting-pot theory, the, 244

Mexican War, the, 52, 53, 146–147
Mexico, and the grant of land to Austin, 146; the War with, 147; 162
Migration, seed, 14–16; human, 17; dominated by soils, 46
Missions, founding of the California, 52
Mississippi River, the Louisiana Purchase and control of the, 143–145; increase of commerce on the, 144–145
Mohawk Trail, the, 165
Money, disputes over the value of colonial, 60–62; "wild cat", 212
Monongahela River, shipbuilding on the, 142
Montesquieu, Charles, quoted, 54
Moral code of the frontiers, the, 133–134
Morality, the problem of, and sectional welfare, 204
Morris, Gouverneur, proposes a canal across New York, 185
Muret, Maurice, on present-day European hatreds, 124

Napoleon I, quoted, 31, 43, 125
National evil, the most serious, a psychic evil, 246
National Road, the building of the, 183–185
Nemacolin's Path, from the Potomac to the Ohio, 165
Newberry Library, collection of old diaries in the, 169
New England, influence of the soils of, 35–39; the urge of emigration in, 71; the township system of, 93–94; feeling in, regarding the War of 1812, 203
New England Confederation of 1643, 63; causes of its formation, 66–67; membership of the, 67; objects of the, 67; duration of the, 67; influence of, in international relations, 67; its successes and failures, 67; as a precedent, 68; 78
"New Viewpoints in American History", Schlesinger, 35 *note*
New York, the stone roads of, 183; and the development of transportation facilities, 185–187; builds the Erie Canal, 187–188
Nicknames, the wealth of suggestion underlying, 23
"Night", the, of prior generations, 5–9
Nitti, Francesco Saverio, on the American business man, 230
North, the, as a manufacturing section, 211; its demand for tariff protection, 211; and internal improvements, 212; and a stable financial system, 212; and the Civil War, 217–218
Northwest Territory, 106
Novelists, realization of local color and tradition of American life by the, 25

Office, the need of better men in public, 228
Ohio, admitted as a State in 1803, 106; demands improved means of transportation, 183–185; and the construction of canals, 188–189
Ohio, Basin, rich soils of the, 55, 86
Ohio Company of Associates, circular of the, quoted, 45; and the Western lands, 103–106
Ohio River, shipbuilding on the, 141–142, 144; production of wheat in the valley of the, 144
Old Bay Path, the, 165
Opportunity and Power, a vision of, 58–68
Ordinance of 1787, the, and the territory northwest of the Ohio River, 105, 106 *note;* and slavery, 209
Oregon Trail, the, 165

Pacific coast, early ignorance of the geography of the, 51–52
Paine, Thomas, on the handling of the Western lands, 91
Partridge, George E., quoted, 18, 75
Pathfinders, the so-called, 166–167

Patriotism, the provincial basis of, 13–33; the local, of the American, 18; the chief art of, 113
Penn, William, quoted, 44–45; 139
Pennamite War, the, between Connecticut and Pennsylvania, 59
Pennsylvania, early development of transportation facilities in, 40–41; dispute with Connecticut and Virginia over territory, 59; the stone roads of, 182–183
Pennsylvania Canal, innovations in the construction and operation of, 191–192
Pennsylvania Dutch, and the winning of the Revolution, 39
Pennsylvania Railroad, completion of the, 193
Philadelphia, anomalous situation of, 59
Pioneers, the early, 4; the harlequin platoon of, 4
Pitt, William, 77
Plant migration, 14–16
Plantation, the Southern, 207; economic system of the, 210
Political antipathies and disputes in colonial days, 62–63
Politics, business efficiency in, 227; the need of better men in, 228
Polk, James K., 147, 162
Pond, Doctor, a California pioneer, 53
Pony Express, the, 57, 197
Potomac Navigation Company, 181–182
Potomac River, soils of the frontier south of the, 41–42
Poverty, on the frontiers, 137, 138
Printing press, the first, in the far West, 56
Promised Land, the consciousness of a, 72
Province, the regard of an American for his, 18
Provinces, the peopling of our, 17; the individuality of our, 18; "touring" the, 19–20; the exceeding number of our, 23; the Republic a collection of splendid, 232; integrity of our, under changing conditions, 237
Provincial development, American, 12
Provincialism, the distinctive American characteristic, 30–31; becomes sectionalism, 201
Provincialisms, the influence of, 26
Purgatoire, the, 166
Putnam, General Rufus, and the soldiers' efforts to secure bounty-land, 92–93; and the Ohio Company of Associates, 103–106; 141

Quatrefages de Breau, J. L. A. de, quoted, 245

Radio, the, as a factor for unity, 198
Railroad, construction and completion of a, to the Pacific, 199
Railroads, station names on the early, 99–100 *note;* largely located by the old trails, 165
Rainfall, east and west trend of lines of, 42
Raton Pass, 166
Records of the Ohio Company, The, Hulbert, 104 *note*
Religious antipathies and disputes in colonial days, 62–63
Republic, forebodings for the future of the, 3; the story of the American, 127–128; a collection of splendid provinces, 232
Rivers, the marked influence of the, as highways for settlement and communication, 65; Washington's vision of the use of the western, 98–100; hazards of the crossing of the, 171–172
Roads, the stone, of Pennsylvania and Maryland, 182–185
Roosevelt, Theodore, quoted, 131
Rostovtzeff, Mikhail I., 114
Royce, Josiah, 53, 235, 236

St. Louis, early rivalry between Chicago and, 193
Santa Fé Trail, a blizzard on the, 169–171
Schlesinger, Arthur M., "New Viewpoints in American History", 35 *note*
Scotch-Irish, in Pennsylvania, 139
Scurvy, 174
Sectional antipathies, the human character of our, 128
Sectionalism, the rise and causes of, 201–219
Seed, the, in the frontier-building process, 4–12; migration, 14–16
Semple, Ellen C., 34
Shaler, Nathaniel S., 34
Shays' Rebellion, 137
Shipbuilding, on the Ohio and Monongahela, 141–142, 144
Sickness, in the emigrant trains, 174–175
Silver, first effect of the discovery of, 51 *et seq.*
Sink, the suffering endured in crossing the, 172–174
Slavery, soil factors influencing growth of, 36
Slave system, early need for, in the South, 205–206; an economic problem, 206; abolition of the, in California, 206; and the cotton gin, 209–210; evils of the, 214
Slaves, 205–206; the care and maintenance of, 207–209
Soil, the democratic element in, 29; psychology of the, factor, 29; the, factor in American unification, 34–57
Songs, best loved, are of local and homey things, 31–32; of England in the Colonies, 64
South, the, influence of the soils of the, 41; opposition in, to tariff of 1828, 204; crops suitable to, 205; and the slave system, 205–210; economic complications of the, 210–211; opposition to the tariff in, 211; and the balance of power in Congress, 213; burden of the slave system and, 214–215; and the Civil War, 216–218; emancipated from economic bondage, 218
South Atlantic States, the soil factors of the, 41–42
Spain, rivalry between, and France advantageous to the colonies, 66; 89
Spaniards, on the Pacific coast, 51–52
"Spheres of Influence", the, of other Powers in America, 66
Spratling, William, quoted, 42
Squatter system, the, of land ownership, 94
State constitutions, adoption of the, 81; uniformity of ideals in the, 81–82
Statehood, the promise of, 85–95
States, rivalry between large and small, 63; cession of land to National Government by certain, 84–85; Western lands allotted for new, 85, 88–91; abuse of initiative legislation by the, 233
States-Rights doctrine, the, 216, 234, 235
Steamboats, on the Mississippi, 184
Storms, on the plains, 169–171
Sumner, Charles, quoted, 38, 56, 240
Supreme Court, the innovation of a, with nullifying powers, 108
Sutter, Captain J. A., 56
Sweden, in the New World, 66

Tariff, opposition in the South to, of 1828, 204; Northern and Southern differences on the, 211; application of business-like methods to, revisions, 228–229
Tariffs, disputes over the colonial, 61–62
Telegraph, Indian fear of the, 199–200
Temperature, east and west trend of lines of, 42
Texas, and the Mexican War, 146–147
Thackeray, William Makepeace, 246
Tobacco, the Southern soil adapted to cultivation of, 205

Tocqueville, Alexis Charles H. C. de, quoted, 76; on the intellectuality of the frontiers, 136; quoted, 201; "Democracy in America" quoted, 208 *note;* 225
Township, genesis of the, system of New England, 37, 93–94
Trade, rivalry between the colonies in, 61–62; close, relations with England, 65
Trails, the old, 162–177
Transportation, developing and improving means of, 181–200
Traveling, little, in olden times, 26–27
Tunnel, dedication of the Cascade, 200
Turner, Frederick Jackson, on the frontier-influence on American history, 72–73 *note*

Unity, creation of the psychic, in Americans, 56; the struggle for, 63–68; the opportunity for expansion an inspiration toward, 72; the new feeling of physical, 75; the best proof of a genuine spirit of, 79; of idealism in the Declaration of Independence, 82; cession of Western lands by the States made for, 84–85; fundamental, of our country, 114; American, and the Civil War, 123–124, 204–205; the type of, of our frontiers, 132; the intellectual, of the frontiers, 135–137; splendor of the story of American, 161 *et seq.*
Unification, the soil-factor in American, 34–57
United States, becomes a tentative nation, 78
United States Weather Bureau, director of, quoted, 35 *note*
"Upsets" to the philosophy of history, 54, 55

Valley of Virginia, the, 139
Virginia, dispute with Pennsylvania over territory, 59; controversy with England, 205
Virginia Resolves, the noted, 78

Walpole Grant, the, 71
Warming, Professor Eugenius, 14–15
War of 1812, the frontier and the, 145–146; influence of the, on building of the Erie Canal, 187; opposition of New England to the, 203
Warriors Path, the, 165
Washington, George, on the Pennsylvania Dutch and the winning of the Revolution, 39; 46, 69; in search of good land in the West, 71; on the Alleghenies as a line of defense, 86; on the western States-to-be, 96–97; exploring and studying the western territory, 98–99; on the utilization of the river systems, 97–99; letters to Governor Harrison and Henry Lee, 100; on the future population and agricultural wealth of the western territory, 101–102; his optimism a factor for unity, 102–103; outline of inland water routes Detroit to New York, 101 *note;* Rupert Hughes on, 102–103 *note;* his vision of shipping on the Ohio, 141; 166, 167; efforts to improve methods of transportation, 181–182; our first expansionist, 198 *note;* 224, 244, 245
"Washington and the West", A. B. Hulbert, 101 *note*, 102 *note*
Watterson, Henry, quoted, 28
Webster, Daniel, 8; on the Ordinance of 1787, 106 *note*
Webster, Pelatiah, on the disposal of the Western lands, 91–92
West, successive frontiers of the, 127–128
"Western Shipbuilding", Hulbert, 142 *note*
Wheat, the limestone belts of soil and, 39; the distribution of good, soils, 43–44; the origin and introduction of hard, 50–51; the Ohio Valley production of, 144

Whipple, Admiral Abraham, 143
Whiskey Rebellion, 137
White, S. E., "Arizona Nights" by, 130
Whitman, Marcus, 8, 234
Williams, Roger, 38, 62
Winthrop, Governor John, 36
Wister, Owen, quoted, 24, 27, 121, 125–126
Wolfe, General James, 69
Wolfskill, the Kentucky hunter, 9–10

YANKEE, peculiarities and traits of the early, 27
Young, Ewing, 56